CLIMBING I

My Descent in Hell
and
Flight to Heaven

CLIMBING INTO ETERNITY

My Descent in Hell
and
Flight to Heaven

Michele Pulford

REDEMPTION
PRESS

Published by Redemption Press, PO Box 427, Enumclaw, WA 98022

Toll Free (844) 2REDEEM (273-3336)

Redemption Press is honored to present this title in partnership with the author. The views expressed or implied in this work are those of the author. Redemption Press provides our imprint seal representing design excellence, creative content, and high quality production.

Some names have been changed.

ISBN: 978-1-68314-249-2 (Paperback)
978-1-68314-250-8 (ePub)
978-1-68314-251-5 (Mobi)

Library of Congress Catalog Card Number:

Dedication

To YHWH, my Lord God

Thank You for rescuing me from the clutches of death thirty-two years ago in 1984.

Abba Father, thank you for loving me so much that You did not let go of me.

Lord Jesus, for your salvation and abundant life that You have clothed me with.

Holy Spirit, my best Friend, my Teacher, my Comforter, and my Counselor, for never leaving me and for always wanting the best for me and this story.

Lord God, this book is because of You and for You and Your glory.

To my loving family

Charles, you are the love of my life, my husband, my soulmate, my Prince Charming.

Cyle-jay, you are our miracle and our mighty valiant son.

Brontii-ann, you are our miracle and our beautiful princess.

You have all been so much a part of me writing and rewriting and editing and re-editing this book. Your support, love and patience during this long process is the reason why I can dedicate this to you. Thank you.

To Tania

We lost you to cancer on this earth and you are now in Heaven. Tania, I thank you for persevering and pushing and not giving up on your brother and me. I dedicate the love story in my book to you because it would not have taken place if it had not been for you.

To my dear dad, George Aiken

We lost you to dementia in 2016. I love you and thank Lord God for you. I dedicate the victory, I could write about in my story to you because of your absolute love and support throughout my whole life.

Acknowledgments

THIS BOOK WAS SET INTO prophetic motion by the Almighty Creator who said, "Let there be . . ." It was in 1986 when He spoke this book from Heaven onto earth. This book has truly been long in coming. *Climbing into Eternity: My Descent in Hell and Flight to Heaven* into being.

A special thank you to my precious family: Charles, Cyle-jay, and Brontii-ann. You have been my reason to see this book through to its completion.

Our dear friend and the children's God-guard father, Reuben, I thank you for your never-ending support. Throughout and over the years, you have walked with me and believed that my story must reach the ends of the earth. Your support and advice is a true gift and blessing to us. Thank you.

To my mentor from 2002, Bill Hollis, your support and belief in this story and book saw me through the days of doubt and questioning if this book would ever come into fruition.

You told me to, "Get myself up, shake myself off and start all over again." Thank you, Bill, for believing in this God-given assignment that will reach and help many, many souls.

To George across the oceans in the U.S.A. Thank you for immediately seeing that this book is God-appointed and for supporting us with your governing field and portfolio. Thank you for taking up Lord God's call to help bring this Kingdom message to the world.

To the whole *Climbing into Eternity* team, each with your unique, specific God anointings, talents, and gifts, thank you for believing in this God-appointed book for His Kingdom purpose and glory, and for stepping up and stretching out the tent pegs, and stepping into helping make this God-given task happen.

To Sharon and Bianca for being the Nehemiah's for this book.

Inger from Redemption Press, a massive thank you for all your hard work and support and patience with me during our extensive step-by-step editing of my story.

A special thank you to the rest of Redemption Press. Thank you to the whole team for your patience, support, and help in getting my story published in excellence unto Lord God's glory. May He truly bless your whole team as He mightily uses and increases you in the publishing arena.

Contents

Prologue

EVERY PERSON WHO HAS BEEN born and is yet to be born has a story to tell. It is his or her story and no one else's. This is what gives them the authority over it.

This is my story about death and about eternal life. I tell you what happened when I died and how I was given a second chance. I begin with the following verses from the Bible that sum up my story.

> Your vows are upon me, O God; I will render praise to you and give you thank offerings. For you have delivered my life from death, yes, and my feet from falling, that I may walk before God in the light of life and of living.
>
> (Ps. 56:12–13 AMP)

> Where, O death, is your victory? Where, O death, is your sting?
>
> (1 Cor. 15:55)

Since creation, man has been obsessed with what happens when we die. We are obsessed with life after death. While what happens after death is not a popular subject to talk about, it is vital for us to know the truth.

I have written about what happened to me when I died not to incite fear or sensationalism, but to alert you to the fact that there is, beyond any shadow of doubt, life after death. It is called *eternity*. And we are all climbing into it.

I flirted with and entertained death for six years. This resulted in me knocking myself unconscious from major acute anorexia nervosa at the age of sixteen. Even though this experience rattled me, it was not long before I once again went back to my old habits and evil ways.

You will read how I messed up my life even further, taking another poor soul with me. Eventually the pit I dug caused me to arrive dead on arrival at South Rand Hospital at age twenty-two, by my own hand, namely suicide.

I had no relationship with God Almighty, let alone Jesus Christ, thus ruling the Holy Spirit completely out. It is no wonder I had landed in the place of eternal damnation, horror, torment and fire. I have not kept anything back with what I saw in hell. I should warn you now: this is not for the faint-hearted.

About eleven years later, from medical reasons, my body was totally paralyzed from an anaphylactic allergy attack that surged throughout my body when lived on the Makgadikgadi Pans of Botswana, where there was a complete lack of medical facilities. As my lungs collapsed, I found life leaving my body. Slowly the earth went dim; I was dead once again. This time

I was taken to the splendorous glory of Heaven. The life we know here on earth does not remotely compare with where we are going. To attempt an accurate description of God's glory in Heaven into words is like trying to climb Mt. Everest barefoot. It is a lot easier to describe hell to you.

You might ask, "How is this possible? How can a person not only die once but die twice, and then come back and live to tell about it?" I cannot tell you how this is possible, instead I joyfully tell you it *did* happen and God's grace made it possible.

How can I keep quiet about this? God Almighty did not allow me to return to life on this earth only to have me shy away and not say anything. That would not only be tragic, even sinful, but would also have the devil smiling. To be mocked by the ignorant or be misunderstood is but a small price to pay for saving people from the absolute horror of the eternal damnation that I found myself in.

This completely open and transparent story will clearly show you how the choices we make while here on earth determine where we will go once we leave this earth and step into eternity. If I can warn people away from this kingdom of pure evil—the kingdom of darkness—I do so boldly. And if I can show them the kingdom of true abundant life, I gladly do so because this is the true eternal life of Heaven—the Kingdom of Light.

Oh, the glory and splendor of God and His Kingdom! I pray that by the end of this book you will have determined to live a life that is Heaven bound.

The thief comes only in order that he may steal and may kill and may destroy. I came that they may have life, and have it in abundance—to the full, till it overflows.

John 10:10 AMP)

When Jesus spoke again to the people, he said, "I am the light of the world. Whoever follows me will never walk in darkness, but will have the light of life."

(John 8:12)

When I saw Him, I fell at His feet as though dead. Then He placed His right hand on me and said, "Do not be afraid. I am the First and the Last. I am the Living One; I was dead, and behold I am alive forever and ever! I hold the keys of death and Hades . . ."

(Rev. 1:17–18)

For God so loved the world that he gave his one and only Son, that whoever believes in Him shall not perish but have eternal life.

(John 3:16)

Michele Y. Pulford

Part I

My Downward Path

One

"God, I Promise"

"MICHELE! MICHELE!"

Who is calling me? I opened my eyes to find myself lying naked on the floor in the passage, my towel displaced at the doorway of the bathroom.

What on earth am I doing here? What happened?

I heard the voice once again. *Michele! Michele, what are you doing? Why are you doing this to yourself?*

I bolted upright, "Oh, my God! I'm sorry, I'm sorry! I mean . . . Oh . . .!" I froze. I did not know what to say. I somehow knew I was hearing the thundering voice of *God!*

How did I know this? It was not as if I had heard His voice before. But my very inner being was screaming it out without any shadow of a doubt. The voice of God went straight into the very depths of my soul, causing every cell in my body to tremble and stand at attention, all at the same time.

Immediately I wanted my towel. I needed to cover myself up. I had to hide. Oddly, I thought of how Adam and Eve must have felt after eating the forbidden fruit. They must have felt naked and exposed, wanting to hide from that almighty thundering voice of God who was calling out to them.

> Then the man and his wife heard the sound of the LORD God as He was walking in the garden in the cool day, and they hid from the LORD God among the trees of the garden. But the Lord God called out to the man, "Where are you?" He answered, "I heard You in the garden, and I was afraid because I was naked; so I hid."
>
> (Gen. 3:8–10)

> The LORD God made garments of skin for Adam and his wife and clothed them.
>
> (Gen. 3:21)

I knew I was not holy enough to hear that mighty voice. If that was what it was like facing God's voice, I shuddered to think what it would be like to face God Almighty Himself in person. I sat paralyzed with fear. *God will strike me down with a bolt of lightning any minute!*

I knew I was not a good person. No, the truth was, I knew I was *evil* in all my secret ways.

God's voice was absolutely fearsome, yet majestic in its brilliance. It sounded like thunderous waters combined with awesome power, demanding my utmost attention as it struck a high pitch on my nerves.

It reminded me of the time I was at Witbank Dam in South Africa. We stood on the dam wall when three sluice gates were opened to release the build-up of water. As the gates were opened and the water gushed out there was a thunderously powerful roar, terrifying, yet still majestic. It seemed to make the wall and everything around it tremble, as if a controlled earthquake, creating an astute awareness that we are but ants compared to that immense power. We were kept safe by the well-constructed dam wall.

Everyone was tightly clutching onto the wall rails, even the loud-mouthed guys in our group. As my body clenched in fear, I noted the magnificent beauty flowing in the rainbow created from the spray of the mighty water as it thundered and smashed down onto the rocks below.

My experience there made me think of God's magnificent, immense voice. The closer one stands to the sluice gates, the mightier the powerful roar is that runs right through your veins into the very depths of your being. This is how I can best describe the voice of God. It is thunderous glory. The power that bellows out is almost unbearable. But His words, though firm, contain a true and solid concern that is like the melodious beauty that flows out of the rainbow.

God's voice thunders in various ways; He does great things beyond our measure.

(Job 37:5)

Hearing Almighty God's voice should be a time of rejoicing and jubilation. But given the situation I found myself in, it was far from a time of celebration.

I felt guilty and ashamed.

My judgment day had arrived.

By that time, I realized that I had knocked myself unconscious, as I had done a few times before. I had been on a complete starvation binge for just over five weeks. I remember my head spinning while I climbed out of my ice bath, turning into solid dizziness until everything went blank.

Not only was God speaking to me, He was also asking me why I was doing this to myself. Looking up, wide-eyed with fear, I thought my time on earth had come. I had really messed up badly. I knew I had said many times, "I want to die," and "I hate life," but I panicked as a dreadful feeling of judgment lurked around me.

I don't want to die.

Had even God given up on me as I walked my path of self-destruction?

Staring up at the ceiling, I shouted, "God, I am so sorry for everything that I have done. Please give me one more chance. I promise no more nonsense, no more evil. I will do whatever the doctors and my parents want me to do. I will stop starving of myself. I don't want to die!"

While I pleaded with God, I thought, *Too late! I am going to die. I heard the voice of God and I have angered Him."*

I slumped back, again overcome by dizziness and slipping back again into the oblivion of empty darkness. I could not find the strength to fight the darkness as I had done so many times before during the previous four years.

How did I get myself to this point?

—∽∿∽—

It had all started seven years prior on the 24th of December 1973. I was ten years old. Standing in front of the mirror and twirling around in my beautiful, ivory flared skirt, I was full of excitement. That night, I felt especially pleased with myself as we were going to the Christmas ice show. And for the first time in my life I said to myself, "You look pretty tonight."

I had just finished a painful diet the doctor and my mom had put me on. As I had lost a lot of weight, I could finally wear a pretty outfit. I no longer had to wear something for a "fat kid."

The holidays are going to be very special for me, I thought. No one will tease me by calling me "Fatso" or "Nellyphant." No one will laugh at me anymore, not even my sister and brother. I twirled around again, feeling good. It felt so wonderful not to be fat!

A few of my dad's family were also on holiday in Durban and would join us at the ice show and to see Christmas Eve into Christmas Day.

That night we all enjoyed the ice show and took a pleasant stroll back to the hotel. As usual, all the hotel balconies were filling up with people sharing the joyous occasion. The atmosphere was electrifying. We arrived together with the whole family at our hotel balcony. My dad, together with my older married cousin started organizing tables and chairs for our large group.

As the grown-ups were setting up, we children went to look at the lady working the reception desk again. She intrigued us as we could not believe how small, thin, and frail she was. We thought she might be one of Father Christmas's elves.

A doorman who worked at the hotel told us she was so thin and tiny because she had been in a concentration camp during the Second World War. He said, "Hitler was a very mentally sick and cruel man. Although the lady was freed, her body was so badly damaged it will never be able to function properly again."

I knew a little bit about Hitler because I had been taught about him at school.

The doorman had also said, "She has terrible stories to tell us about this place that was hell on earth."

The little lady was old and frail with such sad eyes that, even when she greeted people at the reception desk with a smile, it was as if she was not smiling. Her eyes looked tormented, as if something was continuously haunting her.

After we children watched her and wondered about her life, we went back to the adults who had finished sorting everything out.

The last thing that had to be organized was who was drinking what. After the orders were taken, my dad, who hated jackets and ties, took his tie off and said to my sister, brother and me, "Who will take my jacket and tie up to the room for me?"

I jumped up and immediately said, "I will!"

"Thanks, Shell," he said, giving me a smile. His gesture made me feel good. I grabbed the jacket and tie, headed inside the hotel entrance and went straight to the elevators.

I was smiling inside and felt extra special that night. I loved doing things for my dad. I knew I was not his favorite so doing things for him and seeing that it pleased him made me feel really special.

Another man entered the lift with me. I noticed we both needed to exit at the same floor. The man let me get out of the lift first. This was normal because my dad always let my mom and us girls go first. He was always the gentleman.

I went to our hotel room door thinking, *I'm not going to throw Dad's jacket and tie on my bed. I'm going to go and put it nicely on Dad's bed.*

I went into the adjoining room, placed the jacket and tie on the bed and turned to leave.

Then I saw him. The man who was with me in the lift was now in my mom and dad's room. I panicked. I did not know what to do. He was mumbling and I was too terrified to speak.

I instinctively knew I had to get out.

As the man came closer, his words became clearer. He was swearing and cussing at me, insulting me with terrible names that came spitting out of his mouth in a snarl. I did not know what they meant, but I immediately felt ashamed, stripped, vulgar, cheap, like dirt, and worthless rags. I thought of the reception lady's eyes. I knew then what I had seen in her eyes. It was exactly what I was feeling. Fear!

I wanted to block my ears. The words were ringing in my head as he kept on repeating them over and over again.

I instantly knew he meant me great harm. Terror gripped my heart as I saw the look of hate and disgust in his eyes. He lunged towards me. I turned and ran, pushing him with all my strength—strength that I did not know I had as a little girl—making him fall onto the bed.

As I got to the connecting door, I felt his grip on the back of my neck. He continued to spit those disgusting names at me. I knew I had to get out of the room and away from this man. His grip on my neck was so strong that he managed to pull me up against his sweaty body. As he started fondling me all over I knew I had to try to get to the door. He got rougher, turning me around so my face pressed against his chest. He put his one hand on my head and started forcing me down. My lips were pressed against him as he moved me downward from button to button. The smell of sweat and alcohol was overbearing. Even in my innocence, I sensed this was going to end very badly unless I did something.

Then, suddenly, as my lips reached his opened pants button, he stopped pushing my head and grabbed a tuft of the back of my hair, and yanked my head to look up at him. I sensed he was trying to push my head into his pants where his zipper was open. He did not have underpants on. I had never seen or smelled anything like what was emanating from in there. As the man kept spitting out those horrific words at me, the expression on his face became one of pure insanity.

Horrified, I knew this was bad, very, very bad. I was in danger. *Why is he calling me these names? He is going to hurt me. I have to get away from him.*

For some unknown reason, he let go of his grip of my hair. Anger seemed to overcome him. I kicked him with all my strength and let out a terrifying scream. I do not know if it was my scream or my kick that made him fall backwards. Scrambling about, he tried to get back up onto his feet, but he seemed to be doing it in slow motion. I think it had something to do with the strong odor of alcohol I could smell.

A young couple must have heard my scream and came to my rescue. They saw the man stumbling forward. He pushed his way past them, ran out the door and headed down the passage. They first stood motionless before bolting into action. This sudden action caused me to break down crying.

The young man hollered down the passage, "Catch that guy!" while the young lady came over to help me. I was crying hysterically. Eventually she understood my parents were downstairs.

As we walked, I heard more shouts from people to "Catch that guy."

The lady taking me to my parents told me, "It's alright, they've caught him." I did not want to see him. I did not want to go near him. I was still crying hysterically as more people gathered around me.

By then, my mom and dad realized the commotion involved me. The next thing I saw was my dad leap over a table and grabbed the guy. I was taken to my mom, still sobbing frantically. Someone said, "The police have arrived." Although I could not see what was happening, I could hear the crowd. It scared me, causing my crying to raise a pitch.

My mom then turned her attention to me, which made me feel safe. I wanted to hear her tell me that everything was going to be alright, and that the bad man would be taken far away from me.

Instead her eyes were fixed on mine. "Michele! Pull yourself together! Everybody is looking. Now here! Here is some sugar water. It will help you calm down. Do you really want to destroy this wonderful evening your dad is having?"

"But I . . ."

I saw her lips tighten and I knew what those tightened lips meant.

"You are causing everyone to look! Drink your sugar water! Stop causing such a scene. You are always so full of drama. I don't want to have to tell you to stop this drama scene again. And I don't want to speak about this ever again. Do you hear? Is that clear? It is already so embarrassing . . ." She carried on reprimanding me while forcing the sugar water into my hand.

I did not want to destroy everyone's evening. But I felt so hurt and rejected by how my mom was treating me. I picked up the sugar water, not to drink, but to sob silently into it.

The incident faded away as quickly as it had started, and was supposedly forgotten—perhaps by everyone else, but definitely not by me. I felt so hurt that I was not taken seriously.

Everyone listened to my mom who told them, "It's all fine; nothing really happened."

They enjoyed the rest of the Christmas Eve, as if nothing had happened, as my mom insisted they should. No one from the family came to speak to me about it.

This was devastating to me. *Doesn't anyone care?* I heard my mom repeatedly telling everyone, "She's fine."

I was not fine.

Not even the policeman came to ask me anything. They spoke to my mom and left it there! No one came to ask me what had happened; after all, I was only a child! The adults had worked out for themselves what had happened. The story was that the couple had stopped the man from hurting me.

The nightmare felt as if it was still happening. I let out another agonizing scream, this one a silent one, deep inside. I numbly sat and watched everyone laughing as they shared Christmas Eve together.

—⚏—

This was the first night of my new life. I began to pretend, pretend, and then pretend some more. I said to myself, *No one really wants to know what is going on inside you. They want to hear you are fine and all is well. Well, if that is what they want, that is what they will get. And they will live to regret it one day!*

At long last it was bedtime. My brother and sister were excited about their Christmas presents. I tried to explain to them the trauma of what had happened, but they brushed it off and said I was just being totally dramatic and over-imaginative. I immediately kept quiet and knew I would have to deal with what had happened to me by myself. Deal with it I would!

That night while everyone was sleeping, I lay awake trying to reason out what had happened to me. The way the man had touched me all over and pushed me down against him made me feel dirty and disgusting. Then there was that horrible sight and smell from his open pants. It vividly came back to my mind and I burst out crying.

Why? Why did this man do this to me? What have I done wrong? I was horrified to see and smell what was behind that zipper. I silently sobbed in shame. This became a reoccurring nightmare for many years. As I lay there curled up and crying, it dawned on me, *It's all my fault. All of it.*

The *why* had been staring at me all the time. It was obvious.

Earlier on that evening, I had told myself I looked pretty. I even felt pretty and twirled around in front of the mirror. *I have no right to think I am pre*tty. I must be all those things the man had called me! That was why he had to punish and hurt me and spit out all those horrible names. I must be a shameful, ugly, fat, dirty, and disgusting pig. I had to be punished for not only forgetting it but for daring to think I was pretty.

At that moment, I made a pact with myself; I would remind myself every day what that man had called me. Those names were too vile and X-rated to write down on paper, but they had been written and stamped deep down into my soul. They were the new blood that flowed through my veins.

That night I hit myself as hard as I could in my abdomen until I cried into my pillow from the pain. I did not want to wake my sister or brother. Then I decided I would punish myself because I had done something wicked. I had called myself pretty and twirled around in front of the mirror. I had giggled with joy. *How could I have been so stupid?*

The last thing I added to my list was that I would hate men. *One day when I am old enough, I will hurt them.*

I determined to become better in everything that mattered to men: cleverer than they were, and fitter and stronger too. I was especially going to get my kicking perfect. It was my kick that saved me from that terrible man. I was going to become mentally more powerful than men. I wanted to learn how to destroy them. I would use my mind to keep them away from me. *They will never touch or hurt me again. Even if I have to kill them to keep myself safe, I will!*

By this decision, made in the stillness of the night, I invited hate and evil into my life. I did not know how much that invitation was going to cost me.

Immediately after I did this, I felt a jolt in my body and I heard giggling inside me. The giggling did not come from me, I was very sure of that.

I said aloud, "Is anybody here?"

I looked over and saw that my sister and brother were still sleeping.

Once again, I was sure I could hear and even feel giggling, but I brushed it off thinking, *It's all in my mind; I am being stupid.*

To seal this vow in my life I gave all the resolutions to myself as a Christmas present! The only man who would not be included on the list was my dad, because he had come to my rescue and I loved him.

The next morning, I woke up no longer just a ten-year-old girl, but a bitter, hateful person with a purpose to hate men and even kill them one day.

Look to the right and see. For there is no one who thinks about me. There is no place for me to go to be safe. No one cares about my soul.

(Ps. 142:4 NLT)

Two

Learning to Control

I WAS NEVER REALLY A child again. My personal Christmas present to myself the night before opened the door for hate to steal my childhood. The giggling I heard and felt left a telltale residue in my eyes. Just like the lady in the hotel reception had a broken heart and fear shining from her eyes, I believed I also had something lurking out of my eyes. At ten years of age, I harbored a hateful cynicism about life.

I was old enough to make some very serious decisions about my life, and stick to them, compelled by the lurking evil and hate that burned inside of me.

From that Christmas Day on, I continually reminded myself who and what I was. I repeated to myself everything that man had called me. I allowed all of it to become the mantra of my life.

By the age of eleven, I truly believed all of it. I not only hated myself, but I was completely repulsed by myself.

Control and discipline entered my life on a large scale. I started a heavy exercise routine and cut down on the amount of food I ate. I also began to study more. I was determined be fitter, thinner, cleverer, and more powerful than any man.

To ensure this would happen, I figured out I would have to mentally become a monster. I had to start training myself to use my mind to control. That was the only way I would be able to squash and defeat men.

How did I come to this conclusion at such a young age? I do not know. It somehow became the most important tool of destruction in my arsenal.

Slowly, I began to control every thought. I purposely produced and zoned into thoughts until I had accomplished what I set out to do. Eventually, I had worked out I could move objects with my mind. But this was not what I wanted to do. I wanted to be able to "bend a man" as if I were bending a spoon.

I shudder to tell you this, but I started practicing mind games on children. Once I got it right on children, I could move on to men. I believed this was the only way to become more powerful than men.

It was a cruel game that worked like this. I would see how long it would take me to get a child to cry without touching him or saying anything to him. I would always be a few meters away from the child, using my mind to zone into his mind to make him feel so scared he cried. With every outburst of tears, I felt more powerful.

This fed my hate and determination to destroy as many men as possible. I didn't want to make a man feel scared, but to feel bad, embarrassed, confused, and humiliated about himself, so much so that he would want to hide away, and a blackening depression would be ignited within him. I firmly believed that if my mental power could get a man into that state, he would never be able to hurt me with his mouth or with what lay behind his zipper.

To remind myself who and what I was, I continued to beat myself up and burn myself, making it look like an accident by the stove or iron. This way I was never questioned.

Because of that fateful Christmas Eve, I thought no one would ever notice if I did burn myself severely. *No one bothered to care when that man hurt me the way he did on Christmas Eve. And rightly so, because I deserved it. You filthy, disgusting, vile, fat pig dung! How could you think you were pretty?*

I would beat myself up all over again in the silence of my room where no one could see or know what was going on in my head. To others everything looked fine. It was what they wanted that Christmas Eve, so that was what they were getting now.

Then one day, it all seemed to blow up in my face. My mom became hysterical in the dining room, ranting and raving at me about my eating habits.

"Do you think I'm stupid?" she asked. "Don't you think I know what you are doing?" I had not been eating my food but playing with it or hiding it in a napkin under the table. After eating the tiny bit I did eat, I would go to the toilet and make myself sick.

I chose to ignore her and pretended not to see how upset and concerned she was. Instead, I focused on my sister Sonja and brother Gavin who were sniggering in the background. I did not say anything back to my mother. I just said to myself, *You guys have no idea what I am up to. It has nothing to do with eating. You are all just a bunch of idiots!*

From that day on I alienated myself completely from my family. It was not very hard to do as Sonja and Gavin had always ganged up against me from the time we could talk. The only time they were ever friendly to me was when they wanted me to do something for them.

I began to show my contempt for them outwardly as I wanted them to know I wasn't ignorant of their cunning ways. This united them in ganging up me. I was pleased I had more reasons to alienate myself from and hate them. It was as if I were an alien to them; there was just no relationship between us at all. None. They despised me and I used this to counterattack them.

My mouth became poisonous and my hate grew to such great depths within me that it was impossible for me to be kind, even to others. How could I care for others and show kindness when I purposely despised and hated myself? I was trapped inside the darkness within me, suffocated by hate.

> The entire law is summed up in a single command: "Love your neighbor as yourself."
>
> (Gal. 5:14)

Only my father was exempt from my hate. I tolerated my mom but she also became a target of my contempt. She made that easy for me to do because of her famous bouts of physical and verbal abuse. As a result of my terrible attitude, stubbornness, and the contempt I started showing after this incident with my mom, I was zipped off to see a psychiatrist.

I was very cynical and upset about this. Just because I was not acting normally (according to their ideas of normality), they found it necessary to take me to someone for professional help. *Huh? You are three years too late! I was hurt when I was ten, not now that I'm thirteen.*

My parents had no idea what was going on. However, I was quite happy with the way I was handling myself. I was fitter, my marks were above those of the boys in my class, and no boy could handle the mental games I played with his mind. I loved the power. The boys who came across my path were wary of me because I had "something" that kept them at a distance. I thought of males as pathetic with one-tracked minds. They were weak and I hated them with every ounce of my being.

I was quite happy with the way I had dealt with the hurt I had experienced. What could a stupid psychiatrist do for me now? But still, I had to go.

"Michele."

"Yes, Dad?" I always responded quickly to him.

"Your mother and I would like to talk to you."

Here it comes, the psychiatrist's report.

I had given the psychiatrist all the answers I believed he wanted to hear. How did I know what he wanted to hear? Easy! Mental power! At first I thought reading the psychiatrist was going to be a tough assignment, but I found him easy to read. He was merely a hindrance to my plot, and I referred to him in my mind as "Scoundrel."

Dad said, "It has come to the psychiatrist's attention and he has confirmed his fears that you have an eating disorder called anorexia nervosa. Michele, this is very serious and he has advised us to view it as such because it can lead to your death."

Now they are overdoing it! I gave Mom and Dad a dead blank stare as Dad continued.

"The treatment in South Africa is limited as not much is known about the disease (this was back in the 70s). He has advised us to continue taking you to therapy because he believes the quicker we help you deal with this the better."

I don't need help. I've been my own help all this time!

I was angry because I believed I still had a long way to go on my goal of being thinner and fitter than any male who crossed my path. Under no circumstances was I going to stop my plan.

By then I was doing four hours of exercise a day and I was only half way there. I had determined by the time I reached my teen years I would to be up to eight hours a day. And that age was just around the corner!

Scoundrel could go and jump in the lake as far as I was concerned. I immediately started wishing harm would come his way. I really hated him for trying to destroy me with his lies. I didn't need help! I was controlling my eating well.

"But there is nothing wrong with my eating."

Immediately my mom got very worked up and said, "I see you playing with your food and pretending to eat. You hide food in your closet in napkins . . . and what are you doing when you go to the toilet?"

I felt a bit sorry for her, but I allowed the bitterness and contempt in my mind to take over. *It's too late for your attention now. I don't want it. Anyway, they are all just jealous they don't have the willpower I have to deny myself food and not even feel hungry or even crave it.*

My family had just officially become part of the enemy. Instead of fighting back, I just said, "If you say so," then smiled and walked off.

While this set my mom off, I did not care at all. All I did was turn around and stare at my parents. Enemies are not there to please but to destroy, or get them to become your prisoners. This was exactly what I aimed to do. I already had a plan of action. I'd eat just enough to make them smile and then go and get rid of it in the toilet immediately afterwards. That should get them off my back. In the meantime, I could still drop my weight.

My "pretend to be happy" attitude was making me very moody, but I kept these moods to myself. Inside, I despised everyone even more as my hate grew more intense. I believed this was a good thing. Why did people smile at others in any case? They were probably just trying to please somebody else and did not even mean it.

Adding an additional self-punishment to my list, I now only allowed myself four hours of sleep a night. Sleep was a luxury I did not deserve. With this extra time I could do five hours of strenuous exercising a day. As time went by, I felt in control of everything, almost felt invincible, and despised everyone else as weak, pathetic beings.

—ɷ—

By then, my brother's friends had fallen victim to my mind games. My brother used to tell me, "I hate you. I know you're up to no good. I don't know what you are doing, but I know you're doing something."

I was confident he would never find out, so I didn't care. Seeing his friends freeze and look around nervously when I entered the space in their minds gave me a feeling of great power. In my growing hate, I felt males were such false showoffs that they deserved to be brought down a step or two . . . or three . . . or more!

The only reason I talked to boys was to see how far I could manipulate and humiliate them. I often wondered if, once scorched, the boys would expose me. But I was never confronted by any of them.

Then the unexpected happened. Mark, the boy I had chosen as my next target, introduced me to his best friend Charles. Meeting Charles had an overwhelming effect on me. When Mark introduced Charles to me, my eyes locked into his amazing, deep-ocean-blue eyes and I felt like a helpless girl again. That feeling did not please me one bit, especially when all we had said to each other was "Hello."

Somehow, I was prevented from pouring out my well-trained hate on him. This made me so angry with myself.

I told my friend, Vanessa, "He is the one I'm going to marry."

Vanessa laughed at me and said, "Don't be crazy! You said you hate all men and you'd rather kill a man than marry one."

I ignored what she said as the voices within me were screaming at me and telling me, *Take back what you said! Now you have to give yourself double punishment tonight!* I knew they were right. What I had said to Vanessa was treason to my purpose. "I didn't mean it. You know how I hate all boys."

Deep down, I knew I did not hate this boy. He seemed so different; passionately quiet and not as boisterous as the other boys. When he looked at me, I felt his deep blue eyes give off a direct reflection of his intense, deep thoughts.

This worried me as, by then, I was able to zone in and read people's thoughts. After training myself to control my mind and hook into another person's, I could see and hear what they were thinking.

But Charles worried me. He seemed to be in intense deep thought that I was not able to zone into and read. Something seemed to be stopping me or blocking me from doing so. This had never ever happened since I had been able to climb into people's minds and thoughts.

What is going on? Why can't I get into this guy's mind? What makes him different from the others? This did not please me one bit. It made me feel weak and vulnerable to him. I had failed my regime of control when it came to Charles and I needed to teach myself a lesson.

That night a big punishment was due. I beat myself up until I could literally feel the bruising inside my abdomen. This time I had to burn myself with the iron, the stove, and the curling iron. Usually it would be one of the three, but that night it had to be all three.

After the burning, I went ballistic with my exercise routine. Every day I lived by the fitness rule of no pain, no gain.

That night I literally tried to break my leg, but failed. I believed I had lost my normal control of situations and had messed up badly. The verbal abuse that I gave myself carried on for what seemed like hours.

After torturing myself I did the unforgivable: I thought of those deep ocean-blue eyes again! *What is wrong with me?*

The voices inside me were screaming, *Focus, Michele, focus!*

"Yes, I know," I answered them. I just did not know how to focus because of my inner feelings. To make it worse, I secretly did not want the warm feeling I was experiencing to go away.

This caused me to start beating myself all over again until sunrise. There was no sleep for the wicked that night.

News came, which I considered to be bad news. Charles and his family were moving to our mining town. A warm surge ran through my body when I first heard the news, but that was soon replaced by distress mingled with anger. I would have to be very discreet when it came to choosing my next victim to play my mind games on. Thank goodness I was good at acting, because now, more than ever, I had to hide my intentions. I did not want Charles to see what I was really all about.

I learned Charles had a twin sister. Charles and Tanya had a very special relationship and I was determined never to do anything to come between them. I really admired the way they looked out for each other, something Sonja and Gavin and I had never done.

Charles and Tanya joined our group and eventually we became good friends. He did not suspect my dark secret hate for males. Oh, he knew I had bad eating habits and that I was a fitness freak. Everyone in town knew this.

—⚏—

Everything seemed to be going as planned until one day I stood on the scale and nearly had a heart attack! I weighed a whole 38 kilograms (83.77 lbs.). I was horrified at this because I should already have been down to 33 kg. (72.75 lbs.). I cried out in agony, "I am fat! I am a fat pig! No, I am an elephant! A whole 38 kilograms! I'd rather die than be so grotesquely fat!"

At that time I was exercising five and a half hours a day. I needed to push it up to seven and a half hours. I also needed to figure out what else I could do to get myself down to my goal weight of 30 kg. (66.13 lbs.).

Charles had distracted me, which could not be tolerated! How weak and pathetic I had become. No more! I had to do something about this excess fat I felt I was drowning in.

The voices came to my rescue. They always had immediate solutions when it came to me accomplishing "my plan." Or was it their plan? Back then I really believed I was putting my own ideas and schemes into practice. But when everything backfired on me and sent my world crashing to pieces, those voices in me gurgled out with glee.

They told me, *You must purge at certain times every day, even if you don't eat; do so until blood or bile appear.* This way I would know there was absolutely nothing in me that could possibly be digested into fat.

Initially, I was scared when I first saw the blood. I eventually got used to the sight of it and even convinced myself that it gave me power. Eventually, I grew to like it and relish in it. I would feel like the invincible Superman after my blood splattered out into the toilet bowl. The bile tasted disgusting. It was bitter and burned my food pipe, throat, and stomach, but I convinced myself that the purging of bile was good and vital if I wanted to get to 30 kilograms.

The whole purging process made me feel powered up and in full control of my body and everything around me. The only thing I could not control were my feelings for Charles; self-inflicted punishment was not doing its job as far as this was concerned.

I truly thought I was superior to others. I saw others as weak-willed because they could never say no to food and luxuries, and yes to discipline. When it came to fitness, I looked in disgust at all the laziness I saw around me. In South Africa in the 1970s, daily exercise routines were uncommon.

Weighing in the mid-thirty kilograms, I didn't feel sickly and weak, I felt excellent. I had loads of energy all the time as well as the willpower to never detour from the daily regiment I had set for myself, which included the punishments. No one ever suspected a thing. I concealed the burn marks; the bruises were mostly on my abdomen, an easy place for concealing. I would hit myself there because I believed it was the womb that made us women weak. I truly hated and cursed mine.

Three

Mind Games

ONE DAY, WITHOUT ANY WARNING, my mom said she was taking me to see Dr. Zimmen, a gynecologist. And not just any gynecologist but my best friend Yvette's dad! I hated the mention of menstruation and cycles and ovaries and wombs. Why on earth my mom wanted me to get involved in this nonsense I really did not know. She did not tell me why. I think she thought this approach would stop me from destroying myself.

Dr. Zimmen asked me, "Has anyone ever hit you in your stomach?" There was no way I was going to tell him abdomen-hitting was part of my punishment routine. As he examined my arms with a questioning glance at the burn marks, the voices in my head were going crazy. *He knows, he knows! Somebody has told him. It's your friend. She told her father.*

I continued to look at Dr. Zimmen while I shouted silently back at the voices inside me, *Yvette doesn't know what I do. And sometimes, voices, you are so dumb.* I could feel them drill a hole of anger right through me so I told them, *Keep quiet,* while giving the doctor a dead smile with gritted teeth.

I casually answered, "I am so careless when I cook," and ignored his disbelieving glance. (In the seventies there were only disbelieving glances. Now, something like that would not be ignored. It would be reported.)

I thought, *I am not here to discuss burn marks. And there is no way Dr. Zimmen will ever find out!* I quickly added, "You can ask my mother."

Mother nodded in agreement. It was true. I was always "accidentally" burning myself when I cooked, my mother had no idea they were intentional accidents. Maybe she closed her eyes to it, or maybe that was why I was having this conversation with Dr. Zimmen.

I did not dare play mind games with the doctor as he was, after all, my best friend's father. I hated that I couldn't, but I really liked Yvette and cherished our friendship. Yvette had no idea what was going on inside me. The voices were wrong.

Dr. Zimmen told us my internal organs had been damaged and I needed to be hospitalized for X-rays and tests. The results showed major hormone deficiencies, extensive damaged tissue, and my ovaries were not visible at all. Maybe that was why I had not started ovulating. He seemed concerned when he said, "You might never be able to have children."

This did not bother me, in fact it was good news, because I did not want anything to do with womanhood at all. Having babies was a no-go for me. They were not part of my plan. Whenever I saw a pregnant woman, I would feel sick to my stomach. To me, that rounded stomach represented the weakness and vulnerability of a woman. In this state her guard would be down, making it easier for a man to hurt and destroy her.

It got around school that I had been in the hospital and that I could never have children. In the seventies in a small town this was a terrible thing—almost a curse. Apparently, a nurse told her children about this "poor girl in your school."

I was constantly teased about this. I wondered if the teasers really thought it bothered me. The only good thing I found in this was that those poor, insipid, and petty boys who were teasing me gave me more fuel of hate to use against them.

What easy victims of prey some of those boys were! It was easy to bring them to their knees without saying a word, or even getting close to them. Fools! Zoning into their minds was like playing with putty. I had become an expert at silent communication.

Some girls even told me they wished they could be like me because then it meant they would not have to worry about birth control and getting pregnant.

Mortified, I wondered how they could talk like that. How could they give in to the guys? The guys did not honestly feel anything for the girls. The girls were exposing the guys to their most inner selves. They were degrading what we as females stood for and making us look subservient, weak and like easy bait.

Thinking how men could just use girls made my hatred towards males build up inside to such an extent that it surprised me. *One day I'm going to strike out and let males know exactly what despicable disgusting losers they are.* I used this vile hatred and anger to generate more hostile energy. A volcanic determination grew within me.

———ɷ———

This created great conflict within me over Charles. I just could not hate him, no matter how hard I tried. What made it more difficult was that Charles was very happy with us just being buddies. He never tried any boy-girl stuff, ever. Maybe if he had, I would have been able to class him as a typical guy, but he never gave me any reason to.

My dog, Black-lass, did not share my feelings for Charles. Whenever Charles and I would hang out, my dog would never leave my side. If Charles sat near me, Black-lass would promptly sit herself right between us. I laughed because this happened every time. My dog always let Charles know she was number one in my life (and she was).

It was not only his good manners that never allowed me to feel hate when I was with Charles, it was also that I could never read any his thoughts. He always seemed to be so deep in thought. I did not know how to resolve this conflict, but I did not have to worry. We were moving away.

Everyone said, "Don't worry you are only eighty kilometers [about fifty miles] apart. You will still be able to visit and you will see each other at school." I knew it would not be the same. That left me with feelings of resentment. Deep down, I had genuine, serious feelings for Charles—even though we were just buddies.

Once again, my family told me I was just being dramatic. "You're only fifteen, for goodness sake!" At least they did not offer me sugar water, but I felt like spitting at them with a tongue full of venom. I was hurting like I had been hurt on that long-ago Christmas Eve. My feelings were once again ignored, set aside as foolish and overdramatized.

Not even Charles' twin sister Tanya seemed to understand. Nobody did. This made my walls come up even thicker and higher.

Charles was so casual about it that I became angry with him over it. I stamped him in my mind with a "learn-to-hate" stamp. I felt Charles was rejecting me and it hurt me worse than that man had in the hotel. *I will never allow this to happen to me again.* I vented my venomous anger on myself, my family, and any guy who got in my way.

My mental powers seemed to have gotten stronger because now it took just a few minutes to crush a guy. I would zone in on his mind and make him feel ashamed, uncomfortable, uneasy, uncertain about himself, and totally worthless. He would be left feeling exposed, depressed, and would withdraw. It was as if I had hit him with a hundred-pound hammer. This gave me a feeling of immense power and as if I was completely in charge. In my mind, it ensured that no man would ever be able to hurt me again.

I knew guys did not like having these negative, low self-esteem feelings that weakened their defenses. It was good they never knew what hit them as the invisible forces of hate and anger came from my mind and went into theirs. Oh, they knew it was from me because of the deadly stare I would lock them with, but they did not know how to fight it off. They would shuffle and get jittery and sometimes half-heartedly laugh, hoping I would ease up and join in laughing and calling it a joke. To me it was not a joke. I was at war and I had discovered a great weapon against their male egos.

I had come to recognize this involved invisible forces and this made me feel powerful. However, the voices inside were quick to remind me *they* were the ones with the actual power to get into peoples' minds. I did not know what the difference was. I thought those voices were just a different part of me and really believed it was just me doing it all. I thought I had developed a new hidden talent or some form of magic power.

Meanwhile, much to the devil's delight, I had become his pawn.

> For our struggle is not against flesh and blood, but against the rulers, against the authorities, against the powers of this dark world and against the spiritual forces of evil in the heavenly realms.
>
> (Eph. 6:12)

This may sound like a sci-fi plot, but it is not—this is real.

I was an innocent child, a harmless soul on the 24th of December 1973, but by midnight I had thrown in my lot with the devil, without even realizing it. After feeling so rejected, I had invited hate into my life. The devil and his demons got their foot in the door. As my hate grew, so did an overwhelming anger, which turned into more hate. I felt rebellion welling up inside me, causing me to focus all my revenge on the object of my hate and anger.

This hate and bitterness that gave the devil access to my life. God cannot operate without His love being present. It is the same with Satan, the devil: he cannot operate without hate being present. Just as love comes in different forms, so does hate. I had the right requirements that the devil could use.

The dangerous thing was that no one suspected a thing. I played the "goody-goody" part and made sure I looked totally harmless and sweet. I was a good student, a good leader, and eager to please . . . the list could go on and on.

I knew people thought I needed to be taken care of and that I was somehow a victim. I used this fact to my advantage and that was evil.

As for my mind games, I did not know how long these destructive effects would last in guys. I never stayed around to see if they would pull themselves together after a while, if it would last for a period, or even permanently scar them. I shudder now in shame. How cruel! How absolutely cruel and sick my deeds were. I did know the guys always tried to avoid me after becoming prey to my attack.

My brother Gavin also knew that there was something fishy about my stare. I brushed his accusations off with a smile. After all, he had no proof. As long as he did not get in my way, he was safe as well.

At times he said to me, "You are evil. One day I'm going to find out exactly what you are doing and then I'm going to tell everyone."

I was still only a teenager. Was it really possible that I could be so evil? I am not going to lie. From the tender age of eleven, deep, deep, down inside me, I knew I was training myself for the ultimate prize: to murder a man. I can't explain why or from where this came. It came with my hate. It was just there, I never questioned it but relished in it.

These mind episodes I used against guys were just a means to my ultimate goal. But meeting Charles made me stop thinking about murdering a man. As soon as he was out of the picture, there was nothing stopping me.

Who would have won if I had murdered a man? Me? No! What would I win? The only one truly winning would be the devil. A life would be taken and I would be caught in the devil's chains even more.

I did not see this then. I fully believed I would be the boastful winner with more power. Without a doubt, the devil needs humans to do his dirty work, even innocent children. Unfortunately, once in the devil's hands, a child no longer remains innocent.

Did I really believe mind control was my idea? I kept the voices inside me a secret. Deep down I knew this was not the norm but dark and evil.

There were two main voices I came to recognize. One was a very low-pitched voice and the other was a very high, squeaky-pitched voice. The low-pitched voice was the depressive one, that usually made me feel worthless and sorry for myself, and told me I had to destroy myself.

The other, the high-pitched voice, was so aggressive it made me want to take revenge on anything and everything that stood in my way. It was High Pitch that continuously told me I would have to eventually murder a man to stop the torment inside of me. I did not know then that demons could audibly speak to people as well as become a part of that person. If you give them the opportunity, they will grab the chance!

Be self-controlled and alert. Your enemy the devil prowls around like a roaring lion looking for someone to devour.

(1 Peter 5:8)

The night I invited hate into my life, I didn't know that the voices had come into me. I did not put two and two together as I was only eleven years old and soaked in rejection. The voices had come to my rescue and made me feel I belonged and did not need anyone else, or their sugar water. If someone had told me then I was treading on dangerous ground, I would have brushed it off. I had an agenda: to hate men and destroy as many males as I possibly could.

I was not aware of what schizophrenia was back then and remained ignorant about it for a long time. The voices talked to me and told me what to do, but I believed it was all me—a different, new, and stronger me. I had allowed these voices to surface and become a major role in my life, thinking they would help me to achieve my goals.

As it happened, they did.

At first I had one goal, to destroy males. The voices even promised one day they would show me how to murder males in self-defense. This excited me. It filled me with more hate and determination to use as my driving force, leaving me feeling totally invincible.

However, the voices soon instructed me to a second goal: punishing myself, hating myself, and pushing myself and my body until its breaking point to prove I could murder. I had to have complete control of my emotions, never allowing anyone in. This would build up to complete mind control of myself and others. I had to be in control of situations. I had to become a master schemer and manipulator. I was never allowed to play. Not even in a type of sports because the voices made me believe that playing was for weaklings.

I was destructive on the inside, yet hiding it on the outside. This wasn't intentional. It started off as a means to help me deal with my emotional trauma of hurt and rejection. I was suffering an emotional breakdown. Instead of getting help, unknowingly I gave in to the devil with my pact of hate. He became my help!

This inevitably went from demonic bondage to demonic possession (the voices). Medical terms might call this multiple personality disorder, a type of schizophrenia, while the Bible calls it demon possession.

The important thing here is that no one knew there were different Micheles. Most of the time when I would act out of sorts, others would blame it on my eating disorder. Not even the psychiatrist picked this up. He, too, blamed my moodiness on the eating disorder, claiming it was the root. Sadly, it was only a fruit. This all worked out to my advantage because neither I, nor my misdeeds and terrible attitudes, were attributed to anything but the eating disorder and never questioned.

We must never only look at the natural or physical aspect in this world. We must always look beyond. This is not being mystical or melodramatic, this is reality. Many times, it is not the physical that has to be sorted out, but what is beyond the physical, in the spiritual or unseen part of everyday life.

One of the devil's greatest attacks on us comes in our minds. Actions come from thoughts. You cannot touch or see thoughts; however, this is every person's continuous battlefield.

> For though we live in the world, we do not wage war as the world does. The weapons we fight with are not weapons of the world. On the contrary, they have divine power to demolish strongholds. We demolish arguments and every pretension that sets itself up against the knowledge of God, and we take captive every thought to make it obedient to Christ.
>
> (2 Cor. 10:3-5)

I believed the voices to be a good and protective weapon. Never once did I ever think that it could lead to disastrous consequences. At that point, training myself to take a life was not an evil act, but a necessity. The idea of murdering a man became an everyday thought in me. Telling lies to hide what was really going on inside me was an everyday occasion. Lying meant nothing to me. It was just a means to an end to get to my goal. While in the natural world everyone was looking at me as an eating-disorder case, in the unseen world I was a psycho in training to destroy and eventually kill.

I was living as two very different people, or rather, two very different teenagers. Frightening, but true!

Following a tragic incidence of violence, we've all heard variations on these questions: "How could something so innocent turn out to be so deadly?" Or, "What made her turn to suicide?" Or, "What caused him to go on a shooting rampage?"

Or, "That family seemed to be so perfect, so happy. What happened to cause everything to go so wrong?" Or, "He always appeared to be so shy and quiet and decent; why did he do that terrible thing?"

The devil, that thief, is the one who gains when people act out in violent and evil ways. He wraps you in his web purposed to steal, kill and destroy.

> The thief comes only to steal, kill and destroy; I have come that they may have life, and have it to the full.
>
> (John 10:10)

I was in a web all right, not a web of life but a web of death. Even at the age of ten, I only had two choices to make. One leads to abundant life and one leads to death.

Parents must understand their children need help in understanding their choices. Children can only do this correctly when they have been shielded and guided by their parents.

If my mom had understood this she would not have been so worried about what all the onlookers would think, she would never have given me sugar water or told me never to talk about what had happened. Never! As strict as she was, she loved Gavin, Sonja, and me and wanted what was best for us. I do not blame my mom, as I do not think she knew or understood this. Unfortunately, her ignorance left me feeling totally rejected and unloved, leading me to believe the devil's lie that my mother did not love me.

Thus I chose the path of death and not life, unbeknown to everyone . . . even me.

Four

Loving the Power

ONE DAY I CAME FACE to face with the question of all questions. *Could I ever use my mind power on my brother?* I was soon put to the test.

It was an afternoon after school, and as usual, Gavin and I had an argument, but this time he did something that I took personally. He was allowed to tease me about my weight and how I was a weird freak. This never upset me because I believed everyone was just jealous of my discipline and control. Unfortunately, he attacked my acting abilities by saying I was going to be a disaster in the operetta at school that evening.

I fumed. *No male, absolutely no male, criticizes my acting and singing.* This was the one area I wanted to succeed in and felt I was good at. I let my venomous tongue loose with insults.

He fumed and took one step forward, grabbed me by my throat and lifted me up, leaving my feet dangling in the air. His other hand was forming a fist and I knew he meant me harm. His anger scared me and I felt helpless.

Then it came to me in full force. *No male will ever make me feel helpless ever again!* I began zoning into his mind, channeling as much hate and anger into his mind as I could.

The voices in me were in a frenzy shouting, *More, more, harder, harder.* In my anger, I obeyed their bidding. Gavin stood there in a daze. He suddenly let go his grip around my neck, staggered backwards and then fell. He looked up with such despair and dismay . . . and with such hurt. I was shocked, and he was devastated. I could see a depression of some sort come upon him.

I felt a tinge of guilt, but brushed it aside by convincing myself he needed to be taught a lesson. Depression and insecurity were a small price to pay for wanting to harm me.

Feeling immensely powerful, I said to him, "Now that you know, are you going to tell the whole world?" I laughed and continued, "What are you going to say? Who is ever going to believe you?"

I do not think he ever told anyone what really happened that day. What could he tell them? His friends would think he was delusional. He got up, staggered to his room and slumped down on his bed.

For me, it was a job well done and I continued to push my feelings of guilt away. Now I knew I was safe, no matter which male was out to hurt me. I would be able to overpower any man threatening me in a physical or emotional crisis. My hard work had paid off. It felt like a mission accomplished. I would not have chosen to test this on my brother, but I convinced myself he had pushed me into doing it. Things between us went from bad to worse.

I instinctively knew I would always have to be on my guard with Gavin as he would want to get back at me for what I had done to him. I could feel his anger and resentment towards me. I had managed to make him hate me even more, which meant my sister would eagerly join him. He would not even have to explain to her why, because when it came to me they were always united. I had purposely caused this complete rift between them and me, as I had never forgiven them for laughing at me and saying I was just being overdramatic on that Christmas Eve.

I was a walking time bomb ready to explode. It was so well hidden that no one suspected a thing. As I looked deathly skeletal, I pulled the wool over people's eyes.

—⁓—

It is easy to be fooled by those with anorexia nervosa. Many seem to be very fragile and helpless, but the opposite is quite often, but not always, true. When I hear people say, "Oh, she has an eating disorder," they usually have stereotyped her under the category of eating problem. I cringe at this because there is such a big difference in the spiritual realm between the different eating disorders.

Anorexia makes a slave of the person, controlling the mind, will, and in turn, actions, or lack of them. The obvious results of anorexia are the anorexic body, as well as the ostracizing of oneself from society, together with obsessive-compulsive behaviors of never-ending exercising and calorie counting.

Bulimia also makes a complete slave of the person by controlling the flesh, desires, and emotions. It eventually results in some of the following being produced: swollen neck glands; addictive, unstable, erratic behavior; and wildly swinging moods from neurotic outbursts to catatonic depression.

With both anorexia and bulimia, there is the physical aspect that has to be treated, but that is not where the main battle lies. Both of their wars are not against flesh, but against principalities, powers, strongholds, and arguments.

Both anorexia and bulimia lead to total destruction in various forms. They not only destroy the person, but both slowly destroy those who love and care for that person too. Their destruction devours everything and everyone that is in the path and only stops at death. What can parents, husbands, wives, siblings, friends, or even doctors do when they must war against an unseen stronghold inside a person?

Death is not only when the physical body dies. It can also mean death to a marriage, a job, a relationship, a family unit, a dream, a life purpose, a destiny, and to whatever else the devil (the thief) can bring death. When you hear a person saying, "I am living in hell here on earth" most times it does not start off like that. This "living hell" usually starts off as a form of protection, a pleasure, a surging power, a game, or a peer pressure tryout, a false hope, sometimes even a "good thing." The devil is a deceiver and can come camouflaged in whatever nicety or deception or destruction is necessary. Anorexia and bulimia and all its hooks are but one of the millions of chains he can enslave us with.

—∿—

I fell hook, line, and sinker for the deceiver's path of protection and acceptance, and am ashamed to admit I loved and reveled in the "power" I had come to know because of it. Deep down, I was aware of the evil behind it, but I decided that this power was good and necessary to my cause. It was power to be alien and hostile to all around me, power to deny all emotions and all food, power to exercise six to seven hours a day, power to have only two hours of sleep a day, power to physically punish myself and not feel any pain, and power to get into the mind of a guy and destroy him through controlling his thoughts! I knew I was able to do this not only because of me, but also because of the voices inside of me.

It first started with the hate of men, but then it spilled over into the rest of my life. I began to hate everything. This hate became the fuel that enabled me to do all the things I was doing. Normal ways of living (eating, playing, working, and sleeping) suddenly became loathsome and disgusting to me. This caused me to start judging and condemning everything around me. I was truly disgusted with people who had no discipline, which included almost everyone in my eyes. I saw them as weak and pathetic. It was as if I had curdled inside and become completely sour. This became like an acid that slowly ate away any sweetness that was left within me.

Eventually, I believed I was superior to everyone around me. Other people made me sick. And men went beyond this. They were not worthy to breathe the air of this earth. I saw them as the real dogs of the earth, scum of the earth!

One of the first things that destruction will steal is joy. Nehemiah 8:10 says, "The joy of the Lord is my strength." Joy in one's life has immense power to help overcome many problems because of hope, and this is the last thing that Satan wants.

As a young child, I always used to laugh and smile, but by the time I was twelve I had replaced these with bitter sneering and cursing snarls. I had opened a massive door for the devil to get his claws in. I had made myself an easy target for him, the roaring lion. When a person feels like they are in hell on earth, how can they stand up and fight? They can't!

> The strong spirit of a man will sustain him in bodily pain or trouble, but a weak and broken spirit who can raise up or bear?
>
> (Prov. 18:14 AMP)

I had become bitterly unbearable. No wonder I say I had curdled inside. Vileness was living inside me. There was no space for love, peace, joy, or goodness to grow. The real evil was that I looked so helpless and fragile and stuck in an "eating disorder" that people had no idea what was going on inside of me. I was not even a fully-grown teenager yet, but it was as if poison was my new blood.

A tree is identified by its fruit. Make a tree good, and its fruit
will be good. Make a tree bad, and its fruit will be bad.

(Matt. 12:33 NLT)

The devouring in my life had begun at the age of ten, and
by the age of fourteen, I can honestly say without being overly
dramatic, I was deadly. My self-hate had grown, as well as my
hate directed to others.

My thinking was dangerous and evil. Sometimes, when I
was talking to a boy, I would find myself thinking about what
it would feel like if I could stab him over and over again. Yet,
at other times I would find myself wishing I were dead, and
fantasize about committing suicide. I believed that life was a
waste and I would be better off dead.

Then there was my other life where I was a successful student at school. I had been seen as a potential leader right from
grade eight after being chosen to attend attending a leadership
camp. After the first one, I was nominated every year to go to
these camps.

This eventually placed me on the list to become a prefect,
a student monitor, which was a "have-to" achievement for me.
I do not know why I was made a prefect when I was obviously
acutely anorexic. However, I did not care because I believed I
would be able to use this newfound "legal authority" at school
for my benefit—especially when it came to hurting or humiliating boys who got in my way.

The only negative thing was the true Mt. Kilimanjaro in
my life, my weight. I was still struggling to get under the 30-ki-
logram mark. This was not good because my target for that year

was to get down to 25 kilograms (55 lbs.). The more weight I had lost, the more power I seemed to gain; getting down to 25 kilograms meant I would become even more powerful.

I believed more power meant a greater ability to hurt men. The struggle to lose even more weight became the main cause for me to punish myself even more. Pain was my joy and delight because I used it as a sign that I had managed to destroy my womb. My abdomen was permanently bruised, the burn marks increased, but I covered them up and no one really noticed. Most people probably assumed I wore long, baggy clothes because I was trying to hide my weight.

Five

The Accident

MY DAD WAS PROMOTED AND transferred to the big city of Johannesburg. Because I had become a prefect, it was decided I would remain at the school I was attending. I had no problem with my mom and dad moving because that did not interfere with my goals.

Sonja was away at college and Gavin, being the youngest, would go with them to Johannesburg. I had been invited to board with my friend Bridget's family. I was so glad because hostel life was not for me as it would interfere with my routine, discipline, and punishments.

My parents bought me a motorbike to help me with transportation. Bridget and her family did not interfere with my eating and exercise routines. They found it hard to understand, but they just left me alone. It was good for them that they did or else that would have caused problems.

I was excited because it was my final year of school—1980—and my goal of achieving at least four distinctions was within reach. It promised to be a very good year.

When my music and singing teacher told me about her church and invited me to visit, I wanted to impress her because I had my eye on the leading role in the operetta that year. I convinced Bridget to go with me. One Sunday evening in February, Bridget and I went to the service.

At the end of the meeting, the minister gave the altar call. I wanted to get that role so I decided to go up, hoping to impress the music teacher. Bridget also went with me and we both said what they called "the sinner's prayer." We were told Jesus was now our Lord and Savior and that we were now Christians. I actually felt good—until we got back to Bridget's house.

While she was sleeping, I beat myself up. The voices reminded me I was what that man had called me on the Christmas Eve of 1973. I was a disgusting, vile pig. I was evil, unlikable, unloved, and not worthy to be alive. *They are so right! What was I thinking? How could I let the church people fool me like that?* Filled with vengeance and hate, I beat myself up so much that I winced for hours and wasn't being able to move in my bed.

When Bridget woke up she was a totally different person. She said, "I've been saved! I have Jesus in my heart!" She talked about wanting others to know Jesus was her Christ and her Savior.

"Are you as excited as I am about finding Jesus?" she asked me.

To me she sounded like an alien from Mars! I had no idea what she was going on about, which left me totally confused.

I began to feel very depressed at times, especially when I saw how joyful Bridget had become. I truly wanted to believe I was a good person because of Jesus, but the awareness of how bad and disgusting I was resulted in me hitting or burning myself. I convinced myself that Bridget was living in some weird dream. One day her bubble would burst and she would feel bitter and twisted like me, and realize those church people were lying.

At long last, there was one week left of the first term and then Bridget and I were going on a leadership course that involved river rafting. Every year, Bridget and I would represent our school as leaders. However, this was the first time we were going to experience river rafting and we were both very excited.

The evening before we were to leave on our adventure, I wanted to go and visit my friend Yvette. She was the one person who I was wary of, and yet, I felt drawn to her. Not only was she pretty, but she was always, always kind and loving towards people. When I first saw her sitting across the class from me, her sweetness sickened me. But it eventually pulled me in. She would upset me so many times just because she was so kind. She always had time for people, so much so that I'd help her with her studies. Why would she give up her time to sit and listen to others carry on and on about their lives and all their problems? I saw these people as pathetic weaklings and all I could offer them was disgust.

Even though I despised Yvette's kindness, I really liked her as a friend. Today, I realize that she was a person of compassion, but I did not know this back then. It didn't make sense that we were best friends. Yvette was always loving and giving, while I was a hardened, bitter and hateful person. What a combination! I often wonder how she put up with me.

Yvette was not going on the adventure with us and that is why I wanted to visit her before I left. At her house, Bridgette said, "Don't go on your motorbike to visit Yvette." She kept on saying, "The Holy Spirit is telling me that you must not go."

This really upset me. Inside I had these thoughts going around in my mind. *What's going on? What does she mean by the Holy Spirit was telling her?* She had never been so determined before to stop me from doing something.

When I said, "You're just jealous," she immediately dropped the subject and left it alone. I left the house all upset because I only wanted to have issues with men, not with Bridget.

It had just finished raining when I got on my bike to go and I was thinking about how fresh everything smelled and wondering about Bridget's warning. Suddenly, I saw a car coming straight for me.

He can't see me. It was too late to do anything. The car hit me on my right side, which sent me flying in the air, over the car. Landing on my face, I felt a tearing pain searing through my right leg and cried out in pain.

Hearing the noise of the collision, people streamed out of their homes from all directions. I heard shouting to each other about which one was going to call for help.

"I recognize her. She travels this road every day," a voice said.

A man with a strange accent repeated over and over, "I didn't see her. I'm sorry! I didn't see her."

A woman came running up with a glass saying, "Here, drink some sugar water to help you with the shock." That was not what I wanted to hear. I went from crying in pain to rage and anger. Sugar water! *She just better not come near me*, I fumed silently.

Then I heard Bridget's voice and the voice of Mr. Hitchens, her father. He insisted on being taken over to the driver to smell his breath. His anger helped cool my anger towards the sugar water lady. The driver of the car seemed very confused about being grabbed by Mr. Hitchen, who demanded he open his mouth. Bridget's father calmed down within seconds after the driver allowed him to smell his breath and talked calmly to him.

Bridget was with me when I heard the ambulance sirens. Noise and confusion seemed to reign. Everything began spinning. I wasn't sure if I felt like screaming or if I was screaming when I suddenly felt the prick of an injection. Within seconds, calm descended over me and the pain receded into the background .

After the paramedic cut my jeans open, exposing my leg for all to view, I heard panic in the voices of those around me. "Oh, my gosh! Look how thin she is. She's only skin and bone! Like a skeleton with plastic over it!" The crowd did not seem to worry about the bone protruding out of my leg. They were more interested in my weight!

Don't start now, I thought, *I am in too much pain to attack.*

I was rushed off by the ambulance to the local hospital. Mr. Hitchen reassured me he would contact my parents immediately, and they would meet me at the hospital.

My parents were at my bedside when I woke up. I was in pain but all I could think about was finding the man who did this to me and making him pay big time. After another pain injection I floated off to sleep.

—ᴍ—

The next morning when I woke up, my face was full of bandages and hurting. My leg, which was in a cast from the tip of my toes right up to my hips, caused me immense pain. My mood matched the pain, as I was upset about missing the leadership camp.

To my surprise I had an early visitor. None other than the man who did this to me! I could not believe it. I did not even have to go and look for him. He was right here in front of me. Was he going to be sorry! I was ready to channel every ounce of anger and hate that I could get from the fuel banks within me to zone in on this man. I imagined how he would cringe and fall apart as my mind tore him up inside, leaving him as devastated as he had left me.

I was stopped dead in my tracks. Something was preventing me from zoning into his mind. There was something different about this man. He seemed to be covered with protection preventing me from harming him.

To get into someone's mind, I always looked straight into that person's eyes, then locked in and zoned in until I was there.

When I did that with the man standing in front of me, I could see something around him. I did not know if it was light or energy. To make it worse, I could literally see a light in his eyes.

There was definitely something there. I just knew I had to back off. I sensed danger for myself. I did not know what danger, but I knew it was something that would expose my evil ways.

This made me dislike the man even more as I felt so powerless against him. He seemed to be totally oblivious to my scorn and unaware of this protection around him.

Confused, I wondered what I was fooling around with when I used my mind power to destroy. There were a lot of things I did not understand.

The man in front of me seemed to me to be glowing. He also seemed to be solid and firm, not false and flimsy, as I had perceived so many males to be.

Why am I so wary of what is inside him?

I had no idea then that Christians are told to put on the full armor of God. Today I know how vitally important this armor is. My wariness about attacking this man with my mind was caused by this protection surrounding him. To make matters worse, next to him stood his smiling wife, who I could see also had the same thing around her as well!

I wondered, *Who are these people?*

Therefore put on the full armor of God, so that when the day of evil comes, you may be able to stand your ground, and after you have done everything to stand. Stand firm then, with the belt of truth buckled around your waist, with the breastplate of righteousness in place, and with your feet fitted with readiness that comes from the gospel of peace. In addition to all this, take up the shield of faith, with which you can extinguish all the flaming arrows of the evil one. Take the helmet of salvation and the sword of the Spirit, which is the word of God. And pray in the Spirit on all occasions with all kinds of prayers and requests.

(Eph. 6:13–18)

This invisible barrier I could see around them made the voices inside me frantic! They were yelling at me, *Pull away! Pull away from them.* It was eerie.

This protection was real and alive but completely invisible, yet, I knew it was there. I actually felt fear, something I had not felt for a very long time. It was usually me putting fear into a guy's mind. I did not like receiving my own medicine.

I was really dumbfounded by what was going on, but had to suppress these feelings as the man was standing right at my bedside, way too close for comfort. I felt stifled, as if I were the one being strangled. I got very worked up because I could not get myself to attack him with hate and anger. I just had to lie there like a helpless mummy and did not like it one bit.

He smiled kindly and shocked me by asking, "Please forgive me for the accident."

I was dumbfounded. Here was a man asking me to forgive *him*? This did not fit into my image of men. He went on to explain he was a pastor from America and had only been in the country for two weeks.

A minister? I thought, *No, no! Why can't he be a villain?*

He seemed to know what I was thinking. "I belong to the Baptist Church and I am here as a missionary."

Minister or no minister, he must suffer, I tried to convince myself.

As I lay there, the voices inside me began yelling at me. *Leave him alone. He is trouble,* one said.

Pull yourself together. Stop being such a weakling and teach this man a lesson, said the other.

No don't! said the other voice within me. *We will be exposed.*

Who on earth are we?" I wondered.

My thoughts were interrupted by the minister's voice. "Let me introduce myself. I am Pastor Pete. I know you are Michele and I am so pleased to meet you. I am sorry it is in such awful circumstances." And then with a broad smile he turned towards his wife and said, "This is my beautiful wife Mom Susan."

She smiled at me just as warmly and said, "Hello, Michele. I am so sorry that we have to meet in circumstances like this, but I am truly so pleased to meet you."

So nice, so sweet and I just did not know how to do either sweet or nice. I suddenly felt like the sugar water the lady had offered me the night before.

Then Pastor Pete took my hand and did not release it. He held it in both of his hands. This was not a wise thing to do with me as I automatically panicked. He noticed my startled reaction.

"I am so sorry. I didn't mean to scare you. Do you mind if we lift you up to the Lord in prayer?"

As he said this, sweet Mom Susan took my other hand in her hands.

I lay there startled, thinking again, *Who are these people?* I did not do "touchy-feely" things very well, but I gave a tiny nod. Not only was I in shock with this, my thoughts were racing. *Who is the Lord? Is he God? But there is the Father, Son and Holy Ghost. So, who is Lord now?"*

The voices inside me were screaming as if they were being burned. I was so confused. What was going on? I did not like these people holding my hands because I felt as if they could see right through me. I started to wiggle my hands out of theirs, but as I did, they simultaneously let go of my hands.

But it was not over yet! They then each put a hand on my shoulder and stretched their other hands towards me with their palms facing me. To make it even worse, they started praying out loud. I was sure even the people in the next ward could hear!

What is going on? I had plans of annihilating this man, but, instead, he and his wife were right here in control of the situation and praying for me.

Then he said it. "In Jesus' Name."

Why did he say that? It left me feeling so uncomfortable. I mean, after all, it is God we are talking to . . . so *what has Jesus got to do with it? I know He is the Son of God and all of that, but why do people have to say "in Jesus' Name"?*

I must have repeated "in Jesus' Name" out loud because Pastor Pete thought I was responding to his prayer.

"Ah, you must also be a Christian then."

What on earth made him say that? I mumbled something, uncertainly. I mean, that is what they told me at that church when I went forward that night. "Now you are a Christian."

"So tell me, where do you fellowship?"

Why is he using such weird words? What does he mean by fellowship? I looked at him. He must mean which church I went to. So I told him.

"Well Michele, this is such a blessing to hear where you stand in your faith."

Now he says blessing and faith. Where is this man from? Jupiter? Mars? Definitely not America! He is so weird! How does he know where I stand? I mean, I don't know where I stand and here he is telling me he does.

My mind was reeling from all the questions spinning around in my head. What made it worse was he seemed to know what was going on inside of me. It was not very nice being on the receiving end. It left me feeling exposed, and yet too weary to react.

He seemed so genuine and kind. It was strange for me to be thinking any man was kind. This was way beyond my perception of males. He really appeared to be kind, concerned, and gentle. No way! Something must be wrong as men just aren't like this at all. The exception was my dad who I knew I could trust.

Charles is also like that. Shocked, I wondered, *Where did his name pop up from?*

Yeah, but then he dumped you and moved away, a voice inside me reminded me. I felt like crying at this point because Charles was still a very sore point in my life. I tried not to think about him, ever! And now, of all times, I was!

The pastor saw I was upset and must have thought it had to do with the accident. He said, "We have already got you on our prayer chain and we confidently trust the Lord for a full recovery."

This is getting out of control! A prayer chain? What on earth is that? What is with this man and his wife and his words and his concern and his genuine kindness towards me?

This was really more than I could handle. I gave him little nod, not knowing what else to do as I felt totally confused and helpless. The strange thing was I was not at all angry with him for this helplessness.

I was very aware of the invisible protection around him, so there was no way I was going to take him on mentally. The strange thing was that I did not want to either. He reminded me of Yvette.

Yvette, Charles, and this couple were very kind and concerned and interested in the wellbeing of others. What was with these types of people? Why were they always serving other people, and why are they always willing to help others without thinking about how it might put them at a disadvantage? And allowing others to take up their time?

I much preferred "normal" humans, who were always ready to argue, fight, criticize, condemn, mock, put me down, or ignore me. They were much easier to handle because I knew I could attack them. All these gentle, kind, and loving people were overpowering and left me feeling weak. The mind control over people I enjoyed seemed to disappear out of the window when it came to dealing with them.

Pastor Pete must have noticed I was deep in thought and feeling very, very uncomfortable.

"Well Michele! I am sure you are longing to sleep, so we are going to go. Please remember that you are in our prayers continually. If you need any special prayer, just let us know. Mom Susan and I will come by tomorrow to see how you are doing. We are so grateful you are out of surgery and everything is stable. Goodbye, see you tomorrow."

Thank goodness! He was just too much to bear. I just wanted to be left alone so I could go over this visit in my mind. There were so many questions for which I did not have the answers. This was something I did not like at all.

I had got so good at scheming and manipulating when necessary that I was not used to not being in control. Pastor Pete and his wife had definitely been the ones in control in their visit. I liked the feeling of power and being in control, so this was not something I was going to sit back and take lightly.

I had to find out what it was that these people had that left me feeling so exposed and vulnerable. Why was I unable to strike out at them? I felt at their mercy. But if I was at their mercy, why did I not feel threatened? Why did I sense they did not want to hurt or destroy me and actually seemed really concerned about me?

No, this must be a lie, I thought. *They are just hiding their true selves from me. I bet you if I give them a chance, they will destroy me. It is a trick!*

Then it dawned on me that during the four years of friendship with Yvette, I had never seen her be mean to anyone, talk about anyone, harm anyone, or seem to think badly of anyone. I could not say she was hiding anything at all. She was truly sincere and kind.

Pastor Pete and Mom Susan seemed to be exactly the same. Why were they like this? I could not understand it. It could not be because they were Christians, as the other people I knew who said they were Christians were pretending, just like me. They schemed, hurt others around them and always seemed to be fighting among themselves. And they did not say, "In the name of Jesus!"

That saying left me feeling so uncomfortable. Come to think of it, even Bridget had started saying it. *Why do they have to say that?* I went up to the altar the same time that Bridget went up. I did the same as she did that night in church. Why was she saying "In the name of Jesus" all the time? *I don't say it!* And Bridget had also started becoming "nice!"

I did not know it then, but this was love, true, abiding God-given love. "And now these three remain: faith, hope and love. But the greatest of these is love" (1 Cor. 13:13). This was what I sarcastically classified as "nice and sweet." It was this love I could not fight. All my schemes, bitterness, stubbornness, rebellion, unforgiving ways, and resentment, which came from so much hate and anger in me were all at the mercy of this love.

This power of love made a joke of the power I felt after using my hate. One touch of genuine love and it took every ounce of me to stop the walls I had built around me from tumbling down. I enjoyed feeling powerful and full of hate. This love was something I could ill afford.

I just knew I had to stay away from it if I wanted to keep all my vileness hidden. I had no desire to get rid of this darkness within me. It was my weapon of protection against my enemy, men. I had to destroy the enemy, before they could hurt or destroy me. I firmly believed the mission of men in life was to hurt and destroy females. I believed, given the chance, every man would do what that man did to me in the hotel room.

Pastor Pete really upset me because men are not supposed to be kind and genuine and concerned. I mean, how on earth was I supposed to fight against this? The only thing I could do was to retaliate, which I hated having to do. It was the first time a male had ever beaten me at my own game. He did this without lifting a finger or doing anything vindictive against me.

I eventually convinced myself that Pastor Pete was just pretending because he did not want to get into trouble with the police because of the accident.

To add to all my confusion, the voices inside me were saying, *Leave him alone. He will expose you. He is sly and trying to catch you out.*

No he is not! He really is concerned about me as a person and my well-being, I answered them.

No, he isn't! He does not care about you at all. He is being so nice because he is scared that you will sue him for your injuries.

Rubbish!" I defended.

No, you're rubbish and don't forget that. You are rubbish. You are rubbish!

Those words kept boring into my mind. Feeling defeated, I could not argue with that statement as I knew it was true, and this clawed right into me. To cover up any form of rejection, I told myself, *Anyway, what are you doing arguing with yourself?*

I could sometimes almost feel something inside me smile when I was being deflated. This was one of those times. It made me think there was something else living inside me beside myself.

What a stupid thought!

The following morning, after a tormented night, I decided that Pastor Pete was acting all nice to try and get the charge laid against him dropped. After convincing myself of this, I felt better because I felt my sense of power returning.

I also decided I needed to get out of this town, far away from this scheming man and his wife. I was going to tell my parents I wanted to go home to Johannesburg. I would get them to see things my way, I always had. I just had to dangle the carrot of helping me get better in front of them and they would agree.

Just then the doctor, my parents, and my sister came in my room. *This is not a good sign.*

The doctor said this to me, "Michele, unfortunately, your cast has become full of blood, which means the leg is still in a bit of trouble."

Leg in trouble? Please! What has my leg done to get into trouble? Run away? Why can't he just tell me what is wrong with it medically. I am sixteen, not six."

"And so," he continued, "we will have to go back into the operating theatre now to sort the leg out."

Inside I heard screaming because I was not going to be able to leave right then and get away from the kind and sweet Jesus people.

Six

The Walking Skeleton

THE DOCTOR WAS PLEASED WITH how the last operation went. Now it was only a matter of healing, which would happen at home in far away Johannesburg.

I was glad to get away from Witbank, but I knew I had some serious new routines and punishments waiting for me when I arrived in Johannesburg.

The thought of me softening as I had in hospital left me in a state of panic, so I added another punishment rule to my routine to remind myself who I was.

Once in Johannesburg, I only allowed myself to bathe in ice-cold water and I had to leave the window open. Bathing with a cast from the tip of my toe to my hip was quite a procedure, which I insisted on doing by myself. I did not need or want anyone's help. Winter was on its way and I knew I would freeze. However, this would remind me every day of what a terribly disgusting person I was. But while I was freezing, I would use up extra calories in my attempt to keep warm. *This will help me lose weight.* Every bit of weight loss counted in my favor.

I was convinced I had put on a ton of weight with all that lying about in the hospital bed.

Regardless of what people said, when I looked in the mirror I would see a big fat house of a person. I felt gigantic and hideous, a whole 33 kilograms (nearly 73 lbs.) heavy, with the solid cast on! This disgusted me. I knew people were just telling me I was too thin because they were jealous of my ability to be so disciplined, and they were not able to achieve the same results. I convinced myself that my weight had nothing to do with it. In fact, they were not concerned about me or my weight at all.

On arriving in Johannesburg, the neighbors were very interested in getting a glimpse of me. I had been in the country until then and so I was also very intrigued about them.

I was surprised to see that Gavin's friends were a lot older than him. Sonja was still studying in Kwa-Zulu Natal and did not live at home anymore.

Seeing that Gavin's friends were older, I wasted no time. This was exciting for me, a whole new ballgame. I started to test my mind games on these new friends of my brother. *This is going to be great.* Now I would be able to see if I had become strong enough to protect myself against young men (not teenage boys) without ever having to use physical force.

This immediately caused the old walls of hate between Gavin and me to resurface. He did not challenge me on this. I don't think he had forgotten what I had done to him. I threatened him then that if he ever got in my way I would not hesitate to attack him again, and I meant it. Things were back to normal as far as that was concerned. Sometimes I would catch him staring at me with complete dislike, and as always, suspicion. I would just smile as I had him right where I wanted him to be, under my control.

The doctors had told me to rest completely because of the extent of damage to the leg, but they didn't fool me. I knew they were just trying to keep me immobilized so I would become fatter! Instead, I made sure that my six-hour-a-day exercise routines, my punishments, and my new ice- cold water bath rules began immediately. There were times when I felt exhausted and dizzy, but I would have a few harsh words with myself, give myself a burn and an abdominal beating or two, and then carry on.

Having a cast from my toes right up to my hips wasn't any fun. I always managed to stifle any desires to just lie back and quit, as that was not a part of my vocabulary. Because of these desires I enforced a new rule. I only allowed myself two hours of sleep a night, as I felt my usual four hours of sleep was just too much! This would prevent me from slipping up.

Many times, my mom would come in to my room in the early hours of the morning and ask me, "What are you doing? Why are you not sleeping?" I always managed to come up with some lame excuse. I would have to exercise at times to keep myself awake and then, when it was time to go to sleep,

I would hobble into bed and literally pass out. Two hours later the alarm would go off. I would exercise to wake myself up and get going for the day. I was very determined not to weaken and not to get any fatter than I already was: 30 kilograms (66 lbs.) was way too much for me to accept.

I had worked too hard for so many years to get where I was. I would rather die than be weaker than males in any area of combat. My mom expressed concern that I was losing more weight, but I was deaf to her comments. I still believed that I was as big as a house. I had checked off 29.5 kilograms, but I was still way too fat. It revolted me. I revolted myself.

My brother's friends in the city were very different from his old friends in the mining towns. In the mining towns his friends accepted me as I was. They did not even mind me riding motorcycles with them to school. These city friends became nervous when I was near, and always seemed to try to sneak past me. I was never able to corner one of his friends to see if my mind power was strong enough to destroy one of them. I began to get frustrated because I was not able to lure even one of them into my trap to experiment.

For this not to become an obsession, I thought, *I'll start once my cast is off. Then I will be able to trap them and they will not be able to sneak away.*

I believed this was a sign of weakness in me and so I added another punishment. I would cut down on my eating even further. That would teach me a good hard lesson for not being able to get a hold of and zone into one my brother's friends.

So I put my new eating routine into action. I allowed myself a teaspoon of peanut butter in the morning with a cup of tea.

I would make my tea out of half a cup of hot milk with honey and the rest tea. I would be allowed another cup of my tea at lunchtime and another at suppertime. For supper I would be allowed three teaspoons of jelly with two teaspoons of yogurt. I felt that was more than enough food for me for one day.

I added ice blocks to my ice-cold baths. I also increased my six to eight-hours of extreme strenuous exercises a day. This was easy to do because of my two-hour sleeping rule. I did not forget the beatings or the burnings. Not a day went by without me hurling all the verbal insults at myself that the man had given me on that Christmas Eve. I had also managed to find my own unique insults to add to the list.

I never relaxed or rested for one day—the voices never allowed me to. The voices, *my* voices (by this time I did not know whose voices they were) would never let me miss anything, ever! If I experienced more dizziness, I would punish myself with more exercises to show my body I was in control. This was easy to do because both my parents were at work and my brother was always with his friends. If they came to our house, they would either be outside working on their motorcycles or in his room, out of my way.

One day I heard one of his friends tell him, "Your sister really scares me." My brother was irritated with that remark and told him, "Just ignore her." This made me feel extremely good because I knew then they were aware I was around.

One day I called Elsie our domestic worker to the bathroom because I needed more soap during one of my two ice baths a day. I had a whole twenty-two hours of being awake every day and so two baths would take up the time and help burn calories. When she opened the bathroom door and saw me sitting on the side of the bath with my back towards her she burst out hysterically and ran away.

When I had finished, I found her and asked, "What's wrong?"

She started speaking in English mixed with her African language. She said, "You are like a ghost! You are cursed and are going to die! You are a walking skeleton." After that incident, she stayed clear of me. I did not understand why as I believed she was exaggerating. I went to check in the mirror and saw she was wrong. I was still so fat. It made me furious at my body. I hated myself even more and became so angry with myself that I just wanted to die.

My parents were stressed over me, but that did not bother me at all. After six weeks, I went back to the doctor in Witbank for a check-up. They changed the cast and sent me back to Johannesburg for some more rest.

I convinced my parents I had to get back to school because it was my last year and I did not intend to fail. To me failing would be not getting my four distinctions and a scholarship, which I had worked for since the beginning of high school, five years before. I had to get them because this would put me above many of the guys. This was my aim, to be cleverer than males. There was no way that I was going to allow a silly leg injury to ruin all my hard work.

My parents took me back to school. It wasn't as if they were blind; they saw my condition and did care. But they didn't know what to do to save me. Perhaps they allowed me to manipulate them in the hope that what I was asking for might save me. I convinced them that letting me go back to school would save me and they put their faith in that.

Putting our faith in a human being is the biggest gamble we can make. I do not say this to be cruel, but to be honest. My mom and dad did not understand this then and believed me when I said going back to school would save me. They were so desperate that they grabbed onto that without stopping to ask how that would save me. I had been destroying myself for six years so how would I suddenly stop and change if I went back to school? It was an empty promise. My mom and dad put their faith in that empty promise. I was cruel. I say this because I knew if I gave them an empty promise, it would work—which it did.

But my manipulative act backfired. Returning to my old school was a disaster. Everyone saw me as a victim and a loser. I continually heard the whispers of "shame," which was a nightmare for me.

To make it worse, I was called in by Mr. Orchans, the guidance teacher, who was also in charge of the student monitors. He looked very grave as I walked in and I knew it was not going to be good. I assumed he was about to tell me the school had decided to take my monitor badge away. I was wrong. He had called me in to inform me I had missed so much schoolwork that they were not sure I would be able to pass matric—to graduate. He said I should rather go home to fully recuperate.

Shocked was putting it mildly. I was crushed. I was shattered. It seemed I was getting my own medicine back in triple doses. I walked out in a daze. I played the victim of the school's negativity to my parents. Once again they followed my lead in the hope that it would save me.

I went back home, leg still in a cast. There I joined Damelin College, because I did not intend to fail. I intended to get my distinctions and with that a scholarship.

With my strict daily regime and me catching up all the schoolwork I had missed, two hours of sleep seemed way too much. There were times I did not sleep for two or three days. I dealt with the dizzy spells just as I dealt with my eight-hour exercise routine, my ice baths, my punishments and my eating plans. I was too busy to start working on my brother's friends. I had distinctions and a scholarship to obtain. I would have to wait to try to destroy one of his friends during the ten-day winter break coming up.

It was time for my cast to come off. This had been the second cast since the successful operation and I was tired of lugging it around. Even though it was lighter than the first one, I was looking forward to having it removed. Back we went to the country doctors and off came the cast. At first, I was in shock at the sight of my leg, but eventually I got used to the scars and the bump protruding from where the bone had come out. It felt great to be so free and light.

I started the holidays with great enthusiasm. Even though it was a short holiday school break, for me it was just a normal Wednesday. My alarm rang at its usual time, four a.m. I woke up and started my exercises to make sure that I would not laze around, or worse, fall asleep.

It was still very dark outside, with frost forming a layer on the grass. I would exercise outside because I believed I needed to use more calories just to keep my body warm. I was freezing with only a T-shirt and shorts on, but this was part of my way of becoming stronger-willed than men and I ignored the shivering. To give in to the cold would be an absolute sign of weakness and that was too disgusting to contemplate doing.

Later, I heard my mom and then my dad get up and follow their normal morning routines. I heard my parents going off to work followed by the sound of my brother's motorbike leaving the driveway, as he went to see one of his friends. When I heard his bike's high revs in the distance, I smiled. I was alone.

I loved being on my own. I had grown so used to it from childhood that I was very possessive of it now. After finishing my three-hour session of exercising, I allowed myself breakfast: half a teaspoon of peanut butter and a cup of tea. I then proceeded with schoolwork that I was given to do by the college. By the time the term started, I would be up to date and ready to start preparing for the distinctions I had to acquire.

At about ten o'clock, I gave my body its normal mid-morning snack of water. As usual, I was struggling to concentrate by this hour. That meant it was time for my next round of exercising. After my workout, I had my usual ice-cold bath, which was no longer punishment for me but normal. The only part I had grown to hate about bathing was the prone position. I could never get comfortable. I was always sore because each vertebra along my spine had a swollen bruised callous on it.

One day, after my bath I got up and grabbed my towel when I began to feel dizzy. This did not worry me as I was quite used to these spells. But this time it was different as the dizziness did not leave me. Eventually I felt myself falling forward and blacking out. When I woke up, I realized I had fallen out of the bath and hit my head against the basin. I panicked and quickly unlocked the door. Deep down I knew I was getting dizzy spells because I was starved. One doesn't get a bruised callous on every single vertebra for nothing. Who was I trying to fool?

Once again dizziness overcame me. It felt as if something hit me and sent me flying. I sank back into the empty oblivion of blackness. This time it was a complete shutdown. I felt hollow inside, absolutely nothingness, and so very alone. It felt awful.

I was so scared because there was no one to hold my hand in this consuming black monster. I say black monster because this black hole was alive. It was gnawing at me, eating me up. I could hear it gnaw, gnaw, gnaw, bit by bit! I cried out, but no one was there. Inside this black monster, I screamed that no one had ever loved me and no one had ever cared. The emotional pain went searing through my whole being as I heard my sobs echoing out into the pitch darkness.

The voices that had become part of the black monster were repeating inside me, *No one loves you. No one cares. No one loves you. No one cares.*

Then High Pitch jovially shrieked out, *Die, you must rather die. Die, you must rather die. No one loves you. No one cares. Die, you must rather die . . .*

As High Pitch was saying this, I felt the black monster consume me, pulling me deeper into the hole. I knew I was looking at death and I was aware there was absolutely no one there for me. Oh, it hurt so deep within me, so very badly, as I realized how utterly alone I had always been. I felt terrified that I might die inside this black monster and it just did not matter to anyone.

The voices in me told me, *Give up . . . nobody loves you or cares.*

They were so right. I was so very alone in this world.

The truth was, I hated being alone. I was so very lonely and it really hurt. Deep within me, I knew I was not only starving myself to death because of my hate for males and my will to become better and stronger than them. It was also because I was hurting deep, deep down inside. This produced such consuming self-hate because my hurt feelings represented weakness. Whenever I needed someone to hold me tight and safe and love me, I was given sugar water instead because I was not worth the effort or time. They wanted me out of the way. Maybe it was better for me just to go.

A memory came to me of being placed alone in a dark black closet, Sister Paulina's favorite punishment for me. I was four-and-a-half, turning five, when my parents whisked me off to join my sister at a Roman Catholic convent. I was in the pre-juniors dormitory with about forty beds. One night I was scared so I silently walked along the dark corridor to Sister Paulina's room and went inside crying.

She jumped up from what she was doing in a fuming rage. She started screaming at me, grabbed my arm and dragged me back down the corridor, but she didn't take me to my bed. She took me to the linen closet room with its shelves piled up with white sheets and unlocked it.

"I'm going to teach you a lesson for being such a bad girl!" she said, and locked me in the dark closet with the light off all night. I was petrified, cold, and so lonely. I was too scared to cry in case I awakened the "ghosts."

Sister Paulina decided to make a habit of this routine so I would never be a bad girl again. That hurt me so much and left me feeling rejected, alone, scared, and confused. What had I done to Sister Pauline? I went to her room because I was scared and wanted her help. Why did she call me a bad girl? Was I bad because I was scared and I was crying?

After that I just shut down. It had left a scar on my little five-year-old heart.

I decided that I was a tough girl and would never go crying to anyone ever again. I did not speak to my parents for the rest of that year. Years later, my mom told me it had really scared and worried them when I refused to talk to them.

My thoughts of that spooky black linen cupboard and being a bad girl were interrupted by High Pitch screaming in my mind, *You are such an ugly, disgusting, and vulgar fat pig.* According to High Pitch, that was why no one had ever loved me or wanted to be near me. I was just not worth it.

I let out a long, loud wolf-like howl, but it bounced off the black monster back to me. No one else heard me except the voices.

The voices then gurgled out to me again, *You are just not worth it.*

I agreed. *I know.*

Seven

Voices

I DO NOT KNOW HOW long I stayed in that state, but I do know what brought me out of the terrifying blackness!

Michele! Michele, what are you doing? Why are you doing this to yourself?

I heard the voices inside me shouting, *Do not listen!*

What? Are you crazy! How can I ignore this glorious and mighty, yet fearful thundering roar speaking to me?

I had always felt that no one knew what was going on inside of me. How very wrong I was. The second I heard the thunderous voice vibrating throughout my whole being, I instantly felt exposed and wanted to hide away.

This is the voice of God. My mind and every cell in my body was instantly crying this out to me. Why on earth were the other voices telling me not to listen? I could not run away from this thunderous, all-powerful voice. No one can!

I also realized, *God knows everything about me. Everything!* I had no qualms or doubts about that either, as my inner being shouted out that all my darkness lay exposed before God, even my very dark secret.

Now strangely aware of my inner self, I could feel the voices inside of me tremble in fear. Just like when I had felt them giggle, I could feel them tremble. It literally felt as if these voices were little people inside me who were scared out of their wits.

Psalms 69:5 (AMP) says, "O God, You know my folly and blundering; my sins and my guilt are not hid from You."

God's mighty thunderous voice seemed to fill the whole house, and together we shook from this thunderous encounter. I say the house was shaking with me because of the fear shaking within me. I was beyond shock. As God spoke, another part of me shouted within to "stand to attention," "bow down" and "fall on my face" all at the same time, as this was God Almighty talking.

I responded by blurting out, "Oh, my God!"

This outburst made me believe this was the end for me! I had just used God's name in vain. I stammered, "I'm sorry, I'm sorry! I mean . . . Oh, oh, oh!" I did not know what to say. I had expected a bolt of lightning to flash down through the roof and strike me down.

I was more terrified of this happening than of the black monster eating me up. At that very moment, I really thought I was going to die for using God's name in vain.

Then, as if in the third person, I heard myself begging God to forgive me. I began making promises that I would change, and all I would do if He gave me another chance. I could not believe how I was spewing out all of those promises. I even screamed out my dark secret and promised God that I would never ever talk about murder again.

The voices in me were screeching by this time, but I did not care.

My mom had always told us, "Don't make promises if you can't keep them." I had used empty promises as part of my manipulation plots all the time. I did not know then that the Bible also clearly tells us not to make promises that are not kept.

I heard myself promising, "I'll change."

"I will never use mind control ever again."

"I will begin to eat . . ."

While making all these wild promises to God Almighty, I wrapped a towel around myself. Then I dropped, scrambling on my hands and knees to gather my clothes and put them on so I would no longer feel so naked before God. However, even with my clothes on, my nakedness before God lingered in my soul.

Suddenly, a whirlwind of dizziness overcame me again and I felt myself hitting the floor as I slowly started sinking back into that black consuming monster. Once again, I was in the terrifying pit and all alone. Nobody cared. I remember saying to myself, *God is too angry with me. I am going to die.* I let out another anguishing howl and, as before, it bounced off the black monster and came back to me.

After what seemed like an eternity in that black monster, I woke up in the hospital. I looked around and saw I was hooked up to a multitude of tubes, even one in my nose.

God heard me and is letting me live. What about all my promises I made to God? I was already trying to forget about them as cynicism made its way back into me.

Everyone who approached my bed was so serious. *It can't be all that bad. I'm alive.* Why I had to have all the tubes going into me was a mystery. After all, I had only become slightly dizzy and fallen out of the bath. Yes, I had looked death in the face and that alone nearly scared me to death. However, I did not die. I was still alive.

Even though I had also come face to face with how very alone and lonely I was, I had already boxed up and hidden that realization somewhere deep down within me, never to be reopened! I felt the whole incident would be best forgotten. God had given me another chance, so I could just forget what had happened.

I cringe now when I think of how dishonoring and ungrateful I had been.

It was surreal to see my mom and dad walk towards my bed with grave faces. *What is wrong with them?* It was as if someone had died. I felt a lot better already and was ready to go home and carry on with my life as usual.

My parents told me that I would have to remain in hospital because I was very seriously sick and could die. The anorexia nervosa had reached a lethal stage.

Not this again.

My mom picked up on my attitude and got all worked up. "Michele, your starving caused you to slip into unconsciousness and you could have died!"

My dad could see how upset she was and how indignant I was. He gave me one look and said, "Stop this foolishness and apologize to your mother for your insolence."

"Sorry. But why does everyone have to be so overly dramatic?"

My dad in his quiet, yet very serious tone said, "Enough!"

I kept silent.

Dr. Johannes, my gentle family doctor who I really liked, came in and spoke to me, along with another doctor. "Do you know how serious your situation is?"

What situation? Just because I had a big dizzy spell and fainted, my situation is suddenly critical and I can die?

Dr. Johannes sensed the tension around my bed and softly said, "Michele, you slipped into unconsciousness because of starvation and could have died."

No, I thought, *I could have died earlier on because I had said God's name in vain. That is what really happened.* Who were they trying to con? I did not buy it at all; I just did not. After all I thought I was still as huge as a house!

I tried to forget about thinking I was going to die when I slipped back into that black monster. My hair stood up as I remembered how terrifying and lonely it was. I then said to myself, *No, I've already boxed that all up. I'm not going to go there ever again! Get rid of the word lonely; it does not exist.*

Obviously, the five-week period of starvation I put myself through might have been too long. *No!* I determined. *I'm still having my half a teaspoon of peanut butter and a cup of milk tea. It's more than enough food for a day.*

Then it hit me! I suddenly knew what the doctors and my parents were trying to do. They were all trying to weaken me so they could win and get me to do their bidding. Did they really believe that I could not see through their trickery by trying to scare me by telling me that I could die?

No, I am not going to die because I have just faced death and God let me live. No matter what they do, I will not fall for their tricks.

High Pitch yelled, *That's right. It is a trick. They want you to become a pig. A big, fat, roly-poly pig! Fight them! Fight them!*

Hearing High Pitch made me tighten my lips, empty all of the air out of my lungs and stare straight ahead of me. I felt a hand on my shoulder and then heard Dr. Johannes's calm voice. "It's okay, Michele. You can breathe in. We're not going to hurt you."

He had the nurses bring a full-length mirror and place it in front of me so I could see how emaciated I really was. They saw me as just a skeleton with skin on, but when I looked into the mirror, I saw a big, fat, ugly pig staring back at me. There was no skeleton anywhere in sight. *Why are they trying to do this?* When I didn't see a skeleton reflected in the mirror, those around me seemed upset.

My mom then asked, "What about the fact that you are being fed with tubes? Would they do this if it weren't necessary?"

"Exactly," I yelled back. "How could you do this without my permission?"

I felt I was already at an age where sticking a tube up my nose without asking me was a big mistake. *Someone is going to fry from my mental attack*, I determined. At that point, I was even ready to use my mental powers on my parents if I had to. I had forgotten the promise I had made to God that I would no longer use mental powers on anyone.

Putting my hands on my head, I shouted, "Leave me alone. Just go away."

My mom cut through with, "No! Not this time, my girl. This time you will do what we say."

But they didn't know I was not telling my parents to go away—I was telling the voices to go away.

High Pitch screamed within me, *They are trying to trick you. They are not worth listening to.*

You're right, I said to myself. The voices were once again my friends. *These people are trying to trick me into caving in. That won't ever happen!*

The voices chuckled with glee.

These people must really think I'm stupid. There is no critical situation here. I feel absolutely fine. I was still shaking inside from the black monster, but now that it was gone, I thought I was fine. But I knew deep down that everything was not fine. *Why would I have promised God I would start eating?* I knew that my situation was not very good at all.

A desperate urge came over me to talk to someone about what had happened when I stared death in the face inside that black monster and thought I was going to die. *Perhaps Pastor Pete and Mom Susan would understand!* I had a sudden longing to talk to them about it. They would understand just how terrified I was. They would believe me if I told them I thought I was dead and stuck in a consuming black monster of harsh emptiness. I knew this would be impossible as they lived too far away. A part of me felt relieved at this, but another part of me felt heartbroken.

"Michele," Dr. Johannes said, turning to me with a kind look on his face, "You have a very critical case of acute anorexia nervosa. After some serious discussion, we believe that it would be best for you to be institutionalized."

"What! I'm going to a mad house?"

"No, not all institutions are for mentally unstable patients. There are other types of institutions as well. In your case, you need help for your eating disorder. You will only be sent there after some medical treatment here as you are very seriously undernourished."

"Eating disorder? I don't have an eating disorder. It is only a punishment routine that I am on. All because I have the ability to discipline myself and achieve what all of these idiots cannot do.

There was only one solution left for me: let the mind games begin. Once again the promises I had made to God came into my mind, but I was able to push them away. *God will understand I am doing this because they are trying to destroy me.*

Since there were two doctors standing in front of me, I was not sure if I would be able to achieve the results I wanted with my mental powers. I had only worked on a one-on-one basis in the past. Now I had to deal with two minds at once. I called on every ounce of hate and evil in me to zone in on them. After a few minutes, both of them left, along with my parents. Something had taken place, but I did not know what. Both doctors seemed to be heavy in thought, but I was unsure whether I had gotten through to them.

What am I going to do? I was going to be sent off to some mental institution. The thought of going to such a place left me devastated. They would find out about the voices and my games. I just could not go.

Once again, I thought of another one of the promises I had made to God—that I would do whatever the doctors and my parents told me to do. As I had done earlier, I pushed it to the back of my mind as I waited to see if my mental powers had worked on the doctors.

I looked up toward the heavens and said out aloud, "I will, I promise, just not this time." This was asking too much of me. I could not do it! I would not do it! My parents came back in the room and I wanted to object to going to the mental institution, but no excuse came to mind.

I would rather die . . . go back into that black monster.

The voices started jumping up and down inside of me. Were the voices just other parts of me or something worse? I no longer had control of this and I could not risk anyone finding out. High Pitch, in that wiry voice I had come to know so well, said, *No, you won't. We have taken care of that. In fact, the doctors' minds were like putty in our hands.*

What do you mean? I asked him.

But then our inner conversation was cut off by my mom's questioning, judgmental voice piercing through.

"Michele, we have just spoken to Dr. Johannes and he has informed us that, after consideration, you will no longer have to go to the institution. He said you have promised to change your eating habits and will work together with us. He has advised us to take you home and not to interfere with you, as he believes you will get better. He said anorexia is a complicated sickness and interference could make it worse."

I could not believe what I had just heard.

We told you, High Pitch smirked.

Dr. Johannes had told me I was going to be institutionalized after I was treated at the hospital. I had not promised to change my eating habits and to cooperate with them, but now I was going home! I was not going to stay in hospital, and they were not sending me off to an institution. I was very surprised, delighted, and relieved.

I could not believe how strong my mental powers were. "Wow!" was all I was able to say.

High Pitch then blurted out, *Remember! It was not you who did this. We did it and you owe us.*

What did that mean? Hadn't I manipulated the doctors' minds, not the voices? I was trying hard to convince myself I was in control and I alone had the mind power, but deep down I no longer knew. A sense of weariness settled over me. I was so used to being praised for my handiwork, but that hadn't happened this time. I missed being praised by the voices; not receiving praise opened up my wound of rejection.

While I was so glad I was not going to a mental institution, but I was also alarmed that the voices had changed. They seemed hostile and very determined to get the credit for the doctors' change of mind, and they kept insisting I owed them. I had no idea what that meant but it activated another suspicion within me. I no longer believed I could trust the voices. I could feel control slipping away, which was even scarier to face than the institution.

My mom's voice broke into my thoughts. "They are going to do their normal tests that are required for your situation and then together with Dr. Johannes we have to arrange an ongoing outpatient agreement. After which we can take you home."

A nurse came in and angrily took my drips out. She mumbled her disbelief that they were letting me go. She then proceeded to weigh me. I was shocked as I weighed a whole 26 kilograms (57 lbs.). I was fuming with myself. I could not believe I was still so fat. I had determined, because I was sixteen years old, I should weigh 16 kilograms, not a whole 26! How could this have happened? Why was I still so fat? When I got home I would have to start working towards reaching 16 kilograms!

Suddenly I remembered my promises to God. *As soon as I reach my desired weight of 16 kilograms, I'll stick to the promises I made to Him.* No matter how I tried, I could not ignore a nudging feeling that this would be wrong, very wrong! I ignored these thoughts and focused all my attention on what the nurse was doing.

When all was done, Dr. Johannes came to check me out. I had to promise him I would start eating, as well as working together with my parents. He would see me for my check-up appointments.

"Of course," I promised, only because I wanted to get out of that hospital. I felt very nervous about going home as I thought about what had happened at home. The thought of having to go back into the passage of the house where God had audibly spoken to me, and where I had slipped into the black monster, caused fear to rise inside of me. A greater fear lurked even deeper within me as the voices were not sharing this moment with me. Where were High Pitch and Low Pitch? Usually I would have them to coax me along. I felt so alone. They were right; I needed them.

When we arrived home, I went and sat in the living room. This was a big mistake because my parents grabbed the opportunity to have a one-on-one chat with me.

"Michele, you are at death's door," my mom said. "You have to start eating or you will die." I tried to brush off what she was saying. I knew in my heart my parents were right, but I truly believed I was still way too fat to die. At 26 kilograms I thought I was far from being thin, let alone emaciated.

My mom became frustrated with my unresponsiveness and walked out. I wondered what my dad was going to say, and did not have to wait too long to find out.

"We need to work out your eating plan," he said.

This was not what I wanted to hear, but I had no option as I was scared God was watching. After all, the passageway where He spoke to me was only meters away. If I made Him unhappy He might just strike me down, leaving me to face that black monster forever.

The diet plan I was assigned was so much food! Yet, I felt I had no option as I knew God was watching me. I agreed, and, fully aware of the promise I had made to God, I made it my purpose to really try.

But I failed, hopelessly! It was just much too much food for me to consume in one day. The only way that I could be successful at this was resort to plan B. The name of this plan was "Compromise" and it brought in more lies and destruction.

I would eat under the very watchful eyes of my parents but then I would purge until only blood and bile would come out after every meal. This would mean that no food or calories would be left in my stomach at all. I had done it in the past and to start doing it again was no sweat at all.

I was passing the test as far as eating was concerned, but my compromise of purging began spinning a web of lies, deception, denial and habit-forming acts. I was the one being trapped in my own web. I became my own prisoner.

The promises I had made to God did not leave me, and deep down I knew I was falling short. I suddenly became too weary to continue playing mental games on males. I knew it was evil and wrong. Even when I heard the voices screaming and telling me I was a weakling and I had to use my mind for self-defense against all men because they were out to hurt me, I could not do it.

Every time I agreed with the voices and told them I would start using my mind powers again, something deep within me would tell me it was against what I had promised. When I told the voices that I could not bore into any male's mind anymore because I had promised God I would not, they became very angry. I could feel their rage towards me, right down to my core.

I was totally confused. Were those voices I had been listening to and talking to all these years actually my own or did they belong to someone else? If they were just another part of me, why were they now getting so angry with me? Why did they suddenly feel so threatening? What was going on? Was this me or was it not? *It must be another part of me*, I reasoned. To think there were other people inside me was absolutely ridiculous! *No, this is all me and my own power.*

The voices in me raged and shouted in my mind, *After everything we have accomplished for you! And now you say you've been doing it all. Never! You invited us in and we are here to stay! And remember, you owe us!*

What did that mean? I invited them in? How could I owe a voice?

The only thing I was certain about was that my main enemy was no longer men. Yes, I did see them as an enemy, however I realized I had an even greater enemy—myself!

Part II

Hell is Real

Eight

The Anorexic in the Mirror

I STOOD IN FRONT OF the mirror crying. *What am I going to do?* I had promised God I would listen to both the doctors and my parents. This meant one disastrous thing. I had to get rid of the idea of losing more weight, and drop my compromise plan B.

When I knocked myself unconscious from starving I had weighed 26 kilograms. Now I would have to put on the required 8 kilograms (17.63 lbs.) to please my parents and Dr. Johannes. Meaning I would have to weigh up to 34 kilograms (75 lbs.)!

The thought of me being so grotesquely fat scared me. However, I had promised God and I feared Him too much not to try. The truth was I had already turned seventeen, but I would not acknowledge that age because I had not yet reached my desired weight of 16 kilograms.

That was the rule I had enforced for myself and had lived by. For me to break this rule of losing 8 kilograms, and instead gain weight was a significant and major life-changing decision. Only because I had promised God, I would do it. "I know this will please you, God," I continually said out aloud. I did this to convince myself to go ahead and put on the required weight.

I stood in front of the mirror crying because I had eventually reached 30 kilograms (66 lbs.)! A whole fat, enormous, thirty kilograms, a nightmare to me. I had already started to fear what I would look like with another 4 kilograms of fat added to my body. I was tempted to run back into the consuming black monster and never step out. In my mind that was a better option to being so fat and disgusting.

Nowadays, magazine articles feature pictures of the latest star to have anorexia. I have watched people make faces of disgust at the photos, and listened to their harsh judgmental comments towards someone who has been diagnosed with anorexia. The sad thing is many people do not realize how serious this is.

Anorexics can honestly look at themselves and see fat all over. They have become enslaved to a controlling stronghold that has become the dominating force in their mind. It is naïve to say, "She must snap out of her stupidity and put on weight!" or "She knows she is thin and very underweight. She can see it in the mirror!" Anorexics do not see how dangerously thin they are when looking in the mirror. They do not see their skeletal frames. Their self-image has become distorted to such a degree, that it is a huge, nearly impossible task to get them to see themselves as they really are. All they see is bulging fat.

Yes, the anorexic is dangerous, selfish, and stubbornly oblivious, and the condition can end up being fatal. Telling an anorexic any of this does not help. In fact, in most cases it just makes it worse. They are trapped and enslaved to something in their minds that controls their very breath, thought, and movement. A whole new mindset, or to be more dramatic, a whole new mind transplant is needed for the anorexic. This literally needs a miracle. You can replace many organs with surgery, but a mind cannot be replaced. A miracle is needed.

When I looked at myself at 30 kilograms (66 lbs.), I honestly saw a 300-kilogram (661 lbs.) person and not a starving skeletal person. I felt a fat life was not worth living. At 30 kg., I felt I was already grotesquely fat and was heading towards obesity. Inside, I felt the struggle between trying to keep my promise to God and reaching the obese size of 34 kilograms, or reaching my desired weight. I could not see myself doing this. I still earnestly believed if I could get to 16 kilograms, I would then stop losing weight.

Sadly, that never happens to the truly anorexic. They will get down to a desired weight and still see fat all over, and carry on losing more weight, and only stop when they end up in a coma and need to be fed with tubes, or when they die.

Dr. Johannes had said if it ever happened again I would be institutionalized for as long as necessary. I felt I would rather die than have feeding tubes stuck into me or be institutionalized.

As I stood there I told myself, *Because I have stopped the mind games, God will allow me to compromise on my promise of putting on weight.* I had come to realize that not only did I want to be thin to be better than men, but I also needed to become thin, because I thought I was mortifyingly fat and disgusting. I had begun convincing myself God would understand.

Yes, He will understand, High Pitch shouted out inside me. *He doesn't expect you to look so fat. You are grotesque, sick to look at because of all the blubber.*

Low Pitch added, *It is no use. You are disgusting to look at. Give up. God will understand.*

I cringed at what they had said to me, and cried even more because I believed them. I was grotesquely fat. I was a disgusting fat monster and it was no use trying.

They are right. God will understand."

My thoughts were interrupted by, "Michele, it is supper time."

Abandoning the mirror, but clutching onto the depression, I went to the kitchen where I knew my every move would be observed. They had predetermined I would somehow cheat. Did my family not realize I could see them watching me? It was like being in another prison. Being in my own prison was bad enough, but being in the prison they had built for me was sheer agony.

As mom and dad watched me put just enough on my plate to satisfy them, I'd eat what I had to and leave the table. Within ten minutes, I would purge everything out. Sadly, I had now become a bulimic as well, anorexia's competitor.

Some nights when the family had finished eating, I would sneak into the kitchen and find a whole lot of food to binge eat in my bedroom. I allowed myself to eat it all because I knew I would purge it all. I would eat and eat until I was so full I would not be able to stand. My heart would begin beating very fast, my legs would go all numb, and I would start to panic.

I would then crawl to the toilet and purge all the food in order to get my heart to stop pounding and to prevent my stomach from digesting anything. The backs of my hands were already starting to show permanent teeth marks from sticking my fingers down my throat to induce vomiting. I would usually then go and cry out into my pillow. I hated doing this.

The bingeing had started since I came out of hospital. At first I'd do it on weekend nights only. Then I started feeling the need to binge more, so began bingeing every single night almost in clockwork order. Almost overnight, I had become a slave to bingeing and purging, and I did not know how to stop. I had gone from being a starving anorexic to a starved anorexic-bulimic.

Every night I wished to die because of the prison I was in. The prying eyes along with my disgusting secret binges filled me with even more shame and self-contempt. My self-beatings and burnings were not only because of my self-hate, but now also because of how trapped I was feeling. Even though I escaped the claws of the consuming black monster, I found myself engulfed in the monster of desperation and depression.

I wanted to stop the starving, the bingeing, the purging, the exhausting never-ending exercising, the self-torturing, the ice baths, the only-two-hours-a-day sleep rule, the hate, the isolation, everything! I wanted to stop it all. I just did not know how. To my family and everyone around me I was doing so well because I was eating and had put on some weight. Nobody saw the destructive prison I was in, and that I was heading toward a massive downward plunge.

High Pitch and Low Pitch were delighted. They told me if I wanted to break free I would have to go back to my old ways. I did not understand this because before my close encounter with death I had always felt in complete control. Now I felt completely out of control.

You will never be in control again unless you carry on with our plan to murder a man, Low Pitch hurled at me.

No! I can't! I promised God.

Then you will die by our hand, High Pitch spat back.

Yes! You are going to die. Low Pitch added.

No, I won't die. God let me live.

I was not sure about this. I did not want to live, but I did not want to die either. Every night the black monster attacked me in my dreams with the arrow of fear. I was glad to only have two hours of sleep a night, because it gave me more dread than rest. I was desperate, anxious, and imprisoned by the fear continuously devouring me. At times, death seemed the best solution.

Then I heard a soft, gentle voice saying, *Michele, God does not want you to die. He wants you to live a full life. God loves you.*

I put my hands on my ears, fell with my face buried in my pillow and screamed, "Leave me! Everybody just leave me."

High Pitch just laughed and said, *We are here to stay. Remember, you invited us in.*

Don't forget, Low Pitch added. *You invited death in. One day you will have to pay up.*

I did not understand what the voices meant, and it really gave me the creeps. I believed there was nothing I could do except live together with High Pitch and Low Pitch. If I wanted a little bit of peace I would have to become their ally again.

Why are they doing this to me? In the past, it felt as if my voices and I were working together in perfect harmony. But that couldn't be true, it was always me doing their bidding.

Michele, you have to starve. So starvation became my diet.

Michele, develop your mental powers using children. And I did.

Michele, now use these powers to destroy boys. I did that too.

Michele, strengthen yourself so that you can murder a man some day. I willingly obeyed.

Michele, you need to punish yourself. So I did.

Michele, learn how to hate. Kindle that hate. Let the hate consume you and live and move and be this hate. So I knew how to hate and how to scowl.

Michele, you must alienate yourself from others because they are only jealous of you. They are not really concerned about you. They want to destroy you. I became an alien, or as people would politely put it, weird. Isolation became natural.

I believed the voices and had willingly become High Pitch and Low Pitch's human puppet. This did not worry me as I always felt powerful. Now their orders had stopped coming. Why did High Pitch and Low Pitch stop?

It must be the promise I made to God that I would no longer destroy boys and stop with the dream of killing a man one day. Other girls were dreaming about Prince Charming, marriage, and living happily ever after. I was scheming, together with High Pitch and Low Pitch, of getting my personal payback by killing a man or maybe even a few.

I still hated men, but now I avoided them. I still believed men would hurt me given the chance and avoided them. If one approached me and talked to me, I would go into a state of panic and do everything I could to get away from him. Males in a crowd were fine, but I could not be alone with a male. I avoided getting into elevators with them or quiet hallways. A male student could come out from a class and turn the quiet hallway into a trap. I would never go into a public toilet alone. I was too scared a man would follow and corner me.

The voices would taunt me with things like, *Watch out! A man is going to hurt you when you least expect it.* Or, *Look at you, hiding away. You can't even fight your own battles without us. You are as good as dead.*

They were right. I was in such fear that I would begin to panic and hyperventilate wherever I was alone. I would hear the voices laughing at me and I'd cry out to God, asking Him to help me. I would feel strong for a while and then the voices would start taunting me all over again. Sometimes I would go into my bedroom and with music blasting, begin hitting my head on my bedroom wall and frantically rubbing my ears so I could not hear the voices. The voices were driving me crazy. I felt hopelessly powerless against them. Then I'd get angry at my own weakness and begin hurting myself.

Did my parents not see or hear or pick up anything—I do not know. By that time, I had locked myself in my room for so many years they would just leave me alone. I would be in my room, my brother and his friends would pile up in his room, and my mom and dad would sit in front of the television. They truly believed all was well. Our doors often remained shut because both my brother and I had our own music blaring. Many times I used to practice acting in my room. Perhaps that is why my family always accused me of being overdramatic, even when I was trying to reach out in my hurt to them. Can I blame them? I do not know.

One night I heard the voices laughing at me while I was burying my head in my pillow. Something inside me finally cracked. That was it! I sat up and said, "Right, voices! Are you listening to me? You are a part of me and I am in charge. Do you hear me? I am the one who is in charge here and from now on we will do what I decide. Is that clear? I am in control."

Their mocking laughter rang out and bounced off the walls of my mind and landed in the pit of my stomach. I beat my stomach until my arms grew tired.

Good, I thought. *Now that we have that cleared up, I am going to allow myself to have four hours of sleep tonight because I deserve it.*

Even with my stomach rolled up into a painfully tight knot, I fell asleep feeling the best I had felt in a long time.

But I was only fooling myself! It was one thing for me to make a determined decision, another thing to stick to it. Especially when I was trying to do it in my own strength.

Back then I did not know I could ask God to give me the strength to help overcome all my problems. I believed I had to prove to God I could stick to those promises all by myself. I did not realize then there was no way on earth I would be able to conquer everything by myself.

I would first have to walk a very long, long road before I would understand. On this road, I hit a massive pothole and fell with my face head down into the mud. Sadly, it took an extended amount of time for this to occur. And during this lengthy, winding path, I turned other people's lives upside down, together with my own.

As I reveal the next part of my life, I will explain how I got to the point when I heard the following questions being asked about me and comments made.

"Is she going to be a vegetable?"

"How could she be so selfish?"

"How could she have done something so stupid?"

"How could she ruin so many people's lives?"

"She can't be put back in society. The only place where she deserves to be is in a mental institution."

I heard these and many more bitter, but true, words spoken aloud in front of me while I was lying unconscious in a hospital bed.

First, let me tell you about what happened to get me to this place.

College became very intense as I was preparing for our matriculation final examinations.

I heard a voice call my name over the intercom saying Mrs. Botha, our principal, wanted to see me.

In her office, she said to me, "Michele, I see you have made it as one of the candidates for a bursary. I am afraid that due to the anorexia and your weight we must take your name off this list until we get a doctor's certificate stating that . . ."

My head started to spin as I watched her mouth moving. All I heard was a buzz in my ears. I screamed inside, *My weight! There is nothing wrong with my weight. I have already reached 32 kilograms! I am as big as a tent. What more do they want?*

I felt tears flooding my eyes, but I was not going to cry.

Since grade six, I had made these plans of getting a scholarship, and now it had just exploded in my face. I choked on air.

"What is it you want to say Michele?" Mrs. Botha asked.

What was there to say? Absolutely nothing! I had just had the rug pulled from under my feet because of an assumption they made about me having anorexia nervosa.

Don't they understand that I planned and worked hard for this bursary? How can they do this?

I knew I was on my own because my parents and Dr. Johannes would side with them. I looked at Mrs. Botha and said, "I am not anorexic. I am not anorexic!" and I stood up and allowed anger to replace the tears that had filled my eyes.

The voices laughed and sniggered inside me, I walked out of that office more determined than ever before. I would not to let anyone see how hurt and broken I was inside, or to allow the voices to snigger at me.

When I got home that night, I had made up my mind. I told my mom and dad, "I no longer want to get the bursary to study math and science. I want to study fashion designing instead."

They looked stunned. After an awkward silence, my dad asked me, "Are you sure this is was what you want to do?"

"Yes," I answered.

My mother's stare pierced right through me. I could see that this news of mine had hit her by surprise. I stared right back at her, determined she would never find out the real reason why I had just flushed my dream of a bursary down the toilet, as I had done with everything else. I was tempted to ask her, "Do you need some sugar water?"

I was not going to let my parents see or know the pain that was eating through me. But, even with all my determined efforts, the rejection had thrown me right back. All those feelings of rejection from the Christmas Eve of 1973 flooded back into the pit of my stomach.

I ran to get sick until blood spurted out of me. Seeing the blood gave me a sense of retribution and a sense of victory. This had become my way of life. Getting sick until bile and blood appeared was an attempt to replace my feelings of rejection with feelings of power and victory. For a short time I felt powerful and victorious.

I handled the rejection by switching myself off and just going through the motions of life. I matriculated, studied, graduated, and became a working citizen. I had qualified in fashion designing and as an aerobics instructor. I put everything I had into both fields and did what was required of me to do. To the onlooker, I had achieved much and seemed to be doing well. However, inside I was a mess.

Even the voices left me alone to walk this path of existence. It seemed to please them that I hated myself so much. They were still not happy that I had avoided contact with men. I did hate men, but I hated myself even more. Yet no one seemed aware of how much I despised myself.

My eating disorders went from bad to worse, and so did my ups and downs. I had become obsessed with needing to see blood spurt out of me every day. My throat was now cut up from this.

Dr. Johannes was still my doctor even though I was now a young adult. He was still trying to convince me that I was anorexic-bulimic, but I believed he was wrong. I had gone up to the required 33 kilograms (72.75 lbs.). I had promised God and had been accepted by the corporate world. Which meant to me there was no way I could be a bulimic-anorexic.

Dr. Johannes knew how badly cut up my throat was, and often warned me, "One day we will have to institutionalize you and tie your hands up to stop this self-abuse."

My throat was cut up, swollen, and in pain, but that did not stop me. I binged and purged every evening between 10 p.m. and 2 a.m. Then I'd have to clean up the smelly, bloody mess before the bulimic bout was over. I would then have my two hours of sleep and wake up to begin my next day. I was in control of everything I was doing, so I believed nothing was wrong with my life, even on my bad, down days.

But there was a part of me that was desperately searching to get out of this secret life I was living. And yet, another side of me did not want to stop what I was doing. I wondered, *Am I really in control of everything I am doing?*

The fact that I could not have my two hours of sleep unless I had binged and purged and reveled in the blood should have told me I was a slave to this sordid self-destruction. I hated it, but could not live without it.

As much as I was in a prison within myself, I was beginning to enjoy another power surge as I taught two aerobic classes a day. In the early eighties, most of the people doing fitness classes were men. Even though I hated men, I enjoyed being fitter than most of the men going to the gym.

My goal in every class I taught was to get them to collapse from complete exhaustion. There was such satisfaction in this because they did not see me as helpless. *They* were the ones who'd helplessly cry out in pain during the training. They saw me as a wonder woman. No man could keep up with me, and this made my day.

But, I would go home to binge, purge, spurt blood, and sometimes beat myself before having a tormented two hours of sleep. I went from being full of power and the heroine during the day to being low and full of despair at night. I was a loser with the toilet as my throne and my blood as my consoler! My life was empty, totally empty!

—∿—

Then something wonderful happened. I bumped into someone I had known from my teenage years, and she gave me Charles' twin sister Tania's telephone number. All I had to do was phone her to find out where Charles was and what he was up to. I knew she would know everything because they were very close. Even in our teenage years, we had all seen their close-knit bond.

The voices immediately reminded me, *Don't phone! Not only did he dump, reject, and hurt you, but he has also forgotten all about you. He doesn't care about you and never will.*

I know he doesn't care at all. In fact, he really hurt me, but I still have to get him back, I told the voices.

Deep down, I knew I wanted to see Charles because I had secretly always dreamed of meeting up with him again. I pretended I was Sleeping Beauty who had been cast away and that Charles would come to my rescue. I knew it was farfetched, but I reasoned that a girl could dream, even me.

Nine

A Disastrous Marriage

I CHOSE THE MOST STUPID, obscure way of trying to force my Prince Charming to rescue me. *Maybe if I make Charles jealous by dating someone else, he will come to my rescue.*

This did not work, so I plotted and took it one step further. I got engaged to Lawrence, my brother's best friend. Yet my Prince Charming still did not come to my rescue. Charles was aware of my engagement because I had told Tania who instantly told him.

The night of my engagement to Lawrence, I fell onto my bed crying. Charles had not phoned or come rushing to beg me to break off the engagement and declare his love and desire to marry me. I was hurt and devastated by his silence.

I felt no guilt about using Lawrence because I knew he was using me as well. He wanted the South African Defense Force to give him a permanent post in South West Africa (now Namibia), but for that to happen, he had to be married. He was on the rebound and thought his next best option would be to use me.

I knew all this because my brother was furious when he found out Lawrence and I were getting engaged. He tried to put me off by telling me Lawrence was still in love with his previous girlfriend and did not care about me. Instead of this news hurting me, it encouraged me. I knew Lawrence and I were from the same tree—the tree of rejection.

He proposed in the most preposterous way. I should have seen the big red warning signs, but I chose to ignore them because he was a means to an end. We were sitting on a sofa in my parent's sitting room when Lawrence took his watch off and crushed it in his hands. It crumbled into pieces.

He looked over at me and as usual I showed no reaction. This seemed to satisfy him, so he proceeded to tell me, "My psychiatrist says I have what is called 'red anger.'" As he spoke, he studied my every move. At first, he seemed surprised and then pleased when I did not respond.

Which is when he asked, "Do you want to get married?"

I was not expecting that question, but it all seemed so perfect. Getting engaged was a substantially better plan of making Charles jealous than simply dating Lawrence. I said, "Yes."

When Lawrence and I told my mom and dad, my mom looked at Lawrence and said to him, "I cannot stop this because I know the manipulation and stubbornness of my daughter too well. But Lawrence, I will tell you, you will never ever be able to handle Michele. She will destroy you. She is too much for you to take on."

My mother's words surprised me, I knew she was only trying to save Lawrence a lot of grief. Even though she and Lawrence became friends long before I came onto the scene, she did not know about his red anger. If she had known about it, I believe she would have put a stop to the proposal. Although I did want the engagement to be interrupted and not go on, I did not want it to be my mom stopping it. It had to be Charles. He was the hero who needed to rescue me by making known his love for me.

When he did not stop the engagement from taking place, I went to the second phase of my plan. I persuaded Lawrence we should not get married in a church and we should do it right away. We were from different churches and that meant it would take too long. He agreed, and we decided to get married in court.

I had dreamed of the beautiful church wedding Charles and I would have and that we would live happily ever after. I did not think my court wedding to Lawrence would ever take place. The plan was that Charles would hear from Tania that the wedding date was set, and this would shake him, and make him come to me and beg me not to get married.

High Pitch and Low Pitch ridiculed my "stupid wish" as they put it. They reminded me, *Charles doesn't care what you do. He won't waste his time begging you not to get married.*

I ignored them and continued to jump at every telephone ring and wait eagerly for the mail. Nothing! High Pitch and Low Pitch were right. Charles did not care about me at all. This made me bitter and more hateful, which made me more determined to get married and show him.

125

As Lawrence put the ring on my finger and the judge announced us husband and wife, my heart sank low. Charles had not come to my rescue and now I was Mrs. Wellington.

Lawrence was not over the moon either.

Our marriage was disastrous to put it mildly. We were in competition of who would destroy whom first. I was an anorexic-bulimic addict and Lawrence was a manic-depressant with red anger. What a murderous and suicidal union. The question was, what was going to come first, murder or suicide? And who was going to be guilty of what? Lawrence and I were an absolute disaster.

One night, after my bingeing and purging session followed by Lawrence's red anger session, I slumped down on the floor crying. "Oh, God, I want to die. I cannot go on like this any longer. I hate myself. I hate my life. I have nothing to live for. Please take me. Even that consuming black empty void is better than the hell I am living in."

I stayed where I was. No black empty void, although that is exactly what I felt inside. Nothing.

How could you let a man get the better of you again? High Pitch spat.

Low Pitch interrupted, *It is because you won't use your mental powers. Do you have any idea how few people are able to use their minds to destroy others? You are weak, stupid, and blind to the power that you hold at your fingertips because of us. You can destroy Lawrence right now.*

"Oh, shut up and leave me alone," I snapped back and slipped into a heavy depression. I had never been so depressed before. I did not want to go anywhere. How ironic it was!

Lawrence had been in and out of hospital for his depression, and no one had any idea I was struggling with the same issue.

Lawrence did not have a clue what he was getting himself into by getting involved with me. I told myself, *That is the price to pay for using me as a pawn to get a gate pass into Grootfontein.*

I did not know what I was getting myself into either, using Lawrence to try to make Charles jealous. As I lay crumpled on the floor I began screaming. I did not care if it woke up the whole block of flats where we had been temporarily placed in South African Defense Force (SADF) flats in Johannesburg until the Grootfontein transfer came through.

Lawrence lay passed out on the bed, which was the norm after a bout of his red anger.

Strangely, Lawrence seemed to be getting better and appeared to be happy. I was not totally sure what to make of it, but I had a strong feeling he was hiding something from me. I found out sooner than I thought I would.

One night Lawrence walked in and said, "We have to talk." That was better than the shouting, scratching, kicking, and boxing matches we seemed to be having every night. But he looked very guilty, as if he had done something wrong. Or had I done something wrong?

He looked at me and said, "Michele, you are sick and need help. You have a major eating problem. You are skin and bone and you have a self-mutilation problem. If you do not do anything about it, it will destroy you. This is causing you to have major psychological, emotional, and social problems."

"I have psychological, emotional or social problems? This comes from the man who has just stepped out of a mental ward!" As I said this I saw pain cross his face. I felt slightly bad for a split second, but then returned to enjoying seeing him wince.

"It is not the same." He lowered his voice. "I got like that from being on the border for the SADF. I've been declared fit for duty."

I knew I had hit his sore spot as he had just hit mine. However, I had only just begun.

"I am sorry," I jeered sarcastically. "You are fit? Fit for bouts of anger and depression! I wonder what the army would do if they knew what you get like behind closed doors?"

Lawrence knew I had the upper hand here and he backed down and said, "This is not about me but about how sick *you* are. You are slowly killing yourself, Michele."

I looked at him and said, "I know. I don't know how to stop. I want to, but I cannot and no longer want to."

Lawrence never knew how to cope with me, but I did not expect what came next.

"I know," he continued. "I spoke to your mom. She reminded me how she warned me I wouldn't be able to cope. She was right." He paused slightly, and then without looking at me said, "And together we have decided it would be best for me to take you to a psychiatrist. The psychiatrist can help you."

Lawrence had betrayed me.

He was about to do what my mom and dad had done, take me to a psychiatrist. Worse yet, I was not consulted. Once again I was the outsider in my own life. I was like an animal that the humans were deciding what to do with me. To add to this painful insult, Lawrence had consulted with one of the main psychiatrists at the military hospital.

I let out a shrill yell because I believed I had just fallen into a deep, deep trap. "How could you go and do something like that without my permission?" I spat out.

He's out to destroy you, Low Pitch said to me, *Use our mental power on him before it is too late.*

I wanted to. Oh, how I wanted to! But I knew that I could not. I also knew I was trapped, trapped like I had never been before, and I did not know what to do about it.

Since that Christmas Eve ten years before, I had never allowed myself to cry in front of anyone, but I felt the tears ready to come streaming down my face. Even though I felt alone and desperate, I pulled them back.

How could he have done this to me? He had gone behind my back. He had exposed me to total strangers. It felt as if I had been gunned down, causing me to shut down completely inside. I looked at him blankly as he continued. Whatever he said meant nothing to me. I did not care anymore. First, Charles had rejected me and now Lawrence had just betrayed me.

"The psychiatrist has advised that you should be admitted for immediate treatment."

I did not respond to his statement. I saw his mouth moving, but the buzz going on in my mind switched me off from any reality.

I hated him. Oh, how I hated him!

Ten

Committed!

I WAS PLACED IN THE psychiatric ward in the head military hospital in Pretoria and given the rules. I was going to be put on a reward and punishment program. To put it simply, I had to gain about a pound a day until I reached their goal of 23 kilograms (over 50 lbs.). If I did not, I would be punished. However, if I did gain a daily pound, I would be rewarded.

The punishment was not torture or anything like that. If I failed to put on the daily weight, I would get one of my belongings taken away (a toiletry, a book, a piece of clothing, etc.), or a privilege removed (being allowed out of bed to walk down the hospital corridors, different visitors, etc.). Rewards would be that one of the things would be given back to me. I was allowed to choose what punishment I would want it to be, and what reward I would want returned. The psychiatrist would never decide for me. Every day she would let me know if I had gained the required pound or not.

Because of my emotional detachment, I was to undergo special treatment with a psychologist as well. They said the treatment would help me learn how to connect with myself, the world, and express my emotions.

I was told, "We have not treated anorexia in this hospital before and you will be our first case."

"So, I am your guinea pig?" I kept my eyes of hate fixed on Lawrence. The voices inside were going ballistic. I smiled as I heard their idea and agreed in my mind. *Don't play with fire if you don't have a fire extinguisher!*

The psychiatrist smiled back at me as she answered, "No, you are just our first case ever."

Being a guinea pig did not bother me. But Lawrence sitting there looking so concerned and so smug did. My smile tightened and I felt sick to my stomach. *I'm going to scratch his eyes out and then slowly stick a knife through his heart, just as he has done to me.* Lawrence saw my smile and looked away. He knew venom was behind the smile.

After a month, the results were no surprise to me, but what came with it was. I had everything taken away from me and I was put in solitary confinement and not allowed any visitors.

The psychiatrist, Dr. du Plessis, was unable to hide her feelings. She looked heartbroken and gave permission to let me keep a Bible. I did not know what I would do with it.

The cleaner was allowed in my room every day in the morning for ten minutes to clean. My toiletries had all been taken away so I asked the cleaner to help me stay clean. All she could give me were cleaning products she used to wash the floor and bathroom. I used the products as my bathroom soap and shampoo. Due to the harshness of the detergent, my skin, which was already in a bad state from anorexia, began burning, cracking, and then bleeding.

This did not worry me as I truly believed I deserved it all, because of how I had let Lawrence blindside me. I saw this slip-up of mine as a massive weakness and was angry at myself and the world.

While the doctors were unsuccessful in getting me to put on weight, I was being successful in my own goals. I was getting emotionally fatter by developing my anger, bitterness, and hate towards Lawrence.

I had promised God I would not use mental mind games to hurt men ever again. I did not promise Him I would not use another means to give men what they deserved—annihilation. I had many isolated hours to ponder on this. I decided that before destroying Lawrence, I would bring him ten times more humiliation than he had brought me in this place.

I was glad I was not allowed any visitors because I did not want visitors, especially Lawrence. The four white walls staring at me would literally feel as if they were closing in on me, eating me up. When this happened, I would jump off my bed, rush to the toilet and start forcing myself to get sick. There was nothing in my stomach, so the only thing that came out was bile and blood. I *wanted* to see the blood. I was sick of white and found the color red very soothing. At times I would scream out, but no one came into my room. I was not sure if I could be heard or not. This left me feeling alone, rejected, and neglected.

I cried out, "Why am I alive, why?"

No answer. Nobody cared.

The venom in me had resurfaced. Who was I trying to fool? I was not meant to be happy. I was put on earth to expose the vileness of men and kill as many as I could—starting with Lawrence. My revenge would be sweet and deadly. I would make sure of it.

As I obsessed about this, I knew the only way I was going to be able to do this was to get out of the hellhole he had put me in.

Before I had gone into isolation, I had made friends with another patient. Stoney was really funny and I relaxed in her company. She told me many things about herself, and I began to let her into a tiny bit of my life, mainly how Lawrence, together with my mom, had tricked me and put me into that place.

One day, as I was placing my cold wet hand on my skin to relieve the intense burning, I thought of Stoney. I asked the cleaner to go and tell Stoney about the stuff I had to bathe with and how my skin was suffering.

One day the door of my room opened. I saw an arm swing and release a cake of soap that came sliding across the floor. I had never been so glad to see soap in my life. About five minutes later the door opened again. This time a bottle of body lotion came sliding across the floor. I hugged that cream as if it were life itself.

That day I felt like a queen, being able to bathe with soap and then lavish cream all over my skin. I hid the soap and cream so no one would be able to find it if they searched my room.

Oh, thank you Stoney, I thought. *I owe you for this. One day I will pay you back for your kindness.*

Stoney's compassion did not end there. The nurses had told Stoney that things were not going too well with me. I was not putting on the required daily weight. Stoney then organized extra food to be delivered to me. I could then start putting on the required weight and the punishments would stop. From that day on, someone would open my door and slide extra food into my room.

They were so busy trying to get me to put on weight, they did not know I was bingeing. This was what was destroying me, but the psychiatrist and psychologist did not see it. They concentrated only on the anorexia because I was so underweight.

They were also trying to get me to sleep more. More and stronger sleeping tablets were prescribed. But I had made my decision and no one was going to change my mind. I had gone from two hours of sleep to four hours of sleep a day, which was more than enough. I hid the sleeping tablets in the Bible, and at night I flushed them down the toilet.

I thought about saving them and using them to overdose Lawrence without his knowledge, but I had nowhere to hide them. One good thing about being in isolation was I did not have to see Lawrence. Strangely, I missed my parents. They were the only people I would have liked to see— even my mom who had aided Lawrence.

Weeks went by and at long last I had reached my first weight requirement of 40 kilograms (88 lbs.), a whole 7-kilogram gain (15 lbs.), considered to be acceptable. The team working on my case overflowed with excitement. I did not know what the big fuss was about as I felt like a two-ton pig. I felt so fat and disgusting that I did not want visitors. I wanted to stay imprisoned and alone. That way, no one would be exposed to my disgusting fat body. My 40 kilograms (80 lbs.) felt like 400 kilograms to me, and looked like 4000 kilograms in the mirror. I saw myself as a huge and grotesque fat beast of blubber.

One day, Dr. du Plessis came in and told me, "I have a pleasant surprise for you—a visitor!"

Lawrence of course! When I saw him I could only think, *He deserves to die a slow, humiliating death. One day I will make that happen.*

He let me know that as soon as I was better, we could move to Grootfontein in South West Africa. He was really something. He had put me in the institution, but now needed me to get out so he could get into South West Africa.

"Lawrence, you can go on without me."

"I was thinking the same thing because then I can go and get everything ready for you," he said, trying to sound so sincere.

Who is he trying to fool?

My friend Stoney was a major in the SAAF (South African Air Force). Thanks to her, I got some information about Lawrence, more information about his tactics than he would have liked me to know. What she told me threw me off guard at the time, but I had many hours to digest the garbage. While we were engaged, Lawrence had an affair with a nurse from the old military hospital where he had been treated for manic depression. The nurse was married with two young children. This information immediately made me suspicious as to what

Lawrence's extra-mural activities still were. I decided to find out exactly what they were.

I looked at Lawrence and wryly smiled, "How considerate of you to do that for me!"

By the look on Lawrence's face, I could see he was not sure if I meant it. Feeling I had the upper hand, I determined I was going to play "cat and mouse" with him. He would be the mouse and I the cat. Suddenly, I wanted to get out and move to South West Africa to begin this new game. The outcome I eventually wanted was to bite the mouse in half. Eat him all up! And enjoy spitting the furry ball out!

I reassured him, "Of course, yes. You must go and organize your things. I am sure you have a lot to do."

"Are you sure?" he asked looking at me carefully.

Does he really think I would never find out? I was going to make him pay for his betrayal of putting me in this place and humiliating me by his affairs. I would bring him down in South West Africa. My plan was to strike when he was well established and well known in Grootfontein, then his humiliation would be worse.

Though I had a new plan to annihilate Lawrence for what he had done to me, I was still hurt deep inside. He had married me to further his career in the SADF. Then he had me institutionalized after already having an affair. I suddenly wondered what else Stoney knew about Lawrence that she was not telling me.

How could I have been so stupid? How could I have let my guard down so much? I had fallen into my own trap and did not know how to get out.

Oh, pull yourself together and stop feeling sorry for yourself. You are in this mess because you did not use your mind games. You ignored the power that we offered you, High Pitch shouted out.

You know that they are all out to get you and destroy you, Low Pitch added.

The voices are right, I determined. They were all out to destroy me!

Once again, I closed my emotional blinkers. *Me? Cry? Never! The only person who is going to end up crying is Lawrence.*

It was settled. Lawrence went off to South West Africa and I stayed behind, still institutionalized. Eventually, when I was discharged, I stayed with my mom and dad for a short period. Everyone was raving about how successful the treatment was as I had reached a whopping 45 kilograms (99 lbs.). I was to put on another 13 kilograms (28 lbs.) as an outpatient, but the psychiatrist and the psychologist were happy with my progress.

They did not know I was more messed up emotionally than I had ever been. I had entered the institution as a bulimic-anorexic and left it a full-time anorexic-bulimic addict.

My bingeing had now become an all-day affair. I went from one binge and purge into another. I binged and purged as a form of escapism and a means of euphoria. After the euphoria, I always felt down so needed another binge to feel euphoric again. I would force myself at least once a day to purge as much blood as possible. This would always bring relief, satisfaction, and a sense of control. When I was in isolation, I had also started hitting myself on my head, pulling my hair out, and of course, I continued with the abdominal beatings. I could also exercise all I wanted now that I was out.

The hospital staff were so obsessed with getting me to gain weight that they only concentrated on the results from the scale. I had landed in isolation not only because of the punishment system, but because of my nonexistent emotional behavior and my estrangement from society. This had done more harm than good. To sit for twenty-four hours looking at four white walls and have nothing to do but build a bigger battlefield in my mind was not the right treatment at all. This increased my self-abuse and the fire of bitterness and hate, especially towards Lawrence.

I was not going to use mind games on Lawrence. I was out for his blood and would not stop until I got what I wanted. I was going to betray him just as he had betrayed me. I would make sure he would be humiliated, betrayed, institutionalized, and labeled as dangerous, and then I would kill him, in self-defense, of course. I envisioned myself walking into a room where he lay dead and roaring with laughter, hissing and spitting on him in jubilation. The day this was accomplished would be my day of victory and his day of defeat. He would be the first of many men. My time had come.

I chose not to think of the promises I made to God.

I had become obsessed with destroying and then killing Lawrence. I was ready to go to South West Africa to face him and live out my obsession. By that time, I had already dropped 5 kilograms (11 lbs.). I had decided 45 kilograms was just too much weight for me to carry: 40 kilograms (88 lbs.) was more than enough. I still believed I was already as huge as an elephant at this weight.

My mom was no fool. She could see I had no desire or interest to join Lawrence. "Michele, you don't have to do this, you really don't. You can stay here and start divorce proceedings."

I knew she was right, but my marriage to Lawrence would only be over after I had annihilated him.

It was time to move to my new home, the 101 Workshops army base in Grootfontein, the headquarters for the SADF in South West Africa (Namibia) where a few thousand who lived on base. I flew on an SADF airplane commonly known as a "Flossy." If the flight represented my stay at Grootfontein, I was in for one major, uncomfortable, bumpy ride.

The only sweet thing about the whole trip was the accumulated revenge I had ready to pour out on Lawrence.

Of course, he was eagerly waiting for me. His excitement did not fool me as I knew he was excited for one reason only. He would be able to get into the "Swinging Partners' Club." He was in for a major surprise. The only swinging he would be doing was from a noose.

As we arrived in front of the gates of a house, Lawrence announced, "Our home."

What a joke, I fumed.

He acted as if nothing had happened. I felt he had sent me to hell and back again in that institution, but it meant nothing to him. He thought that sending me for "treatment" had been the best thing that could have happened to me and would boast about it. He had no idea how much it had destroyed me inside.

He would soon find out! I could not keep up the facade that I loved him. Any fondness I once felt had curdled and become sour. I knew I would have to keep up the charade long enough for me to corner the mouse. Then the cat would be able to come out and kill.

I was not the only one living a lie. There were times when I seemed mild compared to Lawrence. He had episodes when he was like a total stranger. He would suddenly go ballistic with anger, the red anger he warned me about. After he bashed and beat me with a pan I determined to use my mind power on him. The only person allowed to hit me was me!

God would understand. After all, I was doing it for self-preservation.

Most of the time Lawrence just destroyed objects around him. Only when I got in the way, would he would lash out at me. It was as if he did not even see me. He would start shaking silently, his eyes would go bloodshot, and then he would disappear into another world.

The weird part about these bouts of anger was how Lawrence would wake up the next morning and act as if nothing had happened. I had no idea whether he remembered or chose to ignore his anger outbursts. I began to feel sorry for him and would wonder if I was going a little overboard with my cruel mouth. Those feelings did not last for long. The pity I felt turned into hurt, anger, and determined revenge. I soon realized how I could use his episodes as part of my self-defense ploy.

Lawrence had organized casual work for me in the SADF and we worked in the same unit, known as the "Fish Tank."

There, all my pity for Lawrence disintegrated and my bitter, hateful and toxic feelings for him grew.

One morning Doug, one of the army soldiers with whom I worked, asked to speak to me privately. The soldiers doing their two years of national defense duty were always talking about the permanent SADF staff, so I knew he might have some juicy information, not realizing the juicy information was about Lawrence. He said it would be best if we both walked over to the big stores so we could talk in private.

"In this short time that we have worked together, I have grown to like you."

I cut him short, "No, no, don't say that." I immediately became scared and nervous.

"No," he reassured me. "It's not like that."

I let out a sigh of relief.

"I like you as a person and I can't allow you to carry on working here without telling you what Lance Corporal Lawrence is going around talking about."

Now he had my attention. I had never forgotten what Stoney had found out and sensed Doug knew about Lawrence's extra-mural activities.

"Go on," I slowly replied, giving Doug my full attention.

"He's been bragging to some of the guys at work that he's sleeping with the major's wife. He also said that he's been having an affair with a nurse from the hospital in Pretoria where he was treated."

He hesitated and avoided looking at me.

"Carry on, Doug. You can't stop now!"

Eyes looking down he continued, "He bragged he also had an affair with one of the men he had been on camp with at the Caprivi Strip border post."

Looking embarrassed, he stopped.

This totally shocked me and I staggered. Doug stretched out his arm, asking me, "Are you okay?" He could see I was not. "Telling you was a big mistake. I should have kept quiet. Maybe it's not true."

I stopped him short. "It's fine." I tried to smile, pretending that none of this mattered.

Doug could see I was struggling to deal with all of this and suggested I should go and tell the captain I was not feeling well and would like to go home.

"I did not tell you this to hurt you, ma'am. I told you because I do not want people to laugh at you behind your back," he looked as if he had just robbed a bank. His look told me they *were* laughing behind my back. My hate for Lawrence and men exploded.

I was close to my breaking point, but I looked at Doug and said, "Thank you very much for informing me about this, Doug. Please, do not let Lawrence or anyone know you have told me."

He looked relieved and immediately replied, "No, I definitely will not."

I do not know how I got home that day. When I came to my senses I found myself in the kitchen with the hot iron pressed on my arm. I was beyond any feelings. This was worse than the humiliation and betrayal Lawrence had already put me through. At that very moment, I felt lost and unsure what to do.

He deserves to be mauled with your mind powers, High Pitch said.

"No," I insisted. "I told you God made it very clear it was evil to do that sort of stuff to a person. No! I need to get him back by playing his own game. The difference is I want to do it in such a way it will make him crumble apart into a million pieces."

So, how are you going to do it? Low Pitch eagerly asked. *Remember, he has hurt and humiliated you. Not to mention what he did to you by sticking you in that hospital where you spent weeks in solitary confinement.*

He wanted you in that hospital so he could sleep with that nurse, and I bet other women, whenever it pleased him, High Pitch gloated, knowing that it would hurt me even more.

"He has humiliated me so badly that I am going to first destroy him and then kill him," I told them.

As I sat talking to the voices inside me, I started to feel stronger as I allowed my humiliation and anger for Lawrence to turn into hate. My plans for his downfall became immediate. I was going to come up with a plan to put into action. I had always managed to do this with great success in the past. Scheming and manipulating were my way of life.

I had forgotten how my manipulating had got me institutionalized. It was not so much that he was having affairs that got to me, but rather that he was going around bragging about them. The humiliation that shrouded me was his boasting about sleeping with a man. This made me determine that murder was too mild a punishment. He had made me the laughing stock of 101 Workshops. I was going to get him back. How? How?

I suddenly jumped up with the answer. *I'm going to have an affair on the army base and make sure everyone knows about it.* To ensure ultimate humiliation for Lawrence, I was not going to choose someone in the permanent army. I would select someone doing his two years of national army service, a trooper. That would crush Lawrence's ego. It would be better than any mind game. Not only would I have an affair, but I would also humiliate him at work.

This was going to be sweet, so very sweet. I knew exactly how to get this started. I smiled to myself and said, "Here we go. Let the mouse start running because this cat is going to kill."

The cat and mouse game began. Lawrence walked around feeling all smug about his very active extra-mural activities. He did not know I was being informed about every activity he was up to. Doug was passing on all the stories to me.

I had also gained a new informant, Scully. He was one of the new troopers, and my chosen lover. Scully was part of Lawrence's team and the troopers all knew what he and I were up to. Lawrence was so busy bragging to his troopers, making me the laughing stock of the base, he did not realize they were also laughing at him.

Step one of my scheme was well under way. It was easy for Scully and me to arrange time together because Lawrence flew down to Pretoria on a regular basis. Lawrence had asked Scully, together with another trooper, Dagger, to check up on me. Dagger was our lookout. The three of us, together with Doug, called our group the "Destroying Lawrence Team Force." The guys had no idea what I was actually up to as they had fallen for my victim act.

Besides sleeping with two women at the base and the same hospital nurse in Pretoria, Lawrence also had liaisons with another woman he was doing different SADF training workshops with who was also in Pretoria.

Even though I did not love him, I felt hurt and humiliated. Was I as disgusting as that man had told me I was on that long-ago Christmas Eve?

I tried to ignore this by concentrating on my scheme of destroying and killing Lawrence.

Eleven

"An Eye for an Eye"

THE NEXT THING ON MY agenda was to mess up at work. I knew this would put Lawrence in a bad light, not only at 101 Workshops, but with the whole SADF. I did not have to try very hard because my bulimic binges had become uncontrollable and were catching up with me.

My major fall came when Lawrence went to Pretoria for a two-week workshop. I went on the worst bulimic binge rage I had ever had. I was in a major depression even though I was acting as if Lawrence's sleeping around and my affair did not bother me. But, in my mind, I knew I had become guilty of the lowest of low deeds.

Not only was the toilet my secret throne, I was now an adulterer as well. And I had lost Charles forever. I was convinced I had gone so far there was no hope of going back.

I locked myself inside our house, closed the curtains, and unplugged the phone. I did not let work know I would not be coming in. To outsiders it looked as if no one was home. I had told Scully, Dagger, and Doug I would be out of town. I did not want them to come and check up on me. I knew they were not convinced, but they left it as they could sense I had shut off.

Before I locked myself in, I had spent all the money I could get my hands on for food, food, and more food. I must have binged and purged at least eighty times in those two weeks. I am surprised I lived through it. I kept on thinking about a singer who had had a heart attack and died as a result of a major binge. There were times I wished I would have a heart attack during a binge.

In one binge, I would easily consume a whole chicken, two loaves of bread, each thick piece smeared with everything I could get my hands on, two to three big bags of chips, two to three very big slabs of chocolate, two liters of ice cream, and a few cream cakes. All of this was washed down with lots of liquid. My stomach would be as big as a woman who is nine months pregnant. I suffered great abdominal and back pain. I crawled around on my hands and knees, as my legs would be numb and too weak for me to stand up. My heart would start racing, my head pounding and I would almost black out.

I would then panic and know it was time to drag myself to the bathroom and purge. I would only stop when the bile and blood came spurting out. I needed to see the blood as it brought another type of euphoria.

While this sounds disgusting, this is what I was not only doing but craving to do. This whole cycle would take two to three hours. As I finished one cycle of bingeing, I would go through a period of beating myself and crying out for help, only to have the craving to binge cause me to start all over again.

Why did I do this? At first, I would feel the need to satisfy my craving, and then I would feel euphoric as I stuffed more food into me. I pushed myself harder and harder to see how far I could go. This made me feel powerful and in complete control, until my heart would race and panic would rush in.

I would first feel euphoric while purging, before feeling great disgust and shame. This left me in total despair, until the sight of blood placed me on a new euphoric high. Not long after that, I would hit a complete low. The only way up was by hitting or burning myself. I had also started banging my head as hard as I could. After this, I would drop down completely exhausted and in tears.

I was a wreck and I knew it. I needed help, but I decided I was only going to get it after I had destroyed and killed Lawrence. I would plead insanity. I believed that getting revenge on him would already bring me a lot of help.

The Friday of my second week of binge breakdown, I heard a knock at my door. I peeped through the curtains and saw Scully, Dagger, and Doug. I had been out of contact with people for about eight days by then, and still did not want to face the world. I opened the door slowly and asked, "Who sent you?"

Scully gently answered, "Don't worry Michele. Nobody sent us. We know you are hurting because of what Lawrence is doing to you." They had no idea about how severe my other problem was. They believed like everybody else did that I had a mild eating problem because of Lawrence's sleeping around so much.

"Oh, thank goodness, guys. I am just not able to face anyone right now, except for you, because you know what is going on."

They nodded in agreement. It seemed they had something on their minds so I waited. I looked at Doug because he was the mature one; Scully and Dagger were really boys still.

Doug said, "Yes, we are here because we want to go to Windhoek this weekend and we need a car. We were wondering if you would let us use your car."

This was perfect news for me. The last thing Lawrence would want was his troopers using his car for social purposes. This would make him hopping mad; at the same time it would add to him being a joke on base.

I smiled and said, "Of course you can. After all, I owe the three of you for your support. Please don't let me down." *Like not smash the car up!* I smiled to myself as I envisioned the car falling apart.

Scully, Dagger, and Doug did not let me down at all. My afterthought came true. I thought this stuff only happened in one's imagination and in the movies!

That Sunday I got a knock on my door and saw Scully, Dagger, and Doug standing there looking very worried. I immediately knew it had something to do with the car.

"What happened?" I asked, not sure whether I should be scared or happy. After all, I had wished for Lawrence's car to be smashed up.

"We had an accident," Scully answered, probably figuring it was best coming from him considering our relationship.

"But it was not our fault," Dagger added. "We were driving back when a kudu ran in front of the car."

"Where's the car? And what's wrong with it?" I calmly asked.

"It's outside in the driveway," Scully answered.

The car was smashed up in the front and at the back. The damage to the back puzzled me.

They saw me looking at the back and Doug stepped forward and said, "The kudu flipped into the air after we hit it and landed on the back of the car. We are so sorry. We promise we weren't speeding."

Now that it had really happened, I started thinking of Lawrence's anger. They could see the fear that suddenly took over my face.

"Don't worry," Scully added. "We already have a plan and the other guys are organizing it as we speak."

"What?" I asked, not sounding very convinced.

"We're going to take the car to our panel beater workshop and get it fixed there. (That was the workshop where they fixed the SADF wrecks that came from the army base camps at the border of Angola.) By tomorrow, the car will look exactly as it did before."

"Are you sure you can do this? Is it allowed? Won't the major stop this?" I asked.

"Don't worry about that. The guys have already said they will all put in their bit." Scully said.

"And Corporal Wellington won't ever know the difference so you don't have to worry about that either." Dagger did not sound convincing.

Doug could read my uncertainty as I looked at Dagger, so he added, "The guys won't let you down. They are already waiting at the workshop."

"Please make sure you get it fixed so it looks exactly as it used to. Lawrence is coming back on Wednesday."

When they left, I stood transfixed, feeling as if I had been hit by a tornado. I was not sure whether I was caught up in it or not, as I did not know how events would turn out. If the guys managed to pull it off and restore the car to look exactly the same as it was before the accident, I would be saved from the tornado approaching.

Every soldier, trooper, and permanent staff person on the army base would eventually get to know the secret concerning his car, which would embarrass and shame Lawrence. I could not have planned anything better than this. This freak accident would involve every department in getting it fixed within thirty hours, which would get the whole base laughing. It was as if all of this had been written for a movie script.

I should have been jumping for joy because of this, but I was not.

When I saw the smashed up car it hit me. The car seemed to reflect my own life. I realized I was like the car, a total wreck, and in need of outside help. I was out of control and my plan to get revenge on Lawrence was consuming my life.

I went to the phone and spoke to my mother. She agreed to help me.

Scully, Dagger, and Doug brought the car back and it looked exactly the way it did before the accident. The car's makeover was perfect and was finished on time.

At the airport the next morning where I had gone to pick up Lawrence, it felt good to know I was the one holding all of the secrets now.

As the front door to our house closed, I immediately got down to business. "Lawrence, I have something very serious and important to tell you."

"Can't it wait for later," he said. "I missed you. I haven't seen you for two weeks."

What a lie! How disgusting. His audacity was infuriating. I wanted to hit and kick him until he fell down unconscious on the floor. The bitterness and hate surging through me made me shake. I clenched my lips and fists tightly. I knew he had been with not one, but two women over the past couple of weeks, and now he came back with this lie. *He must really think I am stupid.*

"Sit, this news is important." I saw he wished to say something as well, but I continued. "I have booked myself into Tara Hospital for treatment."

I did not have to hit and kick him anymore because my statement knocked him flat into the chair. He looked flabbergasted. I had no idea why this had such an effect on him. I expected him to eagerly agree to this because it would give him more freedom to sleep around.

"Look here," he said, standing up. "I was going to suggest we go for marriage counseling because your problem has become a lot worse, and my anger is resurfacing. If we go for this counseling it can help us to get better." He smiled brazenly.

What game was he up to? Did he really think I could not see his insincerity? I returned a fake smile, not feeling any guilt for the game I was playing. I believed having an affair, messing up at work with the SADF, and getting the whole base involved in giving his wrecked car a makeover was equivalent retribution for all his affairs that he openly boasted about.

What I had not yet been able to match in revenge was the affair Lawrence had with a man. Lawrence had actually taken me to visit this man and his then fiancé. I was so tempted to tell her, but I did not have proof. I believed Doug when he had told me. I had also asked Scully to find out if it was true. He confirmed what Doug had said: Lawrence had boasted to them that he had slept with a guy while serving in the Caprivi Strip.

I did not tell Scully what Doug had told me. I believed having both of them come to me with the same story from Lawrence was evidence enough for me, but not for the fiancée. It was this deed of Lawrence's that made me decide to eventually murder him.

Pretending we were actually a married couple was enough torture, but marriage counseling was asking too much. I was just interested in revenge. I did not want to improve my relationship with Lawrence.

"An eye for an eye and a tooth for a tooth is what you are going to get from me!"

Lawrence looked somewhat puzzled by my statement. "What do you mean?"

"Nothing!" I snapped.

"Michele, what have you done?"

He had not been to work yet and so he did not know I had really messed up there.

"Nothing. And no, I don't want to go to marriage counseling with you and neither do you really want to go with me. You have to book me a flight to Waterkloof because I have an appointment at Tara next week."

I wanted to add, "*Then you can sleep around as much as you want to.*" However, I couldn't because I did not want him to know I knew about all his merry-go-round sleepovers! Not yet, anyway. I wanted him to find out I knew when he found out about all my other secrets. I knew he would find out about everything when I was in Tara. It did not bother me because I knew I would be safe and far away from his anger outbursts. At least I was hoping I would be away.

Tara Hospital was entirely different from the military hospital where I had previously been locked up in. It was known for its successful treatment of eating disorders. I had booked myself in there because I had lost control of my bulimia addiction. That was all. I liked being the one in control and wanted to get complete control again.

The only information the psychiatrist would get from me was how I wanted to get better from my bulimia. I still believed I was a fat, grotesque, overweight pig. I would brush off the statements of "You are anorexic." I still believed people were lying to me, because when I looked in the mirror I would still see blubber all around me.

I was not alone in a ward in Tara. This suited me because I still had nightmares of the four white walls caving in on me in my solitary confinement treatment. There were about eighteen of us in the eating disorder ward. One side was for the anorexia patients and the other side for the bulimia patients. Where did I fit in?

"Michele, your case is a little complicated because you have been diagnosed with clear anorexia nervosa and are required to put on a minimum of 20 kilograms [44 lbs.], but you are also a high-risk bulimic patient. We have decided you will be put on the side where the bulimic patients are, but you will also have to follow the rules we have for the anorexic patients. This means you have to stay on your bed 24/7, unless you have been given permission to get up."

This was a nightmare compared to the isolation because I was not allowed to do any form of exercise or any form of self-abuse. In isolation, I was free to continue doing my six hours of exercise a day and could beat myself up whenever necessary because no one was checking up on me. Even though I had felt trapped and caged in after a few weeks, I was still able to use up calories.

At Tara, I was not allowed to use up any calories. I could not do anything except eat and bathe. This was a nightmare to me. I regretted my admission to the institution.

When I entered Tara, I did not believe I was anorexic. I was 40 kilograms (88 lbs.) and saw no need to be cured from this as I believed I was already fat. So I closed myself up to dealing with the anorexia. There was progress with my bulimia addiction, because I broke the cycle of non-stop, twenty-four-hour bingeing. The cycle had started to control my life and Tara helped me to gain control, but did not stop it completely.

I knew when I left I would go back to bingeing once a day. The reason why I believed this was because the psychiatrist told me I would never truly be free from bulimia and had to learn how to manage it. He said anorexia and bulimia would be a factor for the rest of my life.

I was totally devastated to hear this. It was as if any hope had disappeared. I knew the psychiatrist was trying to be realistic, but I did not want to hear it. However, I accepted it and felt settled that while I would still binge, I would once again be in control of it.

It saddened me when the psychiatrist told me I would be an anorexic-bulimic for the rest of my life. To me, that was not victory, but failure, and I did not want to fail. I had regained control but that meant nothing. In my eyes, it was failure, despite the psychiatrist and occupational therapist telling me I had made progress. There was no room for half progress and certainly no room for failure.

I signed myself out knowing full well I would not be allowed back to Tara for treatment again. One is only allowed back if you are released with your doctor's full permission and signature. I was not upset with this rule because I had truly lost all hope. I walked out believing I would always be a bulimic addict, which meant weakness and failure.

During my stay at Tara Hospital, Lawrence had started sleeping with our new next-door neighbor as well. Finding out about it, together with my failed attempt at Tara, made me decided enough was enough.

Lawrence had got the last laugh and he had won. I would never be able to keep up with him.

The voices told me, *It's time for you to use our mind power and kill him.*

"I'm tired of all this and did not care anymore," I said aloud to the voices.

They scoffed at me and said, *You are a total loser and deserve to die.*

I agreed with them, which seemed to please them. I did not care. All I could see was how I had become a failure. How ironic! The acclaimed achiever was now the acclaimed failure. It was time to go to South West Africa and face the music of failure over there as well.

Flying back to South West Africa was a time of mixed emotions for me. As I sat in the noisy, bumpy Flossy, I knew I had a major decision to make. I was not sure which way it would swing. I believed Lawrence had orchestrated the entire mess I was in.

Was I going to use mental powers to kill him? Or was I going to sit him down and suggest that we start all over again and go for counseling as he had previously suggested? It would mean I had not failed in my marriage. Deep down, I knew trying to save my marriage was a joke. It was already a failure.

Why are you being such an idiot? Low Pitch screamed out so loud in me that I thought others on the plane could hear. *Lawrence is out to hurt and humiliate you. He has done nothing but destroy you. He has caused you to fail.*

You promised us that you were going to let us destroy him,
High Pitch edged in.

"Leave me alone! Go away!" I replied. I did not care that
the troopers could see I was talking to myself.

We'll see, Low Pitch said. *We'll see.*

After landing at our army airport base, I heard my name
called as I got out of the plane. I was surprised and delighted
to see my friend Leslie waving crazily beside a helicopter that
must have also just landed.

I had not seen Leslie in years and was amazed he remembered me. He was Charles' older brother and we had been in
the same drama group at Witbank High School years ago and
got along very well. We greeted each other like typical drama
students and he proceeded to tell me he was in the South African Air Force.

As we chatted, I asked him about Charles. He was eager to
tell me he believed Charles still had not gotten over me. I did
not expect that answer, but inside I was leaping and doing a
few somersaults.

I hid my excitement by responding, "No Leslie, you are
wrong. He rejected me without even blinking an eye." Inside I
could feel my emotions being torn open.

Leslie said, "Ah! You got engaged and then married. What
else was Charlie to do?"

Save me.

I said good-bye to Leslie and walked away with old emotions festering inside me, making my decision simple. I knew
my mind was made up about Lawrence. I was going to ask him
for a divorce.

CLIMBING INTO ETERNITY: My Descent in Hell and Flight to Heaven

As I walked across the tarmac, I could see Lawrence's six-foot-four frame in the waiting bay, and decided not only did I want a divorce, but his time was up. The cat no longer wanted to chase the mouse. It wanted to kill it. Humiliating and using me had gone too far. It was real payback time. No more playing marriage, no more playing life. I was a failure. I did not deserve to live. However, I was not going to leave this world alone. Lawrence would join me. I had nothing to lose. I had already lost.

I could hear High Pitch and Low Pitch singing and dancing in agreement.

Twelve

Failure

LAWRENCE MUST HAVE SEEN ME speaking to Lesley because his face was filled with disdain. I instinctively felt this was not going to be over very soon. Lawrence grabbed me by the arm and steered me to the car without a word.

Great, I thought. *He is embarrassed because people saw me being so friendly to Leslie. Now he knows how I feel with him sleeping around.* I felt laughed at, embarrassed, humiliated and worthless.

As we got through the front door of the house Lawrence erupted. "What do you think you are doing making me look like a complete idiot in front of everyone? You were flirting with some guy and making it look so obvious." Pacing up and down, he asked, "What on earth is going on?" He ranted and raved like a madman and mumbled things that did not make any sense.

All I did was talk to an old friend. He undoubtedly had spent the night with our next-door neighbor, seeing as she was his new conquest. Or perhaps she was on shift so he had gone to Louise. Or maybe he went to the major's wife. After all she was the first liaison partner he had got on the base. I started to go through all his infidelities in my mind.

When I got to his affairs with men, and I had been told of two, the anger and hate welled up to such a degree that I shouted to the voices, *You are right, it is time and I need your help*!

I locked into Lawrence's eyes with the intent of locking into his mind and destroying him then and there.

A bewildered look came over his face. "What on earth is going on?"

"I'm going to kill you."

He laughed, but then fell onto the floor as if someone had physically punched him.

High Pitch and Low Pitch were screaming in delight, urging me on.

I am not sure what all I said to him as I got carried away. As I bored my eyes into his, I could feel the magnetic waves of his mind and could see his thoughts. I started saying what he was thinking out aloud.

At first, he was stumped. Then with the shock and realization that I could read his mind, he suddenly burst out in rage. I knew the red anger would come next. It did. He went into a fit of uncontrollable anger. I heard him say in his mind, *I am going to teach her a lesson*. This was getting serious.

He started going crazy and smashing whatever his hands got hold of. He went to the kitchen and grabbed and smashed whatever he could find. Then he grabbed the kitchen knife.

Instinctively, I went into a self-defense mode. I zoned into Lawrence's mind with more effort and told his mind to stick the knife into himself. I did not know if it would work because I had never gone this far before.

Lawrence looked so confused. He took a few steps with the knife in his hand. I was not sure if he was going to stab the door or himself.

I shouted out to High Pitch, "Do something!"

Suddenly Lawrence stopped dead in his tracks and slumped onto the floor in a massive heap, the knife still in his shaking hand. He seemed confused and was clearly defenseless. I breathed out a sigh of relief because the raging maniac had been stopped. He was almost like a lost child. I felt a twinge of pity, but bitterness again surged within me. I then remembered what I had said: "An eye for an eye and a tooth for a tooth."

I looked right at Lawrence and said, "You are holding a knife to kill me."

Walking straight past him, I got out the proper cutting knife. This was the perfect time for me to strike Lawrence. Everyone would believe I was only acting in self-defense. I positioned the knife in my hands and prepared to strike. I raised my arms to the highest point I could reach so my downward thrust would be powerful enough to make it a fatal stabbing and screamed out, "I hate you. You had me locked up. You humiliated me."

I began moving towards Lawrence when I suddenly felt something holding my arms back. I could not bring my arms down. Then I heard that soft voice saying, *Don't do this Michele.*

I shouted back, "Let go of me. Lawrence must die!"

As I said this, I remembered my promise to God. It was at this point I realized my whole desire was to murder. Letting the knife go, I looked toward the ceiling and cried out, "Oh, my God, I am so sorry for breaking my promise."

I had broken other promises I had made to God on the day I lay naked on the floor. It seemed like a lifetime ago, but this time what I had done was serious. I had refrained from using mental powers for so long, but all my efforts had been wiped away by what I had just done.

There was total silence. Lightning did not hit me from the sky.

The silence was soon broken by the sounds of sobbing. Lawrence was sobbing like a baby. I never expected this from such a big man, and I was delighted. I started to laugh and sneer at him, forgetting about the cry I had just made to God.

"Your mother is right," he stuttered. "I can't control you. You're dangerous! You're a crazy monster! I want a divorce."

I was stunned as I had not seen this coming. I covered up my surprise with, "You can't divorce me!"

"It is you who has made me like this. This is all your fault!"

"Oh please! You have always had red anger or whatever it is they are treating you for. I am the one who wants a divorce."

"You just don't want people to know I divorced you!"

That was true, I didn't.

"I have already told them I want a divorce. In fact I want you as far away from me as possible. You are a danger to society and should be locked up." It seemed Lawrence had already decided this before his outburst. He must have thought long and hard about this while I was in Tara.

No, no, no! This is not how it is supposed to happen! I screamed in my mind. *I am supposed to be the one who rejects him. He isn't supposed to reject me. No, not again! Not again!* As I said this, I could feel a new wound being gouged in me. It was right next to the scab that was ripped off an hour earlier when I had reminded Leslie that Charles had rejected me.

Where had all my schemes and plans gone wrong? Everything had come crashing down. I had lost the cat and mouse game. I had dug my own grave.

Lawrence was not finished yet. He grabbed my arm once again and dragged me outside to the car. He asked, "How did *this* get here?" as he pointed to one kudu hair sticking out from under the sky-blue paint on the back of the car.

After all the intensity of what had just happened, being asked this was so ironically funny to me that I just laughed. No one else had noticed the kudu hair, but he did. By the look on his face, he already knew how it had gotten there.

What could I say? I just continued to laugh as I realized I had not lost completely after all. He might have won the war, but his victory was not going to be sweet. As I laughed, I slowly loosened my arm from his grip and stepped back, then turned and ran back inside the house as though my life depended on it.

I slammed and locked the front door. I needed time to think. If Lawrence knew about the car then he must have found out about everything, and that was why he was so worked up at the airport. It all made sense now. It meant it had nothing to do with me talking to Leslie. His volcano was already spitting lava before I even got off the plane. Seeing me with Leslie just added fuel to the fire.

Why did Scully not warn me when we spoke on the phone? Lawrence must have gotten to him. Lawrence had started playing his own game. I shouted to him on the other side of the door, "This is war and I won't stop until I see you put into isolation at the same institution I was."

He laughed and said, "That will never happen. You are the crazy one. I will make sure you walk away with nothing but a nutcase certificate."

"Lawrence, remember one thing! I've got nothing to lose! If I go down, you go down with me! You see, I know about all your affairs with the women *and* the men. What I have done to you here on this base is nothing. You are going down with me. I will only stop when you are kicked out of the army and are put into an isolation ward of your own."

"Never!" he shouted and began pounding on the door. "Now let me in! We are finished. I just want to get my things. I won't stay here until you leave the base and go back to Johannesburg. You are sick! You are crazy!"

It was over. I was a failure and I had failed.

—m—

The black cloud that had drifted over me did not leave after I was in Johannesburg and the divorce papers had come through. It seemed to get darker and heavier with every passing day.

I had watered the seed of rejection I had planted in my soul on that Christmas Eve of 1973 with bitterness, hate and revenge. The plant that had germinated from this was failure. I could live with rejection, but I could not live as a failure. I felt there was no room in this world for failures. I was drifting in and out of life looking through the eyes of a starving, heavily-dosed, anti-depressant pill popper. The psychiatrists were on my side and kept the pills coming.

Nobody needed me in their life and I felt the world would be better off without me. How could people stand to look at me when I could not stand to look at myself? How could they stand to be around me if I could not stand to be around myself? That man who hurt me when I was ten years old was right. I was a piece of rubbish, a pig, scum of the earth and I did not deserve to be alive. Why did I not just believe him then and end my life back then? My entire existence, my life for all of these years counted for absolutely nothing.

These thoughts were constantly with me and I always had the same answer. "If I had ended my life then, I would have left the earth rejected. Now I am leaving the earth rejected, a liar, pitied, and a failure."

The voices chimed in, *He is right. You don't deserve to be alive. You are a failure. You are a pathetic loser. Do you know that?*

"I know," I replied. "I am a failure and there is no hope for me!"

You know what to do? High Pitch continued.

"Yes."

Low Pitch added, *You are a worthless soul and a complete failure. You don't deserve to live. You are taking up someone else's space and oxygen here on earth. It is time for you to take your life. It is over because there is no hope for you.*

"I know. I just don't know if I can do it."

High Pitch eagerly jumped in with, *Stop wasting time and just do it. We will help you.*

Low Pitch would repeat, *There is no hope for you. The world is better off without you. We will help you.*

Sometimes I heard that soft, gentle voice saying, *Michele, God loves you. There is always hope in Christ. He . . .*

I always cut this voice off saying, "Leave me alone. Everybody just please leave me alone. Nobody loves me! Nobody cares."

With High Pitch and Low Pitch sneering, I put my hands over my ears. Why I always did this I do not know because the voices were coming from inside me and there was no way I could get away from them.

During those numb days of my life, it made an impression on me that Sonja and Gavin were both reaching out to me. They were even allowing me to spend some time with them. This made such an impact on me because I believed they had always despised me. I was tempted to believe they were genuinely concerned about me, but High Pitch reminded me of the never-ending feud between us. I agreed with High Pitch and told myself, *They are just conspiring together against me and only pretending to be concerned.*

The inevitable day came. It was settled.

I first went for a very long walk to look at the world of which I no longer felt a part.

Going back to my parents' home, I counted all my anti-depressants, tranquilizers, and sleeping tablets and found I had about ninety. I never took the prescribed sleeping tablets as I still believed two hours of sleep a day was more than enough. Before I had decided to start collecting my sleeping tablets, I would throw them away and pretend I had taken them. I had regularly taken my anti-depressant tranquilizers so I did not have a lot. I was not sure if ninety tablets would be enough, so I got a handful of the blue and white Lentogesic pain capsules my mom had in her cupboard and added them to my collection. Now my mixture of sleeping tablets, tranquilizers, and strong painkillers totaled one hundred and ten.

That should do it.

I did not want it said I had overdosed with too few tablets just to get attention. Consuming a fatal dosage of potent tablets would clearly show I meant business. I needed to make sure I would only be found after the medication had gone into my bloodstream and it was too late to pump my stomach. My intention was to die that day, not get attention. I was done with life!

When my mom and dad came home from work that evening, I spent the evening observing them. They had never been very emotional with us children, but we never lacked anything. I pushed away my longing to be hugged by them and told myself they loved me. In a very peculiar way, I loved my parents and knew they did not deserve everything I had put them through over the years. *They will be better off without me.*

The next morning, I made sure I said my last good-bye to my mom and dad.

High Pitch and Low Pitch were urging and encouraging me on. After about half an hour, I proceeded to the bathroom with my bowl of tablets. It was time! I started shoving tablets into my mouth and gulping them down with water, all the while crying and cursing myself.

Quite a few tablets had fallen into the basin and I just left them there. I did not know what to expect so I went to my room and waited. One thing was very clear to me as I lay there waiting. I was alone again. I said aloud, "What's taking so long? I just want to die."

Then it hit me. The room started to spin. I began struggling to breathe and my heart seemed to be pounding out of my chest. My head pounded and I felt sick. I wanted to go and get sick but I could not get up. I think I did get sick because I could feel vomit going up my nose and that familiar burn in my throat. I wanted to try and clear my nose, but I could not move. I was paralyzed and felt pinned down on the floor.

Then I began shaking uncontrollably. I do not know if it was only a few seconds or hours, but it seemed like hours. Going in and out of consciousness, I felt excruciating abdominal pain. Eventually, I pulled my knees up to my chest until I was too weak to do that and just lay like a heap of dirt on the floor.

Once again I realized I had never been loved by anyone.

High Pitch gurgled out, *You never deserved to be loved by anyone and now you are going to come to our house.*

Low Pitch added, *You weren't worthy of anyone's love. When you come to our kingdom, we are going to show you how worthless you really are.*

I did not understand, but I did not care. They were right. I was not worth anything and I did not deserve to be loved.

I heard the familiar, gentle voice saying, *Michele, you are wrong. Jesus loves you. You are so precious and worthy that He died for you. Your mom and dad love you too. Crawl to the phone and get help. You still have enough strength to do this. You still . . .*

I always became angry at myself whenever I heard that voice. I never felt worthy of the things it would say to me. It was always so loving and kind to me, always giving me hope. Those were things I was not used to being given.

I shouted out to it in my thoughts, *Leave me alone. Go away. It is too late. I am a failure, a loser. There's no hope for me! Leave me alone. I hate myself! I want to die!*

It was if the pounding in my head understood what I had just shouted out because it started to pound like a jackhammer. I felt darkness creeping nearer as fear gripped me.

Six years before when I had knocked myself unconscious was the first time, I had come face to face with the consuming black monster. This time, the monster had returned with the jackhammer in full force. I knew it would not stop until it had all of me. The nightmare that had been haunting me silently over the past six years was becoming reality. I was losing consciousness.

Now the pounding had been joined by a spinning, bringing a heavy dark wave with it, causing all light to fade away.

Falling into the blackness, I could feel the black monster breathing. This made me feel all alone and scared. I knew it was too late to try to save myself; I did not want to. I could not move, not even an eyelid. Completely paralyzed, I started screaming inside in unison with the jackhammer in my head as I felt the black monster eating me up inch by inch.

As I lay in this blackness for what seemed like hours, I began to hear my shallow breaths. Struggling to breathe, I was no longer sure if I was still a part of the world. Suddenly, I felt my heart being gripped. My life was slipping away from me. The pain in my chest became unbearable and permeated into my whole body, equaling my emotional pain.

The pain! There is so much pain in dying.

Together with this pain, a sick stench came into my nostrils. I somehow knew it was the stench of death. Death had come with a smile to linger and wait. It had come to linger and wait and smile.

Thirteen

My Descent into Hell

I DO NOT KNOW HOW much time went by. The intense pain running through my body made it feel like an eternity. I later learned they found me around six hours after I overdosed.

In my comatose state I heard a voice from a distance saying, "Michele, wake up! Can you hear me? Michele, can you hear me? Phone the ambulance! Michele, stay with us. Can you hear me? Stay with us!"

Then I heard, "Quick, she's going to die, she is going to die."

All I wanted was to die. I did not understand what the fuss was all about because death was what I wanted—even if it was just to get rid of the pain!

I tried to shout out, *I want to die . . . just let me die!*

This was of no avail, because no one could hear me.

Shuffling, different voices, the banging of doors, and then a siren. It felt as if I was no longer a part of this world. I was not able to pinpoint what it was, but something was completely different. While trying to work out what it was, I suddenly caught a glimpse of myself. I could see myself! I was stunned. *How can I see myself?*

The siren noise stopped and the ambulance doors swung open.

I saw myself being rolled out on a stretcher. A small nurse started running alongside the stretcher shouting with a distinct accent, "We're losing her. We're losing her!" Then it hit me. I had left my body and was looking down from above! I watched my lifeless body on the stretcher surrounded by medical staff running all over the place.

Wait a minute! *I know this place!* It was the same hospital I had been rushed to all those years back when I had lost consciousness and nearly died. I remembered all the needles that had been stuck in me, the tubes running into my nose, my mouth and my arms. I shuddered at the memory. I could not go through that again.

I shouted with all my might, *Leave me to die. Go away!*
No one heard me.

I was hovering above and they were not aware of my presence. I watched as they wheeled me through the hospital doors, doors I knew I would never walk out of. Only my death certificate would leave the hospital! I stopped shouting because it was not necessary.

The nurse with the accent said, "We are losing her!" I watched as she jumped up. I am not sure if it was on my stretcher or on the foot bar of the stretcher, she was small enough to do either. While I was being rolled down the corridor, the sister had started pounding on my chest!

She shouted again, "Help me! We are losing her!"

Why is she bothering? I want to die! I want to be dead! I don't want to come back! Why can't they accept it? Leave me alone.

I saw the little nurse shouting at my body, "Come on Michele! Fight! I refuse to let you go," while she continued pumping my heart.

The next thing, I could no longer see anything from above the ceiling. It felt as if I was back in my body with that consuming black monster. It had been so much better up in the air, out of my body, so I once again started shouting. *Leave me alone. I want to die!*

Once again no one had heard me. This time it was not because I was above everyone. I was locked inside my unconscious body. My screams had hit and bounced off the walls of my mind.

No, no, no! I don't want to live! Why can't you all just leave me and go away! I want to die!

I heard the nurse shouting, "Come on move it! We are not going to lose her!"

I screamed, *I failed. I don't deserve to live. I have to die!*

The same nurse's voice said, "She took a massive overdose a few hours ago! We are not going to lose her! Does everyone hear me? We are not going to lose her!"

I shouted back again, *Leave me! Just leave me to die!*

The pain coursing through my whole body was unbearable. Every fiber in my being was crying out in pain. In the black void, I continued to hear wheels spinning, doors slamming, and people hustling around me.

Then it happened again. I came out of my body and once more I was looking down from the ceiling.

The same little nurse stood next to me, holding my hand, shouting, "Come on Michele, fight!"

A doctor ran in with long strides. He started saying something and then grabbed the pads from a machine. He shouted something out and placed the pads on my chest. He shouted again. I saw my body jump up off the bed and then land down again. I was still limp.

I shouted out from the ceiling, *I don't want to come back. I don't want to live any more. Why can't you all just leave me alone?*

Then it dawned on me. The body I was looking at lying on the narrow bed was dead! It was lifeless. The people who stood around me were filled with despair. But I was not dead! I was looking down at them, watching and shouting from the ceiling! What was going on? How was it possible?

Why did my body seem dead down there while I was very much alive and hovering above near the ceiling? No one had looked up to the ceiling, which meant no one could see or hear me screaming down at them. I tried to touch myself, but felt nothing. But I knew it was me up in the air. It was still my same old voice, which I could hear screaming, and I still had the same feelings and thoughts. Yes, it was definitely me.

I could see my lifeless body and all the medical staff around me. I no longer was using my body's senses to see and hear, yet I could see and hear everything. I no longer felt any pain and realized that the lifeless body down there was not *me*—it was only my earthly body. So much of my living moments had centered on my flesh, my earthly body, as if it was the real me.

How is this possible? What part of me is hovering in the air? I tried to touch myself again, but could not feel my body. I remembered reading about life after death and that humans have a spirit, a body, and a soul. I had left my earthly body and my spirit and soul were hovering above the room. I also remembered how at the time I had found the concept of a spirit and soul leaving the body at death to be ridiculous. How very wrong I was! I realized the earthly body was only the thing that held the real me—my spirit and soul.

What is going to happen to me now? I don't have a body! What have I done? Where am I going? I was scared. Not because I was dead, but because I did not know what was going to happen next.

In sudden desperation, I began to fly. I frantically drifted through the air around the hospital until I saw my mom and dad. Seeing them brought me back to reality with a jolt. I had caused my own death. This also made me get back on the defensive, which helped me get rid of my fear of the unknown.

I hovered right in front of them and said out aloud, *You know it is much better this way. All I ever did was cause sorrow, anger, and pain wherever I went. I'm sorry for everything.*

They could not see or hear me because I did not have a body. I was soul and spirit. I felt a tinge of guilt at the sight of them because they looked totally numb, but the guilt only lasted for a second or so. I had become tired of all the hate. Hate was what I breathed, ate, and lived. I did not want my life back. Within time, they would understand this was for the better.

They would see I was a hopeless cause and a complete failure. When there is only hate and no hope, why bother to live?

Then I felt a massive tug and found myself traveling at what felt like the speed of light, or maybe even faster. The fear of the unknown returned and I felt terrified because a sense of danger engulfed me. I had entered a dark tunnel and once again become aware of how very alone I was.

Where is everybody? Where are all the angels? Why is it so pitch black in here? Help me! Somebody help me.

That stench of death I had smelled since lying on the floor became stronger as I moved deeper into the pitch-black tunnel. I could not see a thing, although the murky evil I sensed in the tunnel felt real and alive.

Where are you God? Where are you? Please, come help me! I shouted this as I realized goodness seemed to be slipping away. This alive, evil murkiness was the consuming black monster's partner.

I tried to convince myself I would soon see the light . . . that light at the end of the tunnel. But I was so very, very wrong. The tunnel started to turn crimson and began to get extremely hot and the smell unbearable! The stench flooding my nose was the smell of death. I just knew I was never going to see light at the end of the tunnel. I was not going upwards to any light. Instead I felt myself sinking into the depths of despair and darkness.

Fiery evil hit me on all sides as I burst out of the tunnel into a deep black hole ablaze with burning flames. A scream curdled out of me. I was burning and totally petrified.

Screaming from the intense pain, I suddenly felt something like a glove covering me. Within an instant I could no longer feel the intense burning flames, even though I could still see them and hear their roaring devouring hunger.

What was happening?

Then I heard the soft, gentle voice. I immediately recognized it as the calm, soft voice I sometimes heard deep inside of me. The difference now was I could also hear a firmness resonating out of the gentleness.

The soft gentle voice had been God all the time!

That day, years ago, when I had knocked myself unconscious, I had heard God's voice. His voice was full of power and might and had sent a great deal of fear throughout my entire being and made me to want to hide.

Now I knew the loving, gentle voice was also the voice of God. As I stared into a fiery hell, I knew with my whole being it was not only God's voice I could hear, but the glove covering me was God's hand of protection over me.

Michele, I gave you my love and showed you the error of your ways, but you chose to ignore Me and walk your own path. The path you have chosen leads to death. The only reason it is not consuming you now is because I have put my hand of protection over you.

I did not know why God had done this, but I was so relieved. Even though I no longer felt the intense heat and burning of the fiery flames, I could see they were still deadly. The hate and evil joining the fiery flames was consuming everything. The fear that had been exploding inside of me, had calmed down on hearing this gentle voice.

Instead of holding onto this I began to panic. I realized I could be stuck in that place forever. If God took His hand of protection away, I would be left in the absolute evil, hateful and horrific terror I was witnessing.

All calm left me and I cried out in fear.

I began reasoning and tried to persuade God. I now shudder at my absolute arrogance, thinking I could reason my sins away. *But God, I tried! I really tried so hard to stick to the promises that I made to You. God, I am not a bad person. I'm not a thief or a murderer. I don't belong . . .*

As I said this to God, I began traveling.

Fourteen

Fiery Horrors

Warning: Below I write exactly what I saw and experienced. There is some graphic detail that some might find too fear invoking or offensive. I am not able to take any of it out as this is the horrific truth of what I was taken into.

FEAR GRIPPED ME. I WAS begging God to get me out of that evil, burning hellhole when I abruptly came face to face with a crowd of people in agony. I also saw demons. Though I had never seen demons before, but I just knew these things were demons. Likewise, I knew the people were dead people who had not gone to Heaven.

I was intensely grateful for the protection around me that was preventing me from being burned and tortured together with the dead people surrounding me.

The dead people were recognizable as people, yet at the same time they were made of an oozing, gray, jelly-like substance, covered with scaly, rotting matter that was peeling off. It would be too kind to call it skin. The matter oozed as worm-like tentacles underneath gnawed on them.

Horrified, I looked towards what had been their faces. As I looked into their eye sockets, I could see behind the sockets and into their souls. I do not know how I knew, but I could see I was looking into their tortured souls.

I will call all the dead people I saw dead-beings. They were definitely dead people but they were rotting things with live tormented souls, and this made up their beings.

God, those are dead people there and they don't have real bodies. They have repugnant, decaying, disgusting, and rotting gray matter covering their bones. And their souls are exposed to those disgusting hideous creatures. This is terrible! This is so cruel.

Michele. They chose this, of their own free will.

Why? Why would they choose this God? No one would choose this. I knew I had not chosen this and yet I was there.

They chose to believe they did not need my Son— they were good people and did not need Jesus. They said I am a God of love.

I had been one of those people. Shamefully, I recalled the many times I said to God, "I know I have broken my promise to You, God, but I know You understand because You are a God of love."

I realized how absolutely dishonoring, completely wrong, and ungodly I had been. I had disregarded God's holiness and taken His love for granted.

I cried out, *I'm so sorry, God. I'm so sorry.*

God answered, *Michele, it is not for me to forgive you, but My Son.*

I had not said anything to Jesus. I didn't think it necessary. Frantic, I asked, *Why didn't anyone come and tell me that? If someone had just come and told me, I would have listened.*

I did tell you, Michele. The cross says it all. You just did not want to truly see or hear.

Oh, my God, what have I done? I am sorry, God. I am so sorry. That kept on going through my soul. I had chosen to take my life into my own hands. I had refused to allow Jesus any right to it. I looked around and let out a howl of regret.

I then remembered how I had invited evil and hate willingly into my life on Christmas Eve and had willingly placed myself under the dominion of hate. I had been given a chance to get out of this grip of evil and hate at the age of sixteen when I had the motorbike accident. Sadly, I had still chosen to cling to my evil ways, enjoying the power it gave me.

God sent people to show me while I lay there in hospital. I chose to treat His way of love and truth with suspicion and reject it as weak. I had even laughed at the pastor and his wife who came to see me and called them Jesus Freaks.

Once again I cried out in regret. I tried to pull away from the grip of the evil with the dead- beings and the hideous creatures that were pressing in on me from all sides, but they just seemed to press in more and more until they felt millimeters away.

The dead-beings were screaming out in fear and looking at me with absolute horror. Begging to get out, their pleas were just met with more torment. They screamed out in fear with absolute horror and hopelessness as they begged to get out. While they looked my way, I do not know if they could see me.

There was no hope in these dead-beings, only fear.

How long are they going to be like that?

For eternity.

As I felt myself being tugged off even further down, deeper into this pit of hell, I started to scream and beg God to get me out.

—⟋⟍⟋—

As I went deeper, the raging fire became more out of control. It was alive and full of consuming evil, hate, and fear. I knew this was where the black consuming monster came from. Even though this monster was a black hole, it had the same consuming breath of evil, hate, and fear. It was birthed out of the live fiery-in-furnace I was sinking into. Petrified, I could hear myself screaming hysterically.

This fiery-in-furnace was like a cancerous amoeba. This cancer of evil and hate was consuming, engulfing, and penetrating the dead-beings. The more they tried to resist it, the more it painfully leeched off them.

I gasped aloud in total shock and fear because I knew if the glove was removed from me I would be in the same hopelessness. Very aware of the hand of God's protection around me, I still had been able to hope. I let out a cry as I realized, if this protection were taken me, there would be no hope and I would be a slave to this fiery-in-furnace of torturous evil and hate.

All around, I felt a heavy, compressed force, as if the forces of gravity were squeezing me. I think it would be like the G-force a person can experience here on earth, only a hundred times worse. I felt so weighed down, so very, very heavy. It was like a pressure cooker, only there was no way to blow off steam. This pressure squeezing in was sheer torment in itself. It was unbearable.

The hand of God was protecting me, and still, I felt as if I would go crazy from the heavy, burdening pressure. I could see how terrorizing it was for all those I could see. I felt certain even the demons could feel the immense force pressing in on them as well.

Another thing weighing and crushing the dead-beings were all the accusations and torture. The demons were constantly hurling insulting accusations. If they were not blaspheming and spewing hate speech, they were accusing the dead-beings. It was burdensome to the dead-beings as they were guilty of whatever the demons were accusing them. This guilt was like another force zoning in on them. They could not get rid of it because they were guilty. This guilt also induced a despairing self-torment that the dead-beings placed upon themselves.

To add to this torment was the horrific physical torment the demons were accosting the dead-beings with.

But what truly made it hell, was that God's presence was not there. There was no love, no peace, no joy, no hope that it would get better. Only evil, hate, howling regret, and a consuming fear of growing hopeless. They all knew this was a place of eternal damnation that would only get worse.

A one-body wave or amoeba had control. It was a massive, dominating wave that seemed to carry the heart of this evil, hate, and fear. When in sight, the whole fiery-in-furnace's pulse escalated, releasing a state of panic and injecting more intense evil, hate, and fear.

As this amoeba wave of fiery larva traveled, it rose up into a hideous, giant ape-like shape. Before crashing over everything, this ape-like amoeba-wave would call out to the dead-beings: *I am god and king; I am lord Lucifer! All will bow down and worship me.* He bellowed out to these dead-beings how much he hated and despised all human beings. And how he hated Jesus the Christ most of all. *I will destroy all who are created in the image of God before they can get to God.* He lashed out with angry, evil contempt at the dead-beings, as he howled, *You are all at my revenging mercy.*

This ape-like amoeba-wave then began to blaspheme Jesus Christ as he came crashing down, releasing his vicious torture of fiery hate and evil.

I knew this ape-amoeba-wave was the devil. He was full of evil eyes and what looked like moving worms that ripped out as live tentacles. If the eyes are the windows to the soul, his eyes were the gates to pure evil. They could draw you in and yet, at the same time, kill you over and over again.

Whenever the devil caused his living amoeba-wave of hate, evil, and fear to flood over the dead-beings and the demons, they all had to praise and hail him, and proclaim, "Lucifer is god and lord."

As he broke over them into larva, it brought more terror to the dead-beings as they saw it coming and they ran in complete desperate horror. Tentacles crawled out of this fiery larva, touched the dead-beings, and began sucking on them. As the tentacles bored into them, the dead-beings released soul-wrenching, anguished cries of torturous pain, and begged for it all to stop. Eventually these dead-beings became so tormented they started attacking one another to get out of reach of the devil.

At the same time, demons were continually attacking and tormenting the dead-beings. The sucking, tentacle-like worms then blew up. The evil, the screams, the crying, the begging, the blasphemy, the threats, together with the spitting accusations and whispers of death all around were hell itself.

The instant the glove of God's protection fell off me, I knew I was going to get a body like these dead-beings and would be terrorized by the devil, this ape-like amoeba-wave of fiery larva and all his demons. Hysterically screaming, I begged God over and over again to get me out. All I wanted was my earthly body made of flesh. I just wanted to go back to earth.

I cried out again, *Oh God, I am so sorry, I am so sorry. Please get me out of here!*

Demons are hideous, disgusting, spitting, grotesque creatures of all shapes and sizes. Their frightening eyes all had the same look as the devil's—pure, consuming hate and evil. The hypnotizing evil that drew the dead-beings into them came from the devil. Their dead-black eyes mirrored the fiery flames eating the beings up, while pulling them in with their destructive, magnetizing evil. The demons were terror themselves and filled with accusing vengeance and violent torture. They tortured gleefully and with such hate, because they also seemed tormented.

The fiery evil and hate among the demons caused them to continuously fight each other and hurl evil hisses and destructive blows at one another. This caused them to attack the dead-beings with even more vengeance and hate. It seemed like they blamed the dead-beings for the fiery-in-furnace they were in.

As I went deeper into what was the core of fiery hell I felt myself being sucked out of the main core and into one of the branches. I started to choke on torturous burning smoke that was alive and very much part of the flame. Burning items smoldered and then exploded into a live, larva-like liquid acid. To me, the burning items looked like coal, but to the dead-beings they looked like gold.

Here the ever-powerful evil of greed was mixed with such intense jealousy, suspicion, and hate. The dead-beings tore at each other just to get at the burning things or burning coal. So obsessed with a need to have it, they did not seem to realize it was junk, and only burning coals.

As soon as they got possession of the burning item, it exploded and disintegrated into live, sizzling larva, which would begin to burn the dead-beings and cause them to let out a wail of agony. After the wails, came screams of complete loss mixed with fury because they had lost the piece of coal. This would cause them to start attacking one another other with vengeance for some more burning junk.

Out of the smoldering blackness, demons came and attacked all the beings repeatedly, accusing them, *Do not commit idolatry. Do not covet. You gained the world and gave us your soul. Hail to mammon! Worship mammon!*

As the demons said this, a massive, fat-lipped demon appeared with fat roll upon fat roll. Its eyes looked squashed because of the greed rolls in its face. Green greed puffed out of it. Out of its mouth oozed slimy green drool. It was disgusting, best explained as thick, infected mucous. It plodded, snorting with dripping drool all over the place as it dropped off burning coals.

As this hideously grotesque thing scuffled all over, the demons shouted out, *Mammon!* and shrieked in laughter.

I cried out, *Who is Mammon?*

This caused the dead-beings to hiss and fight each other for Mammon's coals and the coals to implode into burning liquid larva. Why did they want that hideous, grotesque demon's coals? Nothing seemed real except the total madness in the air and how demented, jealous, and totally obsessed these dead-beings were over the burning coal.

Why are they fighting over burning coal? Can't they see it for what it is? I did not get an answer.

I then thought how obsessed I had always been with trying to keep up with the Joneses. How I had always wanted what others had and how I hated successful people. How absolutely green with jealousy of other people and their possessions I had always been. I despised them and even lied to ruin what they had. I had called out disaster to fall on them, silently cursing them under my breath. I was able to see how I despised and hated any successful or rich person. Ashamed, I gave myself the guilty verdict.

Then, from out of nowhere, the ape-like amoebae-wave hit the tortured, demented dead-beings like a roaring tsunami. As it did, they all had to praise the amoeba-wave saying, *Lucifer is god.* More fear and horror came upon the dead-beings as they hailed the devil because the worm-like tentacles from the amoeba started dropping off. They looked like glowing worms, but the glow was deadly. The fiery, hot worms grabbed out at and sucked the dead-beings with their pouting mouths slithering all over them. As these tentacles sucked the dead-beings, it released a green acid-like substance like snail slime. This caused louder, more agonizing and intense howls as the dead-beings tried to pull these tentacles off. The harder they tried to pull these soul-sucking tentacles off, the more insanely tormented they became. This caused them to release more agonizing howls and wildly run for cover that was not there.

This exposure and insecurity set the dead-beings into another obsessive frenzy of jealousy and greed and they started to attack one another. Despite all the torment and pain they were suffering, they still wanted to possess each other's space and each other's coal. This provoked the demons looking on to join in. The cries of agony, the painful howls of torment and desperation to get each other's possessions bellowed, adding to the hissing hurls of blaspheming accusations, followed by vicious blows from the demons. Coveting, jealousy, and envy was evil and it consumed whatever came in its path.

Horrified, I desperately cried out, *God, I am sorry*. I truly did not realize how evil coveting was.

I then felt myself been pulled out of that green evil madness. Traveling deeper into the torturing fiery core, I felt myself being sucked into a branch that reeked like blood! I could even taste it.

I watched in complete horror as blood gurgled out from everywhere. This thick, fiery-red blood was alive and evil. The dead-beings were repeatedly drowning in it, screaming as this blood devoured them at the same time as if they were sinking in sand. There were others trying to get this thick, stinking blood off them, but it just kept pouring back to cover them. They screamed out in agony as the blood sucked on them like clots of leeches.

The demons that were tormenting them accused them saying, *Do not murder. Do not murder! Hate is murder! Murderer! Murderer!* as they violently attacked the bloodied, tormented dead-beings. The terrified dead-beings howled out in agony, *Damn the blood, damn the blood!* as they tried to fight off the attacking demons.

They did this over and over again. Between the howling and the fighting with the blood, the demons and each other, and the spitting of the blood as it gurgled all over, it was a sheer, violent bloody horror. One of the dead-beings suddenly stopped in its tracks, turned and viciously attacked the dead-being next to it with murderous intent. This dead-being in turn viciously attacked back with even more murderous intent. Murdering hate broke out as each one turned on the other. They were dead but still wanted to murder each other!

I shouted, *I shouldn't be here, God. I am not a murderer.*

As I spoke, I knew it was not the truth. Yes, I had not physically murdered anyone, but in this spirit realm it is not only the physical deed that gets punished, but also the intent of the heart.

I saw how I had chosen and planned to murder men.

Lawrence was going to be the first man I was going to murder, and he was not the only one. The only reason why I had not done so was because all my schemes had fallen apart before I could set them into motion.

I saw how I had breathed and thought murderous hate and nothing else. I had walked around with this murder in my heart since the age of ten, and it had become the norm to me. I saw how hate and bitterness leads to this type of a murderous life which comes alive in the spirit realm and feeds off the devil and his demons. They have a never-ending supply of this evil destructive and deadly fruit. Yet this root would never be satisfied until a murder would be committed, a life taken.

This was why I had taken my own life. It all made sense to me.

As I looked around at all the blood and the murderous, bitter hate, I saw its absolutely-fatal evil and cried out, *Oh God, I am so sorry. Please, God, I can't take this blood. There is so much blood and bitterness, so much refusal to forgive, so much hate, and so much murder.*

As in the previous place, out of nowhere the evil ape-like amoeba-wave full of tentacles entered and smashed all over the blood. The dead-beings and the demons present once again had to hail and say, *Lucifer is god.*

As the dead-beings did this the blood hungrily gurgled out of all the openings, causing the demons to go into a frenzy of murderous torture. The dead-beings begged and screamed for it all to stop, but they were ignored. As the tentacles fell off the devil, they became gross, gory, sucking slurping, slugs. They lashed out onto the rotten grey matter of the dead-beings to suck them. This caused their terrorizing screams of terror to turn into escalating howls of agonizing and torturous pain.

There is so much blood, so much screaming, it is drowning me, I howled out in despair. I stopped as I saw a dead-being run in front of me, chased by a group of accusing, murderous demons. This left me in even more shock and fear. I watched as this dead-being screamed and ran away from the attacking demons, then tripped and fell head first into more blood. As he got up, he began grabbing and pulling at his face and yelling out in a frenzy of pain as the evil of the blood bit into the gray-matter of his rotten flesh.

Even more fear rose within me as I realized who the dead-being was.

That is Hitler! I shouted out.

I knew with my whole being it was Hitler. He was in a disgusting, decaying body, but when I looked into his eye sockets and saw into his soul, I knew it was him.

Once again I questioned, *Is that Hitler?*

Yes, it is, the gentle, but firm voice protecting me from Hitler said.

I shouted out, *God, I am not like Hitler!*

Hitler started coming towards me. I did not know if he could see me as I could see him. I could not believe I had been put in the same place he was in. He murdered millions of people, namely Jews, in the cruelest, most inhumane ways known.

In desperate urgency, I said, *God, I cannot be compared to this sick, cruel, inhumane murderer.*

As I said this I knew I was wrong.

Even though I had not murdered, I had allowed hate, revenge, and evil to consume me just like Hitler had. And like Hitler, I had purposely operated in secret evil and deceit to justify everything I did, every step of the way. Just like Hitler, I now stood in the hellish pit of murder, a consuming, live river of blood that was crying out. I cringed in regret at how I enjoyed the deceit and bitterness of hate welling up inside me. I had used this evil darkness as my energy source and my very reason to live.

I cried out, *Oh, how I have hated and hated!*

I could see how this invisible energy of consuming hate had not been enough. I had known my desire to kill Lawrence was not only to get revenge on him, but to literally spill his blood. I had needed more to satisfy my hate. I also knew I would not have stopped there because my hate had grown to a monstrous size. There would have been other men deserving of this fate, according to my sick, warped mind.

I heard myself let out a howl of regret as I realized my soul was just as vile, toxic, and deadly as Hitler's was. I too stood guilty of hate crime. It did not matter if I was 10 percent guilty or 99 percent guilty; I was guilty and that was why I was in sin's grip.

The only reason why this murderous hate had not been completely exposed in my life was because of the invisible hand that stopped me in mid-air from bringing the knife down into Lawrence's chest.

My hate and desire to see a life taken had been exposed in a different way—suicide. I realized, if not stopped, when the pendulum of hate swings to its fullest, it will either swing to the far left, murder, or far right, suicide. I had been stopped from murdering, but was in hell from suicide.

Oh God, I am sorry for my bitter hate, for cherishing the evil vileness of my soul. I am sorry about the desire to spill and splatter Lawrence's blood and take his life. I am sorry for taking my own life. What have I done, what have I done? Forgive me, God. Please forgive me.

As I was saying this I could hear, *Damn the blood, damn the blood. Hater! Hater! Murderer! Murderer!*

—⁓—

Once again, I found myself traveling through the fiery core of hell before branching off and enter another terrifying level. I had not yet seen anything, however, the smell was worse than the blood had been. It was a sickening, provoking, spirit of sexual lust and vulgarity.

This reminded me of the man who had his hands all over me with lustful intent on that Christmas Eve. I became terrified at what I would see. The sexual, lustful stench became so bad I had already begun to frantically scream and beg God to get me out of that place. My screaming did not get me out. The strong pungent smell began engulfing me. It was the smell of sex and of sordid sickening lust.

As I entered, I let out another terrifying cry at what I saw. What was, and still is, totally horrifying, is that these dead-people, these dead human beings all had both male and female genital organs. It was disgusting, vulgar, and absolutely horrifying.

There were disgusting, vulgar, gyrating bodies all over the place. They were scouring over and into each other like slimy, hissing, yet also snorting snakes, with sadistic, forceful lust. I watched in horror as the dead-beings forced themselves into one another. As this occurred, they would go into shaking, agonizing fits because someone else had simultaneously, sadistically thrust into and violated them. It was not the thrilling sex they knew on earth. Instead it was a terrifying, forceful, vulgar, and sickening violation. I was horrified, mortified, and I could hear my own petrified, terrorized screams.

The dead-beings were doing these violent, disgusting, acts of forceful sex to each other but, when they could, they were also agonizingly begging and pleading for it all to stop as they themselves were being violently and continuously raped. They hated what they were doing but if they stopped for even a split second, they would be attacked and violently raped by the demons watching.

There were hundreds of drooling demons watching and applauding. They all had exposed tentacles with the appearance of male genitals. These tentacles were releasing an oozing substance, producing a pungent sexual, lustful smell that sent everything into a frenzy of mad, lustful sexual acts. The demons attacked one another to get to a dead-being to lust over, rape, and get sexual gratification from. The dead-beings let out agonizing wails and howls of regretful screams. They begged for it all to stop but knew full well this sick, hateful, forced sex would never ever stop.

The vulgar sights, smells, sounds, and the soul-wrenching terror and disgust of the place was beyond definition. [This is a nightmare that took me a few years to get out of my head. As I write this, I do so mechanically. I am not able to go back and fully look at it as I am with the other levels. It is just too much for me to handle.]

Then once again, that big ape-like amoeba-wave of fiery larva came and engulfed the place, this time filled with sexually drooling and slimy tentacles. The dead-beings started screaming and begging for mercy while having to praise Lucifer as lord. This sadistically and sexually provoked the demons even more, causing them to secrete more of the disgusting and pungent, oozing substance all over as they charged about with the intention to violently rape. As they did this, they mockingly spat out, *Adulterer! Adulterer! Slut! Pervert! Womanizer! Whore! Sex! Sex! Drink the sex! Feel the sex! We are that sex!*

They flew in like vultures, attacked like wild dogs, and gleefully guffawed and groaned in ecstasy as they thrusted like humans with the basest lusts. The agonizing, vicious sexual torture and noisy, sexual, lustful gratification began to heighten.

I could hear my hysterical, petrified, and horrified screaming, *No, Noo! Noo! Please, please, get me out of here! God, I did nothing like this. I was never like the sexually-perverted, piggish man who grabbed and hurt me on Christmas Eve. How could I be here?*

As I was shouting, I shamefully began to realize I had committed adultery with Scully to spite Lawrence. Oh, how ashamed I was! How disgusting I felt! How very guilty I was!

I also saw how I had messed up with sexual sin just after the divorce went through. Filled with shame as I looked at all the revolting, disgusting lust, vulgarity, and perverted sex all around me, I saw how destructively evil adultery really was. I fully understood that sex, in all its forms, out of the boundaries of the blessing of God, belongs to the devil. It's a grave defilement that totally defiles spirit, soul, and body.

I stood guilty of this and knew the shame, the absolute shame, as a result. (I know all my sins have been forgiven and I stand totally forgiven for the adultery I committed. But, oh, how I wish I could rip this place of sexual sin out of my memory and totally forget about it all.)

I cried out in my shame, *God, please forgive me. Please forgive me. I am sorry, I am so sorry.*

As I was screaming and begging God to take me out of that pungent smelling, sick, perverted, disgusting, and violent sex, I felt myself being pulled out and again traveling into the evil center core of fiery hell.

—◊◊◊—

I was glad to leave, but dreaded where I would be taken next as I had been guilty of every sin in each place to which I had been taken. Filled with shame, I dreaded seeing what else I was guilty of.

I found myself in a place controlled by an intimidating, controlling, demonic evil, which was worse than the destructive evil I had encountered thus far.

All around were sounds of whispering voices, whispers that drilled into everyone's souls, into their minds and drove them mad. I had just arrived and I already felt like I was going out of my mind.

A very strong, live, electric evil force of control and manipulation slowly drew all the dead-beings toward it like a magnet.

The dead-beings fought with all their might to get away from this magnetic evil as it bored into their minds with a hypnotic effect. This would cause them to go into a trance-like state, making them appear like gray, decaying-matter zombies. As these dead-being zombies got too close to this unseen, yet seen, central evil, it sizzled their souls up alive and spit them out over and over again.

While fighting to get away from this soul-consuming, controlling, magnetic force of evil, the dead-being zombies were also operating out of their own inner evil. I could see that every one of the zombies knew exactly what the other one was thinking and scheming. Nothing was hidden at all. It was one big web of selfish, evil, dominating, and hypnotic control.

These dead-being zombies were not only at war with one another, but also at war against the demons, because the demons knew what they were thinking too. The demons had the power not only to read their minds and to control them, but to also hypnotize them into a tormented state.

The revengeful hate and suspicion the dead-beings had for one another because of the central controlling power, caused fear within each tormented soul. They would not allow one another within half a meter of each other. They would use their minds to attack one another, and at the same time, the demons would use mind control to inflict fireballs of suffering and pain into the dead-being zombie's minds and souls.

As the demons did this, I could see an electric shock wave enter the zombies and travel through them. This caused them to convulse and howl out in pain, as the electric force shot out of their eye sockets, mouths, and ear sockets. They grabbed their heads and screamed and screamed and screamed.

Then that controlling massive ape-like amoeba-wave of fiery larva and evil with live electrified tentacles swept over them, just as it had in all the other places. Once again, everyone had to proclaim: *Lucifer is god. Lucifer is lord.*

This time, the wave rose up higher and turned into the shape of a puffed-up cobra. It stayed in this raised position, swaying from side to side, until it readied its aim and spat. It released what looked like currents hitting and causing the dead-being zombies to bump and fall all over each other. Total chaos and agonizing screams filled the atmosphere as the zombie's minds oozed out into one big central mass of evil, destructive energy.

As shock waves were sent through them, they went into seizures. The whispering tentacles, like electric eels, then latched onto this central mass, shrieking and striking out and grabbing onto the pile of souls, releasing charges and causing them to pulsate and scream in even more torment and pain. These eel-like tentacles then separated as they slithered into the souls that formed the mass. It was as if raw current was running through these zombies, inducing chaos. Every dead-being zombie would go wild trying to get away from the new tentacle. Those who got in the way were zapped down by the demons that enthusiastically joined the tentacles. They burned the dead-beings up with controlling mind power and swallowed their souls with this invisible evil power, torturing them from the inside before spitting them out into a heap.

Demons slithered from nowhere and puffed up into co-bras, hissing and shouting out, *We are stubbornness. We are re-bellion! We are manipulation! We are control! We are fear! Damn the will! Damn the will of God! Damn Jesus! Damn dying to self! Lucifer is our lord! Now it is his way! Bow to him! He is now in control! Damn the will of God!*

As they said this, their snake tongues spat out more electric shock currents that surged through the dead-beings zombies. This sent them shrieking into more painful convulsions. The stench of the burning substance of these dead-beings was like a rotten mass of meat.

The smell of this burning rottenness filled the place and provoked the demons to resume the hissing whispers of the dead-beings' thoughts. This caused a wave of fear followed by more electric shock currents. The dead-beings then came out of their zombie-like state and ran wildly shrieking out in fear and torment while fighting each other off.

The dead-beings also knew if they touched one another, it would cause immense inflicting pain because of the torment-ing current. Hissing, cobra-like snake demons torturing dead humans all sounds like sci-fi material, but this was very real and made complete sense.

What I saw and understood was the evil unseen, yet seen, force of control and manipulation was generating the power to make the deadly, raw electric current. This was an invisible live wire straight from the pit of hell used for one purpose on earth: to make a human conform to what another human wanted them to do. There is another word for this: *occult.*

Control and manipulation come out of the occult. This takes many different forms of disguise in the world, and all of them are from the pit of hell. Yes, Satan is the lord of control and manipulation and he gives these powers to any human who is willing to use them. This invokes a physical realm of raw, evil competitiveness and suspicion causing immense pain.

I gasped because that was who *I* was. I never had any peace because I was always suspicious of everyone and everything. I truly believed everyone was out to get me. I saw how my life had been a cold, vindictive, calculative, competitive game of chess to me. What made this so sick and evil was that I had used everyone who ever crossed my path as a chess piece in my game of control. I switched from one game to another, and coldly changed from using people to knocking out all the new rival pieces.

I had schemed to annihilate, like an electric eel, a spitting cobra. I saw how I had used this controlling and manipulating power at any cost. How I slithered around and raised my hood like a cobra, and spit out the venom of deceit. This blinded people from the truth and I'd manipulate and gain control over them while they were blinded. My venomous strike consisted of scheming, lying, emotional blackmailing, crying crocodile tears, threatening, tricking, calling down evil into people's lives, playing the victim, and whatever else seemed necessary.

I was determined in my stubbornness and rebellion to get my own way. I had slithered into minds, like an electric eel, causing many teenage boys and young men humiliation, hurt and pain—even my own brother. I cringed in shame as

I thought how I had first used children to practice this mind control on until I had got it right.

When I got my own way, I would snigger in power and quietly mock people for their gullible weakness. I had relished in this power of calculating manipulation and control. But as much as I had been able to blind and manipulate people, I could not fool myself. My hidden-agenda smile deceived many, but my eyes mirrored the evil in my heart. I could never get away from what I could see in them.

I had only wanted my own will, my own way. I suddenly understood what the demons' cries of "damn the will" meant. The devil and his demons do not want us to submit to God's will; they prefer us to want our own way, our own will. This is complete rebellion to God and slavery to the devil's way.

Since the age of eleven, I had become this slithering, controlling, self-willed cobra-eel-like person! This had brought major hurt and destruction in people's lives and my own suicide. Once again, I felt shame, immense shame, and guilt. Doing it my way had caused me to become an evil, puffed-up manipulator.

Oh God, what have I done? What have I become? I manipulated people like chess pieces in a game of control! I am so sorry. Please forgive me . . .

I did not finish as I found myself moving still yet deeper through the core of this fiery hell. *How many sins have I committed? How much am I guilty of? What monster am I?*

The places before had been an evil that bored right into the soul and mind, taking complete control. I was relieved to be out and away from the covetous, burning, acid coals, the gurgling murderous blood, and the pungent vulgar, slimy, lustful sex, as well as the raw electric hisses of destructive manipulation.

Now I found myself in a place that suffocated me with an evil that seemed to wrap around and squeeze the soul and mind to nothingness. It was no longer a cobra, but a python. In the mist, I saw floating objects, religious symbols, artifacts, and statues with evil eyes in each one.

I realized those symbols, artifacts, and statues were demons. Out of them rang a soul-wrenching chanting. I was dumbfounded because I recognized so many of these religious symbols, artifacts, and statues.

Shocked, I asked, *Are all religious symbols, artifacts, and statues demons? Are they not from You, God?* Symbols and artifacts from both of the churches I had attended over the years were there. Why were these worldwide, highly-revered symbols, artifacts, and statues in hell?

A condemnation washed over me that I was a failure and would never be good enough, or holy enough. This condemnation had surrounded me all my life. The boarding school, Belgravia Convent, where my sister and I had been placed at the tender age of four-and-a-half years, had ensured these robes of condemnation clothed us. The nun, Sister Paulina, who was the overseer of the babies, continually told me I was bad and evil (she had locked me in the linen closet during the dead of night). It was this same condemnation I could feel wrap around me, squeeze and choke me.

I saw a live black mist, together with religious demons repeatedly chanting out, *We are religion. We are the gods. We are religion. Damn the Spirit! Damn the Holy Spirit! Damn the Spirit of Life! Damn God's Word! Damn the glory of God! Damn the faith! Damn Jesus the Christ! Damn His Name! Damn His grace! Damn! Damn! Damn! Condemn! Condemn! Condemn!*

As they were damning the Holy Spirit, the Word of God, His grace, and Jesus the Christ, the demons went ballistic in their anger and lunged their damning anger out onto the dead-beings closest to them. Then these demons would stop and once again become symbols, artifacts, and statues.

In blasphemous, curdled laughter they said, *We are your gods! We are your church! We are your spirit! We are the glory! Kneel down before us! Worship us! We are condemnation! Give us the glory! We are your faith! In the name of us! In the name of Lucifer!*

As they said this, they dove in and forced these dead-beings to bow before them.

The live black mist slithered into many fat, slithering pythons and wrapped around the dead-beings and started to squeeze them, causing their heads to blow up like balloons. The dead-beings howled like wolves in pain and total terror as they became obsessed and insane.

As this mist eased up on squeezing and strangling the dead-beings, they wriggled free and started running like crazed wild animals, madmen, away from the mist, the demons, and each other.

They clutched their heads and screamed because of the evil humming and chanting.

As the dead-beings fought off the vicious attacks of the religious symbols, artifacts, and statues the symbols turned back into hideous demons and attacked the wild dead-beings. Once again, they wildly howled out horrifying screams of regret and remorse as they were faced with what they had worshipped all their lives.

There was a strong, mocking, religious hierarchy all over as the demons were damning and condemning and viciously hitting the dead-beings with religious artifacts and symbols. This sent burning black mist surging and wrapping around the dead-beings. It would enwrap its burning power around the dead-beings, encasing condemning evil around them causing more choking madman cries to bellow out.

The dead-beings howled out, *How can my church, my god be from hell? How can it be demons? I believed in my church! I put my faith in my church! I trusted the minister! I went to church. I prayed. I was a good person. Good people go to heaven not to hell. I am not supposed to be here. I am a good person. I am supposed to be in heaven. Why? Why? How? How? God where are you? Help me! Help me! I don't belong here. This is for murderers, for cheats and liars.*

As the dead-beings fought off their own religious demons, their questioning, angry frustration and regret echoed in sync with the chanting vibration that rang through this burning place of hell. Their fate was a torturous tragedy when they saw what that they had been worshiping. They cried out, *Why didn't anybody tell me? Why didn't anybody warn me? I believed in my church. How can this be?*

Their trusted religion had mockingly and violently turned against them and confusion, frustration, and realization surged through the dead-beings causing them to wildly run and yell out with more agonized howls of anguish.

Multitudes of demons tortured and viciously hit the dead-beings with their religious symbols shouting out, *Idolaters, idolaters. Fools! Blind fools! Bow down and praise us! Praise Lucifer! The god of religion! It is by the name of Lucifer!* Then with scowling, mocking, laughter they would swarm in forcing the dead-beings to bow down and fall prostrate before them again.

As the dead-beings did this, the demons viciously hit and kicked them, while spitting out, *We are religion! We are the golden calf! Worship us! Idolaters! Blasphemous idolaters! Lucifer owns your soul! He hates souls! He owns you! He hates you! He hates Jesus! Lucifer is your savior! Praise him! Praise us! Damn the Spirit of God. Damn Jesus the Christ!*

Maddening cries of intense physical and emotional pain from the abuse would once again pierce the place, followed with louder soul-wrenching agonizing howls of regret. The dead-beings then turned on one another like wild animals, madmen.

This was when I realized the devil, with all his power and his demons, could not kill the soul. The devil was now the keeper of these souls! Clearly, the devil and his demons hated souls, but they did not have the power to kill a soul. This caused their torturous tormenting intent of hate and anger to grow.

The devil was the devourer of souls, but only the Soul-maker could destroy them. The dead-beings still existed, but in eternal damnation. God Almighty, the maker of the spirit and soul had completely removed His presence from this kingdom of darkness, and this, in itself, was eternal damnation.

The devil uses religion as a cruel, sadistic copycat and counterfeit.

God, I don't understand. Did these dead people believe in You? Did they put their faith in You? I was scared and confused because many of these dead beings had been "good people."

Michele, they believed in their church. They did not believe in Me. They put their faith in their church. Not in Me or My Living Word.

In the other parts of hell I had been in, the people knew they had sinned. They chose to ignore their conscience until, eventually, their conscience became indifferent to their sin. So indifferent that people justified why they were doing that sin. Many began calling it a sickness.

This I understood very well because this was my way of justifying my life.

However, this level was different. The people here had put their faith and their belief in their religion. They had truly believed what they were following and being obedient to was right—that it was God. They had been so deceived that even their conscience had told them the church or religion they were following was right, good—and even more tragic, that it was God.

They had not studied the scriptures well enough to know if it was God. Instead, they had just believed what the church organization, or more tragically, the leaders of the church said. They had listened and followed the church ordinances and their laws and had made their own bibles to suit their own ordinances.

That is why the pit of hell damned the Holy Spirit. I was beginning to see it was God's Spirit that gave life and revealed the truth of God's Word.

When I heard the soul-wrenching howls of regret, I understood why that was more painful to their souls than the violent physical abuse they were receiving. They had not given their lives, souls, and their spirits to God Almighty, but to the devil and his demons. They had truly believed it was God. The god they had given their lives to would be their tormentors, mockers, and condemners throughout eternity. They were not in heaven as they had believed they would be, but in hell.

I howled out for them.

Then out of the mass of wailing dead-beings, I heard a shout of total disbelief and anguish as a crowd of dead-beings cried, *But Satan, we are your followers, we worshipped you and worked our whole lives for you. Satan, we did everything for you. You promised us power in your kingdom.*

This group of dead-beings had been Satanists who openly put their faith in the devil and did everything for him. The answer they got was horrifying. The demons formed a dark, black live cloud as they joined together and honed down on these dead-beings, attacking and assaulting them with their satanic signs and symbols.

The demons let out hideous laughter and shouted out, *Fools, you gullible fools! You are humans just like the rest. We hate you! We hate your souls! We hate your spirits! Bow down to us you stupid idiots! Bow down to us!*

These dead-beings were more devastated than the rest because they had been made such wonderful promises by Satan himself. They were left with the lie of broken promises and eternal torture from the god they had openly and proudly worshipped.

It was not only the demons who attacked and assaulted them, the rest of the dead-beings also began to attack this group shouting, *Satanists, you devil worshippers!*

This caused other demons to mockingly shout out, *And your religion was any better? You stupid gullible fools!*

The demons then attacked, sending the dead-beings attacking the Satanists hurling to the ground in a total vicious frenzy. It was like when a bomb hits its target, destroying and sending all the debris and shrapnel flying.

The demons themselves became wild beasts. I do not know whom they attacked the most, the dead-people or each other. It was clear there was no unity among the demons, each wanted to reign with the religion they were. It was chaos, and the dead-beings were the target as the demons fought one another.

When the ape-like amoeba wave of the devil swept over, the dead-people offered a halfhearted praise to Satan, clutching onto what they had thought to be true symbols of religion. The symbols once again turned into demons that pushed them down and continuously kicked them in anger because of their insipid praise, and forced them to praise the name of Lucifer again.

The tentacles from the ape-like wave then slithered out like thousands of pythons. The pythons slowly wrapped themselves around dead-beings, releasing the deadly black mist. It started squeezing the dead-beings as the demons jeered. As the tentacles squeezed it released more black mist, a burning, fiery, acid-like substance, causing agonizing howls.

Then the pythons released a dominating scream and howl and did not stop until they had pinned the dead-beings down, forcing them to fall prostrate before the ape-like amoeba wave. They had to stay prostrate on the floor until Lucifer departed while roaring out blasphemous remarks, a trail of live black mist following him.

Lucifer's roar caused the demons to lash out in a frenzy of violent vicious attacks on the dead-beings while spitting out blasphemy upon blasphemy. This caused a hurricane of chaos and disunity. As it began to settle down, the humming and chanting of the religious spirits started all over again. The live black mist—the incense of deceit—and the religious demons then started the dead-beings tragic and vicious torture all over again.

At first I did not see what my obvious sin was, but then it became very clear. I saw how I had purposely used the name of the church to play my manipulation games to get control. I had fooled many people by hiding behind being a "good person." I had knowingly been a hypocrite. To the world I portrayed myself as a good, church-going person but I knew I had a rotten core. I shamelessly used church ordinances to get the advantage I needed and to justify my actions.

It was easy to be a white-washed hypocrite because there were so many rules in church. All I had to do was follow the rules. People always seemed to believe the sweetness I used to win them with. They never checked my fruits. I would clothe myself in a "pretty Sunday church dress" when I needed to, but would then resort back to the filthy rags I enjoyed being in.

I had never realized God looks at the heart, not the front I posed. But, in the choking condemnation and fear, I saw my heart—and it was rotten to the core. The sweet smile and church-rule following did not count one iota.

Many of the souls I saw being tortured in this place of religion had repeatedly said they were good people. They had followed their church and put their faith in ordinances believing it was all for God. Because they did this, they thought they would be with Him in Heaven. Their sin was making their church and their religion their bible and their faith.

I was not guilty of being blindly religious; I went one step lower than this. I was guilty of pretending to be religious and playing a good person. This was not tragic; this was pure evil.

Oh, God I am so sorry. Please forgive me. What have I done? God, please forgive me before you leave me here. God, please don't leave me here without forgiving me. Please forgive me.

I somehow knew the protective shield covering me was soon going to be removed. I was frantic, not only because of the eternal hell I would be in, but because I would never, ever, be forgiven. I would stand condemned forever.

Please forgive me God. Please . . .

I began traveling once again.

Fifteen

Guilty

MICHELE.

Yes, God? I said this with great hesitancy, because in all the other places I had said sorry, God had never answered. I would just find myself being taken out of one place and traveling back into the core of fiery hell into another sin I had committed. As much as I wanted to hear God forgive me, I dreaded Him calling my name. I knew this was very serious.

You have been guilty of all. I am a Holy God, a Consuming Fire, a God of Love beyond all measures. You shall have no other gods before Me. But none of these are your eternal damnation.

When God said this I suddenly understood why I had not remained in any of the previous places of hell, torment, and torture. I had been guilty of every sin, but I had not yet entered the sin that controlled my whole being.

Suddenly I knew the next place of sin I would enter. It would be the place I would never leave. I became frantic and started screaming, howling, and begging because I knew what it was. Before I could start begging for forgiveness again, God stilled me.

Michele, I commanded you to love Me with all your heart, and with all your soul, and with all your strength. I commanded you to love your neighbor as yourself. I am your mighty Creator and you have mocked Me. My Word tells you that you are fearfully and wonderfully created. It tells you I knew you when you were in your mother's womb and I skillfully knitted you together. You chose to spit on this and destroy yourself, My beautiful creation. This is the place where you are going. This is your everlasting stronghold, your eternal damnation.

I howled out in regret. I had failed God's first commandment to love Him with all my heart, all my body, and all my strength. I had also failed God's second commandment. I could not love my neighbor at all because I hated myself with a vengeance, which in turn made me hate everyone else.

When I heard that gentle, still small voice tell me God loves me because He fearfully and wonderfully created me, and that I must stop hating myself, I told the voice to leave me and go away. I turned to High Pitch and Low Pitch instead. I would accept them telling me to hate, punish and destroy myself and I would always go and do it.

I cried out as this hit me. I saw how I had mocked and rejected God because of my self-hate, and how this cancerous self-hate grew into hating others.

What have I done? Oh God, what have I done? I gave the devil reason to smile. I mocked You. I killed myself. I am here because of suicide—a suicide because I had failed in my first murder attempt. What have I done? I sobbed in regret.

Michele, I gave you many chances to repent. You did not. I told you to stop hating, and you chose to hate. I am the giver of life. I do not take life. Woe to the one who dares to take a life. Woe to anyone who dares to hinder the abundant life that I have put in place for all.

I was guilty. When I saw Hitler, I saw how I had been guilty of wanting to take life. I was not only guilty of wanting to take someone else's life but I was guilty of taking my own life. I had died because I had committed suicide. Being a hater of and despising life was what controlled everything I did. This was the controlling sin in my life and my final destination in hell.

Howling out in regret, I began traveling to this final place of sin and damnation. I started screaming, begging, pleading, and fighting because I knew my end had come. I could feel and see the eagerness with which the place of my eternal destination was pulling me in. The tentacles from the amoeba wave started moving all around me as if calling me in with an eager sadistic call. Only the protective hand of God was preventing them from being able to get right to me.

This was when I heard High Pitch and Low Pitch joining in with the terrifying calls of these sucking, calling tentacles of the amoeba wave.

I shouted out in utter shock, *It is you!*

When I heard their laughter, I knew they had joined the evil tentacles beckoning as they aided in pulling me further down. I knew their sarcastic, cruel laughter very, very well. I could not see them, but I heard them.

This was when I realized High Pitch and Low Pitch were definitely not voices of mine. They were from this pit of hell and they were demons. The devil had assigned them to me to win my soul for him. These two demons had the task of bringing my soul down into his kingdom forever and they had achieved it!

The devil is the devourer of souls. He is the greatest hater of life because his eternal doom is death. He is making sure he will not face it alone and is doing everything in his power to bring God's prized creation down to the pit of final hell, using his soldiers, and his seed, the demons, to do this.

What a stupid fool I had been all along! To make it worse I had invited the devil in on that Christmas Eve. I again howled out in regret and fear because I knew I was moments away from God's hand of protection lifting from me.

I had invited hate into my life and given the devil and his demons permission to come into me. I had become a slave to High Pitch and Low Pitch. Now these two demons were escorting me to the final place allotted to me for eternal doom. To make it worse these demons would be the scorpion's tail stinging me forever.

I could not say, "The devil made me do it all." Or, "It was High Pitch and Low Pitch who made me do it." They had played a major role in getting me down here, but I had chosen to help them all the way.

When I gave permission, I gave the devil and his seed, High Pitch and Low Pitch, a place to live and reign inside of me. I had literally made them my guardian demons and I knew they would be my main tormenting torturers forever. I sensed how they were eager to start their hateful torment and torture on me. My soul was their eternal prize from the devil, their father, as a job well done.

High Pitch and Low Pitch then showed themselves, bellowing out their guffawing laughter right in front of me.

I let out a yell of horror and disgust.

They were hideous, grotesque monsters. High Pitch was a very tall, thin, crooked, and hunched creature with many wiry limbs all over. He had a hideous enlarged, ridged head with an over-bearing scowl and tight, unforgiving lip. Sadistic bitterness and anger oozed out from him. His mouth was tightly twisted, projecting the message of manipulation and control. His cruel, hateful eyes bored right into my being with the suspicion I had come to operate in.

I now understood why I had called this hideous thing High Pitch. His thin, hateful, high-pitched voice was always telling me to hate and torture myself. It was High Pitch who dominated, telling me I was a disgusting, fat pig and I had to lose weight. This demon also domineered in telling me to hate and not trust any man. He said the only way to be entirely safe from men would be to murder them because then they could not hurt me. High Pitch was the main voice telling me to never forgive anyone. People could not be trusted and that's why they had to be controlled. He was bitter hate. All of this matched the very tall, thin, crooked, hunched, and tight-lipped wiry creature I saw in front of me.

Low Pitch bulged out from behind High Pitch. He was just as disgustingly hideous. An oversized blob-like midget creature, he seemed to release doom and gloom. He was hopelessness and rejection personified. The whole top of his head was a frown, which pulled his lower lip down so it was hanging into his neck. This matched the low-pitched voice always telling me how worthless I was and how nobody loved me and how life was not worth living. His eyes were filled with hate that bored so strongly into my soul that I already found myself wanting to destroy my own soul, even with the divine protection around me.

Disgustingly, he had no limbs, only short stubs all over making him appear like a sick, helpless victim. His helpless appearance did not fool me into pitying him. As I looked at the hate in its eyes, I could see this demon's intent. It was this thing who had trained me and enabled me to play the victim to manipulate others and get control. It was Low Pitch who had bored hopelessness and no reason to live in my mind.

As I looked at these two hideous demons in front of me, I saw how I had become what they were. This sickened me as I had no excuse for becoming them. Shocked, I cried out, *I have been listening to you two sick, hideous creatures doing your bidding all this time? No, no, no, no!*

They screamed, *Yes, yes, yes,* and went into a frenzy of utter delight saying, *Now you are ours! Now you are ours!*

Once again, I cried out, *No!*

But these hideous creatures zoned in, *Yes! You are ours! Lord Lucifer has given you to us. And, remember, you owe us your soul!*

I could hear myself screaming and screaming as they went into another spitting frenzy of delight.

What have I done?

God immediately said, *Rejected My love.*

I released a greater anguished howl of regret because of what I had done to God and His love. I had turned what God had fearfully and wonderfully created, into drudge and slime. Hate, anger, bitterness, self-abuse, anorexia, bulimia, blood euphoria, lies, deceit, schemes, playing the victim, victimizing, manipulation, judging, avenging, purposely hurting others, adultery, the list of everything I had done went on and on.

I was guilty. I could not pretend, deny, or blame shift anymore. I had enjoyed the power of getting my own way, getting even, destroying someone, playing games with people's emotions, always being the controller, and even planned to murder.

I had enjoyed it all. I saw how evil it was. God was right, I knew what path I had chosen and refused to turn away from it.

I did not plan, or enjoy the pit I had dug for myself. I never once thought I would end up in hell. I had not really believed there *was* a hell. How wrong I was. If only! But, it was too late for that!

I was a hater of self and a hater of life, and knew I was traveling down into the place of self-destruction. Panic gripped me because I knew in a very short time I would be stuck in this hell of self-destruction for eternity with the two hideous demons as my main torturers. I was able to feel and see how they were dying to begin ripping me apart. They had no mercy for me whatsoever, only hate. I also knew that while they would all be torturing me, I would be abusing and destroying my self, my own soul, as well, because that was my controlling sin.

What have I done, my God, what have I done? I screamed. *God, please don't send me there, please forgive me,"* I begged in agony.

I cannot, Michele. It is only the blood of My Son that can bring forgiveness.

Desperate, I said, *God, I stood in front of that church with Bridget and said the sinner's prayer.*

Yes, you did.

Can't that save me?

Michele, you acknowledged my Son many times, but most religious people do. You never accepted My precious Son Jesus as Lord and Savior, who died on the cross for you. My Son is the one and only sacrifice and High Priest. I accept nothing else. I am the God who sees into the hearts and thoughts of a man. You did not mean it when you said the sinner's prayer.

God was right. He had seen right into my heart that night in Spring Valley Church. I had gone up to the front of the church and repeated the words saying, "Jesus is the Son of God and He died on the cross for our sins and rose again and is now sitting on the right hand of God." But it did not really mean anything to me. I had acknowledged that Jesus was the Son of God, yes, but I had never really accepted Jesus as *Lord* of all, the One who had shed His blood for me so I could be forgiven.

Suddenly, as if a light had been clicked on, I saw it! On breathing out His last breath on earth, Jesus had come down to this place of hell, to the devil's kingdom, his domain and territory. Jesus had done this so He could finally overcome the devil once and for all, in his domain, and rightfully claim the keys of death from him. This was the final blow against the devil, Lucifer. Now the devil stood completely defeated by Jesus Christ.

I cried out, *Oh, God Almighty, I am so sorry, I am so sorry. I now understand! What have I done? Jesus what have I done to You?*

The fear that was filling me about my eternal fate was replaced with soul-wrenching remorse and repentance. I had missed telling Jesus He is Lord on earth, but I was not going to enter my doom before telling Jesus He is Lord.

I then turned my whole being to Jesus. I knew He was not there physically, but I also knew He would be able to hear me. I shouted with all that was in me, *Jesus, I am sorry! Forgive me! It is only through You! You are Lord of all! You are the Christ, the Savior! You are the only begotten Son of God. Oh, Lord Jesus, please forgive me before I go into my doom! Please forgive me before you take Your hand of protection off me! Please let me hear You forgive me before I enter the place of torture and hell I deserve.*

As I said this, I bowed my spirit and soul before Him. I knew He would see my heart and I hoped with my whole soul He would forgive me. Before I entered the place of my doom for eternity, I wanted Jesus to see I had bowed down and worshipped Him as Lord. I hoped the amoeba-ape, Lucifer, the devil, and all his soldiers were also watching.

I shouted out, *Jesus is Lord!*

The angry, snarling voice of the devil cursed me. It seemed to resonate throughout hell and be followed by the cursing and blaspheming of all the hideous demons present.

I knew I had angered Lucifer and his demons but I did not care. I had seen the truth and this had set me free! My soul had never felt such freedom when I was alive on earth. I felt as if I were soaring like a bird high up in the sky, and not seconds away from burning in hell forever.

I defiantly shouted out, "Jesus, You are Lord! You are Lord!" As I said this, I bowed down in total surrender before His Name.

High Pitch and Low Pitch, and all the demons present, went into a frenzy of anger and started to snort like animals. I knew their attack on me was going to be vicious. I did not care because I had done the most important thing—I had proclaimed to Jesus that He is Lord.

I purposely raised up and stood with my whole being outstretched, ignoring the blasphemous scowling from hell as it became a distant muffle. With determination and a spirit full of praise, I shouted with all my might, *J-E-S-U-S!*

The next thing I knew a luminous, brilliant, white-bright porthole of light came over me and I suddenly felt myself being lifted.

High Pitch and Low Pitch let out a cursing wail as they scurried off in frightened flight. As I continued going up, the evil, waving tentacles and hideous demons screamed and cursed as if in pain as they scuttled away from this brilliant light. Fiery hell was clearly fleeing from the Light. It was as if this luminous, brilliant, white-bright light was tormenting them. Hell seemed to be totally petrified of this Light and began to tremble, releasing an agonized tortured wail.

I gasped out in total amazement and cried in relief.

Part III

The Glory of Life

Where, O Death, is your victory?
Where, O death, is your sting?
(1 Cor. 15:55)

Sixteen

Rescued!

INSTEAD OF BEING ATTACKED AND mauled by the devil and his demons, I was being rescued by a brilliant, white bright light.

I could hear myself crying as I was saying, *Jesus, Jesus, Jesus.*

Then I became still as I clearly heard His voice say, *I AM the Light.*

It was beautiful, Oh, it was so beautiful. I could hear the sound of running water. It rang out in song. I could not see the water. I did not have to. The melodious sound that was quenching my soul was already enough.

I cried out, *I have been saved. Jesus, You saved me. You saved me. Thank You, Jesus, thank You.* Once again, I fell down with my whole being in complete relief, surrender and thankfulness.

Jesus had saved me. He saved me out of hell!

It felt as if the beautiful running water of the Light was consuming my whole being. Even though the Light was so brilliantly white, it did not burn me. Instead, it gently embraced me with a gentle, pure, and enduring love. I could hear myself sobbing in grateful awe. I was still only soul and spirit so I was not physically shedding tears, but my whole being gently sobbed with emotion.

Then something tender and caressing stilled my soul. It was as if the whole porthole of this Light stilled in expectation.

Jesus' voice rang out, *Michele, I love you with an everlasting love. Your sins have been forgiven.*

I could not see Jesus, but I knew He was there. I quietly responded with all that was in me, *Thank You, Jesus! Thank You, my Lord!*

Then the whole porthole of light broke out in a running water melody again and joy entered me. A joy I had never before felt flooded my soul. Joy is just so much more than happiness. It is happiness mixed with thankfulness, excitement, hope, song, satisfaction and expectation.

I heard myself gurgling out in unison with the running water. As I was gurgling and twirling around, I saw a brilliant, dancing, white flame of light. I stilled and watched in wonder. This flame was even brighter and whiter and more condensed than the porthole of light itself. It was so pure, so holy, and so beautiful that I gasped in total awe. The flame descended in dancing movement until it stood in front of me. Then a massive, invisible, yet visible hand picked it up and placed it inside me, just as a surgeon places a pacemaker inside a person's body. As this brilliant flame was placed inside me, my joy was now joined with an inner peace beyond any description.

I once again raised my whole being up and cried out, "Glory, Hallelujah! Glory, Hallelujah!"

I had never said this before, but I knew from that moment on it was my newfound language I would never, ever, stop saying. Jesus had saved me. He had rescued my soul. Death and hell were no longer going to consume me. I was no longer going to spend eternity in the pit of self-destruction. I had reason to shout, *Glory, Hallelujah*!

—⚂—

I then found myself traveling, leaving the porthole of light. I felt the void I was in and realized I was back in my own warm, earthly body of flesh. This time the void was different. I was not in a consuming black monster because I was not alone. The newfound joy and inner peace I received in the light was with me. I was still gurgling with laughter and dancing, not afraid at all, even though I was in a body that was in a coma. I had no reason to be afraid. I had been given a new chance.

I was alive; I was alive inside! For the first time in my whole life, I felt alive!

Thank You, Jesus! Thank You, Jesus.

I heard Jesus' tender and loving voice say, *I love you with an everlasting love, Michele.*

His voice was tender, full of pure, compassionate love. It was the running water I had just left and it was the joy gurgling inside of me. It also made me think of a soft, gentle lamb with soft fleece as pure and white as snow.

As He spoke, the pure dancing white flame that had been placed in me seemed to come alive and it felt as if it was glowing in response to His voice. The glowing of this flame made me glow. I was in a coma, but had never been more alive.

Then I heard the gentle, soft voice that had always told me God loves me say, *Jesus is Lord. Jesus loves you.*

The most amazing thing followed. This voice started singing and I found myself joining in with Him. This was a whole new world for me—a world of joy and praise. Oh, it was so beautiful!

I said, *Jesus, You are the Light.* This was also new to me, yet it felt so right.

I then fell into a sound and sweet sleep.

Sometime later I was surprised to hear people talking at my bedside.

"We don't know how much oxygen her brain has lost. We have to prepare her parents for the worst." It was definitely a male voice, so I assumed it was a doctor.

"We're going to have to inform them we will be sending her to Sterkfontein Hospital if she pulls out of this coma in one piece. Her body is in no fit state," a second male voice answered.

"I agree. Her body did not reach this degradation from a healthy mind," the first male voice responded.

Hello there, I cried out. *I can hear you! I am right here.*

I knew they could not hear me, but I had to try. Did the doctors not know unconscious people in a coma can hear what goes on around them? I tried to raise an arm to show them I could hear, but I was not able to.

Then the first male voice continued, "What a waste of life! So young and yet doing everything in her power to destroy herself."

"I know," replied the second man. "I hope she doesn't go and destroy it again after all our hard work."

In desperation I said, *Please stop it! I am right here and I can hear you. Don't you know I can hear you?*

"Records show she had also arrived in a comatose state six years ago from starvation. She is self-destructive."

Oh my goodness, they are right. I froze inside when I heard the next words.

"Yes. She was discharged prematurely then, but not this time. Continue to keep the restraints on her," said the second voice.

A female voice answered, "Yes, doctor."

What do they mean by restraints? They think I am dangerous? Jesus, they don't understand. They don't know that You have saved me." I could feel desperation in me.

The quiet, gentle voice from within whispered in my ear, *Michele, get some rest. You are going to need it.*

That gentle voice was so comforting, so peaceful and strength-giving that I knew I could trust what He was telling me. I fell asleep and forgot all about the doctors and the restraints.

Drifting in and out of sleep, I vaguely remember hearing my mom and dad's voice. I also remember being visited by the little nurse. I recognized her voice with its distinctive Dutch accent as belonging to the nurse I had seen sitting on top of me when I had left my body. She was the one who had been hitting my chest telling me to fight and come back to them and not to give up.

I enjoyed her visits because they were always so encouraging. It felt as if she was speaking my language and singing my song—that Jesus loves me and wanted me to come back; that He is the giver of life and still had so much planned for me. Her words forced me to fight and ignited my desire and my will to wake up from the coma. I loved listening to her pray for me. As she prayed I would always feel the dancing flame of light in me glow more intensely, and this would give me more strength and desire to come out of the coma.

I remembered how the demons in hell had said, "Damn, the will!" That made me realize the will of humans was something the demons cursed. Our will makes them nervous. The way this little nurse built up my will to fight in prayer was the ammunition I needed.

The joy and peace I had been given in the light never left me. My body might have been lying there in the bed, but my soul and spirit were doing very well. The gentle voice and I had started a wonderful friendship. I knew this was an eternal friendship.

The gentle voice had said to me, *Not only is God almighty, He is also Abba Father.* From that moment on, I no longer saw God as being far away, sitting up in Heaven judging and punishing. I saw Him as my God who is mighty and my Abba Father, my heavenly dad, who loves me as His very own daughter.

This gentle friend started teaching me how to have a relationship with my heavenly Dad, my Abba Father. We laughed, sang, danced, and cried together. We shared and celebrated profound immense joy and unspeakable peace together. Together we sang out, *Jesus is Lord*, and *Glory, hallelujah!* He also taught me a new, beautiful, and powerful language that I did not understand. When we spoke and sang it together, I could literally feel Him glow as He released an immense overflow of love. At the same time, I felt a sense of understanding grow within me. Now that I know it is His language, the language of Heaven, I never take it for granted and am so grateful to be able to share this with Him.

In my comatose state, I got used to hearing people's judgmental talk about me. I couldn't blame them as everything they were accusing me of was true. Jesus had forgiven me and set me free, but there were many people who had not. I knew I had to get out of my coma because I had many people to say I was sorry to.

The first obstacle I had to get over was showing the doctors my brain was fine, my emotions were restored, and that I did not need a psychiatry institution.

Then it happened . . . I opened my eyes and smiled. I looked around and saw I was in a private ward. I was back! I wanted to jump up and sing my joy out to the world, but I realized I could not. I was restricted. I looked down and saw my wrists and ankles were strapped down. I winced as I remembered the conversation when the doctor said I needed to be restrained.

When a nurse walked into my ward, I said, "Hello."

She startled and said, "You're back with us, oh! You can talk!" And then she ran out of the room.

"Where are you going?" I asked.

Another nurse came back with her and she immediately came up to me smiling, asking, "How do you feel?"

Before I could answer, she turned to the nurse and said, "Go and fetch the doctor and tell Nurse Helen she must come here because I have a surprise for her."

The nurse ran off eager to go and tell everyone.

"Can you take the straps off me?" I asked, expecting her to do so.

"Sorry, love, but we have to keep them on for your own safety and ours. Doctor's orders! Maybe tomorrow when you have rested and relaxed a little bit more."

I was sad, but I left it because I was so excited to be back.

Two doctors came in and checked all my vitals. They kept on telling me how lucky I was not to have any brain damage. The next moment, Nurse Helen came bursting through the door. I recognized her right away as the nurse who had jumped on top of me. She had regularly come and told me to fight and not give up until I joined them back on earth. She was beaming from ear to ear and I returned her smile. Then she hugged me and held me tight and said, "Oh, thank You, God, thank You, God!" Holding me at arms' length, she said, "Do you know how blessed you are? We did not think you were going to make it." Bursting out crying, she said, "Please Michele, don't ever do that again. Promise me that you won't?"

I really had grown to love her and her Dutch accent and felt so relaxed with her even though this was our first conscious meeting.

With all the earnestness I could express, "I won't. I really mean it because the love I have found from Jesus has just changed everything for me. Jesus is real."

All who were in the room stopped what they were doing and looked at me as if I had said some forbidden thing. Nurse Helen just smiled and held me tight again; I knew she understood.

"I have been blessed. I have been given another chance by God Almighty to live the right life with His Son Jesus. I was in hell and Jesus came and rescued me. And He . . ."

"Michele, you have just come out of a coma that resulted from attempted suicide. You are lucky!" said one of the doctor's whose voice I had heard in my coma. "It appears you do not have any noticeable brain damage, but we will still run a few tests. Your liver and kidneys seem to be functioning well. But, you have severe acute anorexia nervosa! We understand you *think* you've been to hell and that Jesus saved you. A side effect of a drug overdose is hallucinations."

I recognized his voice as the one who said he hoped I would not go and mess up all their hard work again. I understood his impartial coldness and knew it would be best to remain silent.

"When you have been cleared medically, we will arrange for you to have a mental assessment. This is just to get the paperwork in order before transferring you to Sterkfontein Hospital. You are mentally unstable and need intensive treatment."

I understood very clearly what the doctors were thinking and their concern and plans for me. I knew I had truly been set free. I no longer needed to be in control of the situation. I did not want to get into the doctors' minds and manipulate them.

I did not feel threatened or think they were trying to destroy me because of the way they were looking at me. I knew I would have to face consequences, but I was not afraid because Jesus was with me all the time.

This was a whole new mindset. Not only had I been given another chance at life, a miracle, but this whole new mindset was also a mighty miracle. No more hate, no more evil, no more destruction.

I looked at the doctor and said, "I am sorry."

He looked at me and there was a hint of a wry smile. He then looked at the nurse and said, "Keep the restraints on and put Michele under suicide watch!"

I did not expect this and I felt the tears pricking my eyes. I said to my gentle friend inside of me, *What have I done?*

Michele, Jesus loves you and He is watching over you. He is in control. Do not worry. Jesus will never leave you nor forsake you.

I believed the gentle voice and I smiled and said, "Thank You."

They no doubt thought I was saying thank you to myself or them and that didn't help my case. I could tell by the stares and body language of those standing around me that they thought I definitely needed to be in Weskoppies. Weskoppies' proper name is actually Sterkfontein Hospital. We were told Weskoppies was for the very serious patients. It was where the patients were given electric shock treatments. I did not know if that was true, but I did not want to find out.

I then fixed my gaze on the little Dutch nurse and asked her, "Can I see my mom and dad?"

She beamed and said, "They are on their way, Sweetie."

I laughed inside as I thought how she called me Sweet-ie, even though I had been put under suicide watch and was strapped to my bed and heading for Weskoppies. I had never been called sweetie before or under such circumstances.

Oh, Lord Jesus, I prayed. *Please let more people forgive me as she has. Please let them see me as she does. Please don't let my mom and dad hate me.*

As I was praying this, my mom and dad walked in. Right away, I said, "I am sorry. I am so sorry for what I did. Please forgive me?"

Both my mom and dad had always been very reserved in showing their emotions, but I could see their relief and grati-tude. They came and held me, and we shared a very intense, silent reconciliation. They said, "Let's not talk about it now."

"Please, can I speak to Dr. Johannes?" I did not know why I wanted to speak to him. He had been my main doctor for twenty-three years, since I had been two months of age. Maybe speaking to him would help me accept Weskoppies or even prevent me from going to Weskoppies at all.

As I said this, the doctor who had placed me under suicidal watch immediately said, "I am your case doctor, but if you want to speak to Dr. Johannes we will put a notification in your file."

My mom looked at me and said, "I will get Dr. Johannes here," and smiled. This was an amazing moment for me because my mom had never done anything like that for me before.

I smiled and said, "Thank you."

She seemed amazed that I was smiling at her.

When they all left the room, I prayed out, "Oh Lord Jesus, please help me. The doctors want to put me in Weskoppies and I don't know how to stop this from happening. They don't believe that You rescued me from hell. I don't know what to do. I really need Your help."

It felt so good being able to talk to Jesus as a friend and ask Him for His help, not try to do it on my own. Manipulating and controlling was a game I never wanted to play again.

I then heard the soft gentle voice inside me say, *In Jesus, you have victory. He came so you can have the abundant life.*

I did not completely understand what this meant, but it flooded me with the hope that Jesus had heard my prayer and would help me. This caused the joy in me to burst out together with an unexplainable peace and I drifted into a deep peaceful sleep, even with the restraints on my wrists and ankles.

Seventeen

Dr. Johannes

THE FOLLOWING MORNING, DR. JOHANNES walked into my ward with both doctors in charge of my case. My mom and dad followed. As they greeted me, I could sense how tense they were and knew this was an important meeting. The Dutch nurse, whose name was Helen, walked in behind my mom and dad and gave me a big encouraging smile.

I held onto what my gentle-voiced friend had said to me the night before. Jesus would help me. I still was not sure how this whole new way of life worked and did not know how Jesus would help me, but I believed this.

"Good morning, Michele. I am glad to see you have come back to us," his familiar, kind smile and gentle voice let me know he truly meant it.

I returned the greeting with a smile and he said, "It is very good to see you smile."

"It is good to be able to smile." I really meant this. I had not truly smiled for years and Dr. Johannes had been fully aware of this fact and acknowledged that he noted this.

This exchange of smiles encouraged me and increased my hope. In turn, it gave me the boldness to ask, "Doctor, can the restraints please be taken off?"

"It won't be long before the suicide watch will be over. So far the observation report has been very positive."

I believed what he said and this left me very calm.

He continued. "Michele, Dr. Roberts here is our leading psychiatrist in this hospital and he has recommended you be transferred to Sterkfontein Hospital once you are declared medically fit by Dr. Jenson."

I remained silent, as did my mom and dad, but my eyes did not waver from my doctor. He knew I was waiting to hear what his opinion was.

"Michele, I was your doctor six years ago when you arrived unconscious after having starved yourself for six weeks. You were then required to become an outside patient to get psychiatric counseling. You had to work together as a team to put on a minimum total of 30 kilograms (66 lbs.). You did not stick to the agreement we had made. You are still 20 kilograms (44 lbs.) underweight and clearly not fit. Your rebellion has landed you back here six years later on suicide watch. You are alive only because the doctors successfully performed resuscitation on you. Michele, you stopped breathing for quite some time. We could have lost you. You could have suffered brain damaged. I thank the Lord that you didn't. Dr. Roberts and Dr. Jenson here have also reported you were still suffering from the side effects from the overdose. You were hallucinating yesterday?

"If we as your doctors think it is in your interest that you be institutionalized, then we must go ahead and do so. Even though you qualify as an adult, you are in no fit state to decide for yourself. Your mom and dad have agreed."

I did not know what to say because everything he said was true. Then it hit me! Not everything was true. I had *not* been hallucinating. I had been rescued by Jesus out of the pit of hell and I knew I could not remain quiet about that.

One thing grabbed my attention, Dr. Johannes had said "the Lord." This gave me hope.

I looked at him and said, "Doctor, when I stopped breathing I came out of my body. I was looking down at all the activity around my lifeless body from the ceiling. I saw Dr. Jenson run in and put those electrical pads on my chest."

He looked over at Dr. Jenson who nodded in surprised confirmation. This encouraged me and I said, "I also came out of my body when I arrived at the hospital and was taken out of the ambulance. I saw Nurse Helen jump on my trolley and hit my chest. She started shouting at me to stay with them. She told me to fight. She also told everyone that they were not going to lose me."

He looked at my nurse who nodded in surprised agreement.

All eyes were on me. I noticed my mom's lips had tightened and her hand was repeatedly tapping her leg, her usual way of showing impatience, but ignored it. I was not upset with her response. I had already made up my mind I would not keep quiet. Jesus had saved me and I had confessed Him as my Lord. I wanted everyone to know.

My mind told me that if I said what happened I would be sent to Weskoppies, but my heart was filled with hope that Jesus would help me. I instinctively knew the decision the doctors were going to make about my future rested on what I would say to Dr. Johannes.

Oh, Jesus, please help me. Once again a feeling of immense peace flooded me and I knew He would help me.

"Dr. Johannes," I spoke from the peace that was within me, "You are right. I stand guilty of everything you have just said, except for one thing. I am not guilty of hallucinating."

There was so much I wanted to tell, to explain and to say sorry for, but I knew it was not about what my emotions wanted to say. I needed to tell the truth.

"Doctor, I died and I went to hell. Jesus saved me and has given me a new life. I learned one very important thing when I was there. God created us humans in His own image. I also learned that God fearfully and wonderfully created me for a mighty purpose. I was put on earth for a reason. Right now I do not know what that reason is, but I intend to find out and live it. Doctor, you are right. I am underweight, but I no longer want to be. I have made you and my parents false promises for years. I will no longer do that. I am not going to ever live a lie again. I know Jesus has healed me spiritually."

I paused for a moment. "I want to get medically and physically better too. I cannot do it by myself. I need help to do this and I am hoping you will help me, doctor. I am sorry for destroying myself. I am sorry for all these years of my life that

I have wasted and your time too. I am sorry for thinking I had the right to take my own life. Only the Creator, God Almighty has that right. I am truly sorry. I do not know what else to say."

I had not taken my eyes off my doctor as I spoke. If a pin had been dropped on the floor, the sound would have echoed in the room and down the hallways of the hospital. The silence did not seem to perturb Dr. Johannes. He just looked at me and then smiled.

"Does this mean you've stopped all your destructive stubbornness and rebellion?"

When he asked this, I knew he had seen the destructive stubbornness and rebellion in me over all the years.

"I am done with both. They are from the pit of hell."

"Good. Because that is where they come from." He smiled again and continued, "Does this mean you are now willing to gain 20 kilograms?"

I answered without hesitating, "Yes, doctor. I want to."

"Are you also willing to be institutionalized and receive psychiatric treatment?"

This question filled me with apprehension, but I held on to the hope that Jesus would help me. I said, "Doctor, if you deem it necessary, yes I will. I am committed to becoming well not only in my spirit, but in my soul, and my body too."

Once again silence filled the room.

Dr. Johannes then said, "Michele, I am going to discuss your case with Dr. Roberts and Dr. Jenson. We will return once we have made a decision." He looked at the other two doctors and they walked out together.

While everyone else in the room seemed to be filled with tension, I was not. I was still filled with immense peace. I knew there was nothing I could do except pray.

Strangely, my mom said nothing. She continued to tap her hand on her leg. My dad, as usual, folded his hands behind his back and said nothing. I did not get upset as I had in the past. I knew my old manipulating and controlling behavior had instilled this wariness in them. I also knew I would have to prove to them I had changed.

But first I had to hear Dr. Johannes's verdict. I realized from hearing him talk that he knew Jesus. Jesus was his Lord, too and this filled me with hope.

Once again the three doctors stood around my bed. As much as I was full of hope, I did feel a flicker of butterflies in my stomach. I kept my eyes fixed on Dr. Johannes, as did my mom, dad, and the nurses as we waited for the verdict.

He smiled his usual smile as he addressed me and said, "After much consideration, Dr. Roberts, Dr. Jenson and I have come to an agreement. Michele, I will be taking over your case."

I was not sure what that meant, but I felt good because Dr. Johannes had made his comments directly to me. I felt it meant something. I looked at him without saying a word.

He continued, "I will be responsible for you and your progress."

Then I understood and the butterflies were replaced with tears of joy and gratefulness. I smiled and said, "Thank you."

He continued, "If you break any of the protocol, you will be institutionalized."

"I won't Dr. Johannes!" I was singing and jumping somersaults inside.

"Michele, you have chosen the right road. This is going to be a long and winding road and it will even have a few bumps along the way." He paused, smiled again and continued, "I believe you are going to get through it all. Michele, I have been your doctor since you were two months old, both through the good and very bad times. That is why Dr. Roberts and Dr. Jenson have agreed that I take charge of your case. I am looking forward to walking this road with you. I am confident that the good work in you Jesus has begun, will also be finished by Him. You will also need to get yourself a true, understanding, and a firm-standing pastor."

I did not expect that, but I knew he was right. I was ready and determined to do everything I needed to do to reach my destination. I knew it was going to be a long, and probably interesting road, but ultimately a road to victory.

Dr. Johannes then turned and said to Helen, "Take the restraints off Michele and take all the necessary steps to ensure she gets therapy until she is able to walk on her own."

He then turned to me, smiled and said, "The restraints are going to come off, but you cannot get out of bed until you have been declared fit by the physiotherapist." As I nodded and smiled, he then said something to Helen that puzzled me. "When Michele is strong enough to walk, please assist her to the full-length mirror in the hall."

He turned and looked at me and said, "Michele, we will speak again after you have stood in front of the mirror."

Nurse Helen removed the restraints and we both gave a sigh of relief. She helped me raise my arms as she joyfully said, "Hallelujah! Glory to God."

I repeated, "Yes, glory, hallelujah to God!"

I had said this when I was unconscious. This was the first time saying it in my conscious state and it has never left my lips since then. Glory, hallelujah!

The restraints being removed represented a turning point in my life, a new life I had been blessed with. I was free.

Getting my strength back to walk was a step-by-step process. The time came when I was ready to walk out of the two-bed ward I had requested to be moved into. I was very excited and was so grateful I had legs and I could walk. I realized how blessed I truly was. I could have been brain damaged. So many people had said it, but it only seemed to truly hit home then. God had not only given me my life back, He had given me a better and more abundant life. I would never cease being grateful for the small things as well as the big things in life.

Nurse Helen wanted to escort me on my first walk to the full-length mirror. I still was not sure why I had to do that, but I knew it was important as it was Dr. Johannes's orders.

The walk down the hall was the most fulfilling and joyous walk I had ever had. The other patients in the larger ward seemed surprised to see me walking, but I was just enjoying my ability to walk.

Then I stood in front of the mirror. I gasped and asked, "Who is that?"

With her hand on my shoulder my nurse whispered, "That is you, my dear."

I stared at the young, yet old woman in the mirror. I saw two bony skeletal hands attached to twig-like arms that reached up and touched an equally bony bulging-eyed head. As I saw the bony hands touch the oversized head, I felt my hands touch my face. It truly was me! I stepped back and burst out crying out of sheer shock, horror, and shame. For the first time, I saw what I had been doing to myself all those years.

I had always seen a big, fat pig in the mirror. Now I could see myself as I really was, I wondered how I had never been able to see the skeleton figure before.

I suddenly remembered the pale, thin, frail and sad-looking reception lady from the hotel where I had that Christmas Eve experience. She had survived Auschwitz, one of Hitler's concentration camps.

I was sobbing as I said, "Oh God, my Abba Father, I am so sorry."

I looked at my nurse and said, "I've put myself in my own concentration camp all these years. I've destroyed my body and my soul! What have I done?"

Nurse Helen held me and then escorted me back to my bed where I was grateful to be alone.

I knew she would report this to Dr. Johannes. I would not have to work out what I saw in the mirror alone.

When Dr. Johannes came in the room, his gentle smile reassured me. "Michele, you saw yourself as you are?"

"Dr. Johannes, I am a skeleton. How long have I been like this?

"You were declared with anorexia nervosa since the age of twelve, Michele. You became an acute anorexia nervosa patient since the age of fifteen and have been like this for eight years."

"I don't want to be this skeleton, anymore. Please, help me! I no longer want to be like this."

He smiled again and said, "You are now ready! I've been waiting to help you for a very long time. Jesus never gave up on me and He saved me, too. So I never give up on my patients, even when they give up on themselves."

"Thank you, doctor."

"You can thank me afterwards. You have many, many months of hard work in front of you, but I know you are up for it."

I replied, "Where do we start?"

And so my journey began. I smiled and laughed a lot, cried a lot, ate a lot and learned how to sing and pray a lot.

While I enjoyed every emotion, but the greatest thing I cherished was the joy and peace that was planted deep within me because I knew where I would go one day. I believed, and now I know beyond any doubt, that when my God-appointed time comes to leave this earth, I will not go to hell. I will be joining Jesus in Heaven.

I did not know then that just over a decade after this new life and new start, I would experience what I believed and it would be confirmed to be 100 percent true. Jesus and the angels and Heaven are very real and we will spend eternity with Him.

Eighteen

The Right Road

"MICHELE, YOU HAVE CHOSEN THE right road. This is going to be a long and winding road and it will even have a few bumps along the way, but it is the right road."

Dr. Johannes said those words years ago when I had come out of my comatose state. So much had taken place since that day when I stood shocked at the reflection that stared back at me in the hospital's full-length mirror. I had stared at a bruised and battered death-like skeletal person with eerie, gray saucer eyes placed in an oversized head covered with patchy, wiry straw-like hair. I looked ready to drop down dead.

Now I was standing in front of another full-length mirror. A shudder ran along my spine as I recalled that earlier image. I immediately cut the thoughts out of my mind by raising my hands up and gratefully saying out aloud, "Thank You, Lord Jesus."

I heard my mom checking in on me from the doorway and I gave her an excited smile. She stopped and smiled back

The reflection I was looking at, at that moment, was of a healthy, joyous beautiful bride-to-be. Every bride looks beautiful because the sheer joy and excitement of her wedding day makes her glow. I was glowing.

Gleefully swirling around, I thought of the road I had chosen. It was, beyond any doubt, the right road. There were times when this road seemed so very, very long, almost never ending. It also had its share of sharp, uphill winding curves that did not allow me to see the road beyond. When this happened, I had to shift into lower gear and take the curve with my eyes fixed only on the road just in front of me, trusting there would be no falling rocks or washed away road ahead. I would hear my heart beating in my ears and my voice telling myself not to worry because God is always in control.

There were also times when the road got so steep I became afraid I would stall and start rolling backwards. Those were the times in my life when I would hold my breath and place all my attention on God's promises from His Word. I have also had to slow down to a snail's pace because of the endless bumps of all sizes along the way. A few times I hit big, deep, unseen potholes that caused a lot of damage. Those were the times in my life when I had to stop.

There were also wonderful, smooth travelling sections on the road of my life. These were the times when I had time to stop and "smell the roses." One thing has always remained constant. At no matter what stage of the road I was travelling on, I was never alone. And I will never be alone as I continue my journey. This has and always will be my joy and hope and the security on which I stand.

The split second the bright light rescued me from hell, I heard the soft, gentle, and loving voice, which is part of the light. That voice has never left my side. Jesus is this Light and tells us this in the book of John.

I came to understand that the love, peace, and joy that were steadily increasing within me were somehow directly linked to that brilliant white and beautiful dancing flame that was part of the light that had been placed as a permanent deposit within me. I also came to understand the dancing flame, beyond any doubt, is the gentle voice that speaks and shares every split second of my life with me.

He has become my dearest, most loved, and closest friend. No one and nothing on this earth could ever give me this love, peace, and joy that has flooded into me. Whether I am travelling smoothly, going up a sharp, steep, and blinding curve, hitting and bouncing over bumps, or crashing into a pothole, or even driving through a dark tunnel, my gentle friend never leaves me as I travel this road.

I have grown to trust His love, peace, joy, and holiness. Even when He corrects and disciplines me, He first lets me know how much God loves me. He teaches me more and more about Jesus every day. I have come to know this gentle voice and friend, the dancing flame. I now know Him by name and in person. He is the Holy Spirit. He is that Light, the power that rescued me when I screamed out with my whole soul and spirit, *J-E-S-U-S!*

Many people have said to me, "What a miracle! You died and came back to life! I do agree with this and will stay on my knees, giving thanks to the Lord God Almighty. But I always tell people it is not the biggest miracle I have ever experienced.

The most mind-boggling miracle is that I have this brilliant, magnificent light living within me and He is my best friend. He is also my governor for Jesus, our Lord, on this earth. He never leaves me. Because of this, I know nothing can separate me from the love of Jesus. Nothing!

I do not have to hide the fact I have a gentle, loving-voiced friend living inside me. This is part of the gift of Jesus Christ. Since His death on the cross and resurrection, millions, no billions, of humans have come to know His voice and have Him living inside of them. This no longer makes me a candidate for any psychiatrist or institution.

The Holy Spirit has shown me God's love for every single person. He does this by leading, guiding, comforting, counseling, disciplining, strengthening, and teaching me as He shows me the way. He has turned the Bible into the Living Word for me. He knows me, and what is in my heart, better than I could ever know. Whether He speaks to me aloud or softly, His voice and His intentions are always loving and gentle, even when He is firm. He always wants the absolute best for me.

He delights in us and He wants the abundant life for all of us. My most cherished moments are when the Holy Spirit and I laugh, sing, dance, pray, cry, and counsel together, hand in hand. He has also taught me how to boldly worship God in all things and in all situations of life, all day, every day. He has helped me to get to know God Almighty as my Abba Father, my heavenly Dad.

I never knew or ever imagined this was ever possible. In the church I grew up in, we had to go through a priest behind a screen and do certain rituals and beads to have access to God. Even then I was never sure, never convinced that I or anyone else had really managed to reach God. Doubt was the air I breathed.

For me, there was never any inner revelation or true inner fulfillment. The truth is, I had rejected this cold ritualistic way right from the very beginning. It just did not make sense to me and seemed to make God unreachable.

Yet, here I am! I am now able to talk directly to God and hear Him talk directly back to me in so many ways. God has now become my true heavenly Dad and I have become one of His dearly loved daughters. I stand confident in this.

I no longer have a religion of God, but a relationship with God Almighty, my Abba Father, and my Abba Daddy. What permits me into God's most Holy of Holies, into His glory and straight into His heart is His Son, Jesus. I know I did not deserve this and this is why He is my all in all. By God's grace, Jesus loved and rescued me even though I did not deserve it. He did not reject me because I had rejected myself. Instead, He loved me with all His being.

I stand confident in this because of what I experience through God's Word about His love and grace.

This confidence began in me because of what happened to me when I was in that torturous inferno when I had cried out to Jesus. Instantaneously, that magnificent porthole of light bored down around me and all the agonizing terror, bitter hate, consuming guilt, and condemnation left me. I was flooded with God's love, joy, and peace and the snake of fear that had wrapped itself around me disintegrated.

I remember watching in total amazement how the devil with his demons, and that consuming fiery inferno, and the suffocating and consuming darkness, literally fled, shrieking away in terror. It was as if this Light was now torturing and suffocating hell and all its occupants. The Bible says God Almighty is a consuming fire, and it was this fire that I saw consume the devil's fiery torment.

This was the miracle that enabled me to have my Cinderella wedding day.

Nineteen

Dream Come True

"MICHELE, WE MUST GO. YOU do not want to be late for your own wedding."

My mom's voice had the slight edge she got when something was not running according to her plan.

I smiled because everyone who knew my mom knew that was just who she was. She knew me well enough to know, that if anything, I would be late. I was well aware she was ten times more nervous and excited than I was.

"Just give me five." I was ready, but I just wanted to give my thanks to God once again.

This was a reflection I never ever dreamed would come true for me. I felt like a frog that had been kissed by a prince, and because of this kiss I had turned into a princess. I lifted my head and arms up and looked to heaven and said, "Oh, Abba Daddy, I am getting married to my Prince Charming. Jesus,

You have made this all possible. Holy Spirit, can you feel my joy bursting?"

I swirled around again and shouted, "Thank You my Almighty King and Lord."

Let me tell you the story of how this beautiful fairy tale day came about.

—∿—

About eighteen months into my new life, I got a most surprising, unanticipated phone call.

"Hello Michele, how are you?"

The female voice sounded familiar, but I just was not able to place it.

"Um, hello," I hesitated. "I am fine, how are you?"

"You have no clue who is talking, do you?"

"I, um, so sorry, but no, I don't." I felt bad having to admit this, but what else could I do?

"It's Tania!"

"Tania? Tania!"

"Of course this is Tania, Tania. Which other Tania do you know that would phone you after you messed up so badly?"

I smiled and gave a sigh of relief. She was still the same Tania: no hesitancy or embarrassment because of what I had done, and no condemnation.

It was as if we had just spoken the day before. "Oh my goodness Tania! How are you?"

"I am well. I bumped into Sonja quite a long while back and she gave me your number. I wasn't sure if I should phone you, but hey? How would I know until I phoned, right?"

She was the same old Tania and this immediately made me feel at ease. I asked her about her life and what she was doing.

She gave me a briefing of her life and then, typical of Tania, she got straight to the point. "You really hurt my brother, Michele. Why did you dump him and marry someone else?"

I was grateful for this straightforward talk because it showed she did not condemn me. It was refreshing and enabled me to give her my side of the story.

"I did not dump your brother. Charles dumped me!"

"My brother would never do that!"

"But he did! Why do you think I tried to make him jealous by dating Lawrence?"

"Michele, you married the guy!"

It felt so good to talk to Tania because I could say I was sorry and tell her how I had totally messed up. From that moment on, we renewed our long-lost friendship.

Then Tania got to the point of telling me why she had phoned. She told me, "I don't like seeing Charlie all alone." She had spoken to him and he had not found anyone who could replace what he felt for me. Tania wanted us to get back together again.

This was one thing I never thought would be possible. I did not think that Charles would ever be able to see past my past.

"Tania, Charles will never forgive me for what I did."

"Ah! You still haven't said no! Don't worry. All you have to do is call him. I will work on him."

"Oh, Tania! Only God can get him to forgive me."

"Well, then just phone him so God can get him to forgive you."

"Tania, I can only contact Charles if Jesus tells me I can."

There was an awkward silence! I could tell she was beginning to think that I had gone over the edge.

Before I had accepted Jesus as Lord, I had always thought people who confessed faith in Jesus Christ had gone off the edge and were "Jesus freaks," especially when they tried to convince me. I knew it was important she understood that He was the Rock I now firmly stood on.

I was direct and told her about my faith in Christ and that it was Jesus who saved me from dying when I tried to commit suicide. He had made me who I was at this point of my life. I also told her about my relationship with the Holy Spirit, because of Jesus Christ. Until He said so, I would not be able to contact Charles.

She accepted this and then asked, "Do you love my brother?"

I had buried losing my first love deep within me. This was a loss I did not like reminding myself of. So this question threw me. Tania could hear my reaction and this time, she helped break the awkwardness with one of her friendly, bubbly outbursts. I did not answer because I felt it would make me too vulnerable. She noted my silence on that question and respected it.

I knew she was doing this to help her twin brother. She knew I was eager to find out about Charles so we began speaking to each other by phone at least every four to five weeks.

A new found hope that Charles would one day forgive me was born within me. Tania was my only link to Charles. Strangely, she felt I was the link to her brother's happiness. Every time we spoke, Tania would immediately ask me, "Has God told you to contact my brother yet?"

"No, the Holy Spirit has said both he and I are not ready yet."

Tania did not understand how it was possible for me to hear God talking to me, but she never pushed me.

There were times when she would ask, "Are you sure you are not chickening out. Are you going to phone Charlie one day?"

We had been in the same circle of friends as teenagers, mainly because our brothers hung out and she was nuts about my brother, and I was nuts about her brother. This automatically caused us to develop a friendship.

Tania and Charles were very connected to each other. We called them "chemical-identical twins." No one messed with Tania, knowing they would have to face the wrath of Charles. And no one messed with Charles, because they knew they would have to face the wrath of Tania. When they were apart, they always seemed to know how the other felt or if the other was safe.

Because of this, I knew asking me if I still loved Charles was not just a casual query. She was serious. She made it clear she did not want him to lose out on love and happiness. I was always honest with my answer. I told her I knew that if I did not submit to God's will in this, I would mess up my chances completely and forfeit His blessing.

CLIMBING INTO ETERNITY: My Descent in Hell and Flight to Heaven

Summer and winter went by and we continued to talk. She introduced me to her life and I introduced her to mine. At the beginning of the following summer, Tania phoned to tell me her great news—she was pregnant and over the moon with joy and excitement.

I had never been a part of someone's joy and journey during pregnancy and never thought I would be. In my old life, I had despised pregnant woman and regarded this as a total weakness.

With my new chance at life, I decided that even though being pregnant was a blessing from God and according to His will, I would never be privy to "all that pregnancy stuff." I believed it was because I had been told I would never have children and so I never dreamed of it for myself.

Perhaps I chose not to think about it because I used children to practice mind control on. Whatever the case may be, I chose to stay clear of babies and children. It was because I was scared of them and not them of me.

Tania believed it was something every woman desired. I did not tell her how I felt because I knew she would never be able to understand. I also kept quiet because her joy and excitement really moved me.

She let me know how excited Charles was for her and how she could not wait for the day when her children and Charlie's children would play together. Besides her own family, she had also become part of a very close-knit family with her husband's family.

I eventually let her know I was not able to have children. This threw her. She could not imagine the person she was waiting and hoping for to be with her brother could not give him children. I told her that ovulation was totally impossible for me. The truth was I did not have a desire to have children. It was something I believed would never be for me.

She eventually stopped talking about it when her daughter Lauren was born. Tania said being a mom was every single bit of joy she imagined. She loved being a mom. This increased her desire for me to phone her brother.

This was a request I continually put before God. He would say we were not ready. It was not His appointed time yet.

I had never looked back since being released from the hospital three and a half years earlier. I had overcome and gotten the victory over so very much. With every victory, I increased in my relationship with the Lord and matured. I grew as the Bible says from "glory to glory." I believe there is only one true glory and that is the glory of God. As much as I stand very assertive in Christ Jesus, I am always completely humbled and bowed down in thanksgiving because of the glory of God Jesus takes me to bask in.

I knew that without Jesus, the Holy Spirit, I would not last. My weaknesses would eat me up. Knowing the glory of God as well as my weaknesses, I never questioned why the Holy Spirit was telling me I was not ready to contact Charles.

There was one giant that still shadowed me. When I had been put back into my body, I had been healed of all mindsets of anorexia. I had walked in complete victory as an outpatient with Dr. Johannes. I had put on the required minimum of 25 kilograms (55 lbs.) over a two-year period. I had also overcome many other anorexia-related issues. When I had gained the weight, I went out and celebrated. I thanked God for giving me the strength to do it.

A little while after celebrating, I messed up. I began bingeing and purging.

I cringe as I write this. It did not take me long before I became a bulimic and this eventually led to me becoming a bulimic addict. I believe this was why I had not been given the permission to phone Charles. I had taken one hundred steps back and this was a major burden I did not want to put on anyone.

Every day I would cry out and ask Holy Spirit to help me to be victorious over this addiction, to break the chains that were slowly making me feel like a prisoner again. I had been such a fool to once again binge.

Beside my family and close friends, other people did not know I had bulimia at that stage of my new life. I hadn't told Tania.

One day she phoned me with news that would change everything for those of us who knew her.

I was surprised to hear her voice because we only spoke on Friday evenings.

"Michele, I am phoning to tell you that you really have to contact my brother."

"Tania, I have told you . . ."

"No, no! You don't understand. Something has happened."

"I really need you to contact Charlie. I am paralyzed and I want to see you and my brother walk down the aisle before I die."

"Tania! Don't speak like that . . ."

"Michele! Michele, I am not lying. They found cancer in my spine and so they cut that part of my spine out. Here, ask Brendon."

I had not met or ever spoken to her husband Brendon, but I could hear how choked up he was, "She isn't lying."

I choked up as Brendon gave the phone back to Tania.

I stammered out, "I . . . am . . . so . . . sorry, Tania," I did not know what else to say.

"It's okay Michele, you don't have to feel sorry for me, but I do want you to promise me that you will phone my brother." She sounded lighthearted with no sign of self-pity.

I was blown away by her news, but I could not give her an empty promise. "Tania, you know I can't phone your brother unless God says I can."

"But I am paralyzed, Michele! I have cancer."

I knew I had to tuck my pride and shame away and tell her.

"Tania, the reason why I think that God has not given me His blessing to phone your brother is because I am struggling with bulimia. I am a bulimic addict."

"But I thought that you had been cured of anorexia?"

"I was healed from anorexia but I have bulimia. This is a totally different eating disorder." I felt so selfish and vain. She had just had her spine cut out and I was whining about a stupid, out-of- control eating disorder.

I once again said, "Tania, I am sorry. I just don't know."

"Michele, Charlie can help you with this problem. We can all help you with this eating problem. Please! I want to see you guys walk down the aisle."

After speaking to her, I dropped to my knees in shame at my weakness of bulimia. I looked up to heaven as I silently cried out for Tania and asked God to allow me to phone Charles. I had an intimate living relationship with the Holy Spirit and so I knew He would speak to me. I knew He would counsel and guide me and reveal God's will to me.

He gently whispered to me, *Not right now, but it will be soon.*

I let Tania know. She just accepted my answer and I knew Holy Spirit had stirred this acceptance and expectation of "soon" within her.

Tania loved to talk and so we still spoke about every third to fourth week. Her strength and humor amazed me. It was not I who cheered her up, but she who would cheer and give me newfound hope. Every time we spoke, she would ask if the "soon" had come and I would tell her it was right on *our* doorstep. I said *our* because phoning Charles was just as much a part of Tania as it was of me. I told her this because I trusted and had faith in my best friend, Holy Spirit.

Four months went by. One evening my best friend gently said to me, *Michele, go and phone Charles.*

I had been walking in the hope of hearing this every day since Tania's news, but actually hearing it made me freeze, "Uh . . ."

Michele, go and phone Charles. It is time.

After praying, I imagined Tania's response and nervously phoned.

Because the phone was always placed at Tania's side, I knew she would answer. Whenever I phoned her, she always answered.

The phone rang. "Hello, this is Charlie."

My heart skipped a beat and then started pulsing in my ears! He had never answered the phone before. I had been rehearsing what I was going to say to Tania, but never anticipated this. "Hello, Charles. It's me, Michele. How are you?"

There was an awkward silence that stretched across the telephone wires. Before he could answer, I could hear Tania in the background, "Michele it's you. I know it's you. Is that you on the phone? Everyone, Michele has phoned Charlie! Michele has phoned Charlie! She's on the phone with him right now." I could hear she was ecstatic as she asked, "Charlie, what is she saying? What is she saying?"

As I smiled, I knew Charles was smiling too. We were smiling because only Tania would be so excited. We were also smiling because we knew her perseverance had made this precious moment possible.

Four months later Charles put the engagement ring on my finger. This ring represented so much. It showed how what seemed impossible had become possible. My Prince Charming had forgiven me. He kissed me and I became his princess. It also represented to us and to Charles' family, Tania's strength and her love for her twin brother.

By the time Charles told Tania about his decision to buy an engagement ring, it was three months after that first telephone call to Charles, and she had already been paralyzed for around seven months. Tania was over the moon with his news, but even more joyous when he asked her to go with him to choose the ring. Tania had not been in a public mall since her paralysis, only going out to the doctor and the hospital. Tania knew that for her to help choose the ring, she would have to go to the mall in a wheelchair.

I knew this was something Charles wanted her to be involved in. After all, she was his twin sister. I was in total agreement with him and said I would love whatever he and Tania chose. Tania was thrilled when she heard it would be their choice. She told me she was scared to go to a mall where people would stare at her, but it was too important for her to turn down.

When they got back, Charles phoned me in Johannesburg from Durban where they lived. He said he was really pleased with the ring and I asked him, "What does it looked like?"

He said, "It's nice. It's a ring."

Tania was in the background saying, "Charlie, let me speak to Michele. Michele, Michele . . ."

I could imagine him smiling with me as he gave her the phone.

"The ring is beautiful, but it's a surprise. I told Charlie not to tell you what it looks like. The only thing he's allowed to tell you is that it has a sapphire in it."

I smiled again. I knew that sharing this with Charles was very important for her. It was part of them being twins and I honored it.

"Thank you, Tania. I will see it next weekend when Charles comes up to Johannesburg."

"It was really special going out with Charlie," Tania said, "but I tell you, it was horrible being in the wheelchair. I couldn't meet people at eye level. It was even worse the way they looked at me. It felt as if they looked down on me." Only Tania's love and strength had enabled her to go with Charles to choose my engagement ring.

I left Johannesburg and moved to Durban, Charles' hometown, to be reintroduced to his family. To say they were still wary of me, or what I might do to Charles, was putting it mildly. I really had to show them how I had changed and that my commitment to Charles was real.

—⁓—

On our wedding day, November 11, the door burst open and my mom said, "Your five minutes are up. We must leave now. You are already going to be five minutes late."

As my dad slowly walked me down the aisle of the church, I made sure to catch Tania's eye. We exchanged smiles, nodded, and our eyes welled up.

The most important people in my life were there. Tania was able to join us in this miracle. A few seats away I could see Gavin, my brother. I was walking down the aisle in my sister Sonja's wedding dress. My dad and my mother were seated on the front row. Standing in front of me was the man of my dreams. I looked up and saw Charles' smile.

Holy Spirit, I am bursting. Thank You.

They were the same people I had hurt the most with all my lying and scheming manipulation. I had lost their trust. But, they were all willing to give me another chance, despite the fact I still suffered from bulimia. I knew I did not deserve such forgiving love, but I was so grateful for it. I knew I would have to prove to them in my commitment of saying "I do," that their forgiveness hit God's rich soil.

As my dad placed my hand in Charles' hand, I smiled. *Oh, Abba Father, Jesus my Lord, thank You.*

The idea of organizing my wedding on my own had been risky. My organizational skills are vague and sketchy. I was always amazed when I watched my mom and sister at work. Their perfection for detail, precision timing, and assertive authority to get everything done was truly a beauty to behold, especially when it came to event planning.

With my sister living in Scotland, the thought of having to work with the perfectionism of my mom was unbearable, so I decided to plan my own wedding. My mom kept asking me, "Don't you want me to handle the details?" She was clearly nervous with me at the helm.

But I wanted to do it on my own and wasn't expecting a perfect wedding. God takes the impossible and makes it possible, but my pride of wanting to do it myself stopped this from happening. I dropped the wedding cake the day before the wedding. The flowers did not arrive on time. When they did, Charles had to place them in the church, and at one point, he dropped them. I had arranged for rose petals to be used as confetti and they did not arrive. The photographer did not show up. The daughter of one of Charles' family friends was a photographer and jumped in her car and came to our rescue.

When the church service was over, it was raining cats and dogs. It was decided that those who were part of the photo shoot would go to the photographer's place. On the trek there we stopped next to a beautiful park for photos. We did not mind the rain because rain on a wedding day is said to be a blessing. But when we walked back to our cars, we could see the bright pink papers under our windscreen wipers signaling we had all received parking tickets!

It was a truly memorial wedding day. And we all had parking tickets as proof!

The irony of it is that our guests loved what we had done with the wedding cake and said it was wonderful, creative, and original. Charles and I were so tired by that time, we were just grateful for any compliments on the cake. We had sat up until four that morning trying to sort out the remains of the cake after its fateful fall. Even Gavin and his friend George gave us a helping hand for an hour or two.

Our wedding day may not have gone according to plan, but we would not change a single thing about it. It was the most blessed and rewarding event that ever took place in our lives. Tania always said, "Never take any day for granted. Always remember to let each other know how much you love each other every day."

We still do to this very day. We have been married for three decades. Our marriage and our life does not always run according to plan, but we cherish every day. Whether there is sun, rain, snow, hail, an electric storm, wind, or just a gentle breeze, whatever happens, we live through it with the Holy

Spirit. Every day that passes enriches us and we try not to take any day for granted.

Twenty

New Life in Botswana

WITHIN SIX MONTHS OF OUR marriage, it became very clear to me that Charles' dream from his teenage years to work in another African country was still burning deep within him.

While I am one of the worst with organizational skills, I am really insistent and unrelenting when it comes to helping people take hold of God's purpose and plans and encouraging them not to let go of God's Word that will never pass away. I gave Charles Psalm 37:4 ("Take delight in the Lord, and he will give you the desires of your heart.") and told him to give his dream to God Almighty and believe in God without any doubts. I knew God would be faithful to fulfill His Word to us and it would come into being.

I also told him he must let Tania know he was looking at Botswana, to prepare her and to get her blessing. Tania was sad, but she blessed Charles to go.

By the following spring, Charles had begun working in Botswana. His dream had come true. He had spent his childhood growing up in Zambia but the family had to leave due to the political situation in the country at the time.

Together with their sadness that we would not be living in South Africa, Tania, as well as Mom and Dad Pulford, Charles' parents, had also come to the realization that I would never have any children of my own. I know they put on a brave smile; however, deep down I knew they were saddened that their son would not have any of his own DNA children.

There were absolutely no signs of ovulation present in me. I tried to be upfront about my bad situation, especially because I had destroyed my own body. When I had asked for their forgiveness I think they gave it to me more out of politeness than anything else. I could see the disappointment in their eyes.

Charles and I were considering adoption, but we needed to be married for at least five years before we would start the process. We needed time to grow as a couple and establish ourselves financially. When Tania and her parents saw Charles was happy and content, they seemed to accept it a little bit more and blessed us with our decision.

On the 6th of January 1990, Charles and I were on the road to our new home in Sowa Town, north of Botswana. Charles had signed a contract with Soda Ash Botswana, based in Sua Pan on the Makgadikgadi Pans of Botswana. It was a twelve-hour drive from my parents' home in Johannesburg and a nineteen-hour drive from Charles' family in Durban.

I was both excited and scared. When we entered the new country through Gaborone, I felt unsettled. I asked Holy Spirit, *Oh Lord, what have we gotten ourselves into?*

I had never been close to cows, donkeys, or goats before. After crossing the Botswana border, I was more than shocked to see all these animals on the main road. I kept looking over at Charles to see his reaction, but he did not seem to be disturbed by any of it. It was normal to him.

"Charles, there are goats, cows, and donkeys on the road!"

He glanced over at me with his bright smile and said, "I know. Welcome to Africa."

And so my endless journey of goats, cows, and donkeys began just ten kilometers on the other side of the South African border. The straight and seemingly endless road, produced more and more goats, cows, and donkeys.

About four hundred kilometers into the country, Charles had to slow down and eventually come to a stop. We did not know what the hold-up was, but we were definitely approaching something.

I was thrilled to finally see other cars. But this excitement turned into frustration as we sat about thirty minutes in line of cars. It was over thirty-five degrees Celsius (95 F) and sitting in the hot sun in was no joke. I took off my seat belt because we were just crawling forward slowly.

Eventually, about five cars away, we saw a police roadblock. Our turn came and Charles' driver's license and car license was checked to see it had not expired. Next they checked to see that the car's horn worked. They do this to ensure you can communicate your presence to the goats, donkeys, and cows. At this point, I knew I was an alien in a foreign country! If I wanted to survive and enjoy my stay, I knew I would have to understand a whole lot more about their customs and ways.

My thoughts were confirmed when the police officer looked at me and addressed Charles, saying, "I am giving her a ticket." He took out a pen and a little book.

"What have I done? I'm not even driving," I asked.

Charles nudged me to remind me of what he had told me about a woman's place, not just talking out, especially in the northern parts of Botswana.

He then asked the officer, "Officer, why are you giving my wife a ticket?"

"She is not wearing her seatbelt."

I popped up with, "But we have been sitting in the sun for over half an hour without moving."

Charles took hold of my arm and gently squeezed it. I knew he was reminding me to let him talk. The custom there was women must not speak up, but let the men do all the talking.

"No, Charles, this is the 1990s and I have just as much right to talk as you do!"

My outburst upset the police officer. He looked at me and said, "You are not wearing a seatbelt and you have broken the law."

I could feel Charles' hand gently tighten around my arm as he said, "We are very sorry, officer."

As Charles took the ticket, the officer added without looking at me at all, "You cannot leave here until you show proof that you have paid the fine."

It was at this point I realized that life as I knew it was going to be drastically different in this very hot, very dry, and very harsh country. On the next 400 kilometers (248 miles) I was hot and sweaty and on the lookout for more roadblocks, goats, donkeys, and cows on the road.

The last stretch of our journey began after we had stopped off in Francis Town. Only 190 kilometers (118 miles) left to go! We had no radio signal and we were tired of hearing the same tapes over and over again. When I switched off the radio, I said my final farewell to civilization.

The long straight road changed and we began travelling on a winding, dusty, bumpy, and slippery clay road. It was only 40 kilometers (25 miles) to Sowa Town, but it took us a whole hour to get there.

The town? There was no town. The company, Soda Ash Botswana, had just started building the town. I was glad to see the company had installed water and sewage pipes, but the houses were still to come.

The company had built a little group of townhouses for the families that had already started working for them. They had put a big steel fence around this common area. There were no driveways or pathways so we parked our cars in the spaces between each little townhouse.

Dogs had the run of the place. Eventually we got to know the names of everyone's dogs. The dogs also sorted out who was feeding them. We were in bush, bush and more bush. We were even taught about how to read and understand elephants, just in case! Upon hearing that, I went home and cried and cried. I loved the city so this was the worst-case scenario for me.

Sowa Town at that point had no telephone lines and no television or radio access. The company had been able to put only one telephone in the first office built at the soda ash plant. Every employee was allowed to use it for a personal twenty-minute call every second week. The spouses of the employees were also allowed to make one phone call.

This was how we stayed in contact with our families. This was tough for Charles and Tania. The cancer had started spreading to her brain. All I had to do was look at Charles and I would know how Tania was doing. Whenever Tania was in pain, Charles would have excruciating headaches.

Before we left for Botswana, Tania was experiencing intense migraines, nausea, and vomiting. Even with all this suffering, she never felt sorry for herself. She would look at me and not complain but say, "Being paralyzed really sucks." Her strength kept me from pitying her as she never wanted that.

Charles and I had taken two dogs with us to Botswana: a Labrador called "Kalos" (beautiful, glory) and a collie (sheep dog) called "Shalom" (peace). The highlight of my days in Botswana would come at about 4 o'clock every afternoon. I would hear Ross, a six-year-old boy, shouting, "Aunty Michele." I always smiled because I knew what Ross wanted.

Every day at 4 o'clock, Shalom, our sheep dog, would round up all the children playing outside and bring them to stand outside our townhouse. It was "treat" time. I would fetch the tin of treats and give all the children a sweet. This was a very big event. The closest shops to us were in Francis Town, 190 kilometers (118 miles) away.

Treats were the number one item on my monthly shopping list. Shopping was a big day and an all-day affair. The wives would always go shopping in pairs, for practicality, budget, and safety. In the early nineties, there were no shopping malls in the whole of Botswana! In Francis Town we had a Spar, an OK grocer and a Metro. I missed television and radio, but oh, how I missed the shopping centers and malls!

I thought longingly of sitting in a coffee shop and enjoying a cappuccino or a cold drink out of a glass with lots of ice. But, we had no options for this enjoyment and had to settle for a can of cold drink in a moving car with the air conditioner overworking.

Having Shalom bring the children to the townhouse to get a treat required good planning on shopping days and became a blessing for me. My friendship with the four to six year olds had grown so strong that I became more confident about perhaps one day adopting a little person who would come walking through the door carrying a suitcase. I believe that the Lord had placed our dog Shalom in our lives so this bond would grow between me and the children in preparation for when we would have our own six-year-old child.

The first thing the company had built when breaking ground for the newfound company and town was a tiny airstrip. They set up a portal cabin as the customs office. Whenever any medical issues were verified and signed off by the company doctor, the company would fly the patient in a little eight-seat plane to see a doctor or specialist.

I was still working with Dr. Johannes as he had not been able to sign me off because of the bulimia. This was the out-patient treatment I had committed myself to on the day I had left the hospital after my suicide attempt. Even though I had gained the required weight and kept it on, not losing a single gram in the process, he wanted to examine me on a six-month basis. He'd check my weight, and take blood tests to check the mineral, vitamin and iron levels in my blood.

When time for my blood tests in March came, I was excited for my first flight in the eight-seater plane, although flying was not my cup of tea.

Arriving at Lanseria Airport in Johannesburg, I breathed in the polluted air and smiled. I was back in civilization. The highway and traffic was absolute bliss for me. My mom and dad took me to a restaurant that evening. What an absolute luxury that felt like! Having television, radio and a telephone felt so surreal.

The next day I went to the doctor's office for the usual blood tests. This was the fifth year of this procedure and so it had become the norm for me. It usually took a day or two before the results came back.

I would stay with my parents for three days before returning home, enjoying cappuccinos with my mom and visiting people and places. I had already phoned and caught up with Tania the minute I had arrived at my parent's house.

My first day at their house had not even passed when Dr. Johannes phoned. Usually his receptionist would phone and tell me the results were back and I would make an appointment to go and see him.

"Oh! Hello, Dr. Johannes?" Hearing his voice on the same day the blood had been taken startled me.

"Hello Michele. I am phoning you because I personally want to give you the results of the test I have taken."

I went from feeling startled to feeling anxious. I had been his patient for twenty-eight years and in all that time he had never phoned me personally. As he continued speaking I could sense a smile in his voice so I relaxed.

"I would like to let you know the test is positive."

Strange words. I didn't know what to say. Usually it would be about my iron, Vitamin C or potassium count and things like that. But he had never before said anything about me testing positive.

Dr. Johannes knew by my silence that I did not understand what he was saying. He said, "Congratulations, Michele. You are pregnant!"

"What? Sorry, what did you just say, doctor?"

"Michele, you are pregnant. Can you come and see me tomorrow morning?"

I was stunned beyond belief. I was totally shocked and my manners seemed to have left the room. All I could say was, "Yes."

"Good, see you tomorrow."

Shaken, I went back into the sitting room and sat down. My mom immediately thought something was wrong.

"What's wrong, Michele? Michele? It looks like you've seen a ghost! What's wrong?"

"I'm pregnant."

My mom looked at me in disbelief and said, "That's impossible! Your ovaries look like prunes and you don't even menstruate. The doctors have been telling us that for fifteen years. Because you you don't ovulate at all, you are barren and you can't have children!"

"I know."

Silence. My mom and dad knew how bad my bulimia was. My dad never spoke about it, and my mom never stopped speaking and lecturing me about it.

Then my very logic and statistically-orientated dad said, "Okay. Go and phone Dr. Johannes and double-check. Let us take it from there."

I phoned him. He knew my parents very well. He was one of the doctors who had told them I would never be able to have children. I was sure he was smiling when he heard my voice.

His voice had a light tone as he answered, "Michele, tell your mom and dad I have already double-checked the results specifically because it is you. You really are pregnant! I cannot explain in medical terms how this has happened, but by God's mighty hand you are going to have a child."

"Thank you, doctor! I'll see you tomorrow."

When I told my parents what he had said, they expressed a bit of excitement and congratulated me.

I then rushed to the phone. I could not phone Charles, so I phoned Tania instead. The Pulfords are very expressive so this news took the roof off their house. Tania was not doing well at all and this news of joy for her brother was a fresh measure of strength for her. It was also an unanticipated mountain of joy for Mom and Dad Pulford, too.

Tania ended our conversation, "Thank you, Michele. Please take care of my brother for me, always! Tell him how much I love him."

"Tania . . ." I was as choked up as she was. This was unlike any other goodbye.

When I went to bed that evening, I had still not processed the news. I had the memory of an earlier disastrous babysitting episode. I lay in bed saying to Holy Spirit, "Lord, I can't do this. I will be a disaster. I will fail as a mother. I will never be as good as Tania."

The flight back home could not come soon enough. When I got off the tiny plane, Charles was there to take my bags off the plane and take them through to customs. I could not keep it in any longer. I could not wait until we got into the car.

Out on the tarmac by the plane I burst out and said, "I'm pregnant."

I think Charles had picked up something telepathically from Tania because he smiled. He put the bags down, hugged me, and held me in silence for a while. When he released me, I could see tears forming in his eyes. Sharing the news with Charles and being in his arms helped me to process the news myself. There was a baby, our baby, growing inside of me!

When we got in the car, I looked at Charles and said, "I'm scared I'm going to fail."

He leaned over, kissed me and said, "You won't. I am right here by your side." He said this despite the shadow I had brought over his life and into our family. He never gave up on me. He believed in me, in us, and in our family because God is faithful to His promises.

The reason I believed I was going to fail was because of the shadow of bulimia. That was why Dr. Johannes wanted to see me once he had discovered I was pregnant. He had specialized in obstetrics so he was able to look after me and bring my baby into the world. He had become my general practitioner, obstetrician, and my psychologist-counselor.

The hard truth was, I was an addict. Since moving to Botswana, my addiction had increased until I was having an average of three binges a day. No, it was not Botswana's fault. It was mine. I tell you about my battle with bulimia not for sensationalism but to show the tragic mess I had gotten myself into and was now dragging Charles into.

I had died and gone to hell. I had met and accepted Jesus Christ, the lover of my soul, and made Him Lord of my life. My best friend was the Holy Spirit. I had developed such a close relationship with God, my Abba Father. And after all these divine blessings, I was literally drowning it all in the toilet.

Charles knew I was a bulimic addict, but before this he was not really exposed to my extreme binges because I had been in control of it and was able to keep it from him. Overnight, I had given the bulimia total access and it took control of me, just as the anorexia once had.

Once this happened, Charles saw a whole new side of me that he had never seen or experienced before. Up until this point, he had seen my beautiful personal relationship and bond that I had with God. Now he was seeing and experiencing the torture and prison I had opened the door to as it began to ransack our lives.

This is still one of the biggest regrets and shame in my life.

Not a day would go by when I did not rage and fight with Charles because I was trying to put the blame of my backslidden state on him dragging me to Botswana. If he got in the way of my bingeing, or if I had the jitters because I was craving a binge, the fireballs that came shooting from my mouth were even worse. I became a vile fool.

What made this worse was that Charles was averaging a fourteen-hour day of hard intensive physical work every day, seven days a week.

The company was in the process of commissioning the Soda Ash Botswana mine and plant. All the men were working long hard hours from ground floor right to top management. This had become their baby and they were heart and soul in the project as one team. The men were working from 6 a.m. through the day in the sweltering sun that averaged 40 degrees C (104 F) in the shade until about 8 p.m. to 10 p.m. every night.

Instead of joining this team as a supportive wife and allowing Charles to just flop down and rest at home to build up energy for the next day's work, I attacked him and placed him under major emotional stress and strain.

During my binges, whenever the Holy Spirit tried to get my attention and tell me to stop, I purposely brushed Him off. There were days when I did not even want to pick up my Bible because it would make me think of what I was doing.

My bulimia did not only rule me, but it ruled Charles as well. Whenever he tried to help me, my strong, vile words stopped him in his attempts. If he didn't stop, I physically attacked him, even jumped on his back like a monkey, screamed and lashed out with my nails. Eventually, Charles gave up and just dropped onto the bed out of sheer exhaustion and slept.

Oh, the shame of it!

I would then go to the kitchen and stuff my face. I was like a yelping, grunting hyena–pig. When I finished eating, I would drop down onto the floor and wallow about as if I were an elephant seal. I then shuffled to the toilet to throw up. This sick cycle took about three hours and I would have about three to four of these binges a day. This meant my last binge ended in the early hours of every morning, when Charles was getting his very much-needed sleep.

I was a mess and had dragged Charles into it.

One Sunday evening, I was with my mom and dad and we were watching the TV program Carte Blanche in which Derek Watts took us into the home of a bulimic addict. She had allowed them to film one of her binges. It was disgusting. She too went from a lady to a hyena–pig to an elephant seal, slogging to the toilet to hang over the bowl and vomit.

My mom was obviously feeling disgust from what she had just seen. She turned and said to me, "Do you see what you can become?"

I looked at her in disbelief because I had already become what we were witnessing on TV, but obviously, they were blind to it all. I was doing exactly what the woman on TV had done in my parents' kitchen and bathroom. (Sadly, a year later this woman passed away from bulimia when her heart could not cope with it.)

My mother's reaction showed me how loved ones of an addict can suffer from denial. They do not want to admit to how bad it really is. There must have been times when Charles had seen these disgusting moments of mine and had chosen to deny it as well.

The truly shameful and disgusting thing was that I was a *pregnant* bulimic addict. I could not have stooped any lower. There were times when I would hear my gentle-voiced friend telling me to walk away because Jesus died for this; to walk away because I had the victory over it. I was torn between wanting to walk away, knowing Jesus had already given me the victory in it, and having just one more binge before I stopped.

I am ashamed to say that just one more binge always won.

There were many days I would cry with Holy Spirit because of how I was letting Him down, and, in turn, Jesus Christ. All He would do was love me even more. Every time I would repent and begin afresh, determined to overcome. He would be there as my number one support and belief in me, even though I would let Him down.

All of this put a new strain on Charles. It was not only me he had to think about, but the baby as well.

Dr. Johannes was unhappy with me. I knew he was disappointed in my weakness because this was just plain selfishness towards Charles and the baby. We had come so far since my suicide attempt. I had grown so much in the Lord and in my personal life, and my doctor had been an integral part of all of this.

What I was doing with the bulimia was so destructive. I had reached a point where my legs were permanently numb. The bingeing had already caused the pulse in my legs to drop dangerously low, a sign of bad circulation. Now that I was pregnant, Dr. Johannes told me it would naturally put more pressure on my legs and lower the pulse count even further. I ran the risk of losing my right leg (the one that was so badly injured in the motorbike accident).

My continuous state of bingeing was putting high stress on the baby. I had already started having stress contractions and was placing him or her in danger. Dr. Johannes questioned whether I could carry my baby full term and he was not over-exaggerating. Despite the bingeing, I was still very fit and flexible. Being told about the risk of losing my leg did not really seem possible to me even though my legs were completely numb. The stress contractions always passed and I chose to ignore them.

I was an addict and was acting like one: I was inconsiderate, selfish, hot-headed and reckless. I did not let myself dwell on the fact that I had the fruit of the Holy Spirit in me, because I was not showing any evidence of this.

> But the fruit of the Spirit is love, joy, peace, patience, kindness, goodness, faithfulness, gentleness and self-control. Against such things there is no law.
>
> (Gal. 5:22–23)

—✎—

All of this accelerated at an alarming rate. The fact that Tania's health was deteriorating made my actions seem even more selfish. Her cancer had spread like a forest fire throughout her brain. When I had phoned her to tell her about the pregnancy, she had already been in and out of hospice. Eventually, she let me know she was going to be permanently placed in hospice care.

Tania and Charles' birthday was coming up on the 6th of June. Because of Tania's situation, this had become a very special birthday for the whole family.

One morning in their birthday week, Charles had left for work as usual at 5:30. I didn't expect him to be home until after 8 p.m. that night. I was startled when I heard the front door opening very abruptly at about 10 a.m. I could see by the expression on his face that something was terribly wrong. I knew immediately it was Tania.

"We must pack and leave straight away. Tania is on her last and is waiting for me."

After holding him and praying, we moved in silent motion as if it had been practiced. The way Charles got this information was a miracle itself. He was usually working somewhere on the plant outside. That morning, for some reason, Charles had to be inside. As he walked past the office where the only phone was, he heard the phone ringing and looked into the office. There was no one there so he went in and picked up the receiver. The call was for him! After trying for two days to reach him, his family had taken a chance and phoned the number again.

Mom Pulford worked in the accounts department for the very first Pick 'n Pay Hyper in Durban. Because they had failed to reach Charles for two days, on the third morning Mr. Raymond Ackerman, the big boss, said they must give it one more shot. If Mom Pulford could not reach Charles, he would make his private plane available to pick Charles up. That phone call was their last try and Charles just happened to be there to answer the ringing phone.

The management of Soda Ash Botswana released Charles to leave immediately. We found ourselves on the road within thirty minutes. Charles had to drive most of the way because of the state of my numb legs. I had good control of the lifting and releasing of my feet on the pedals, but Dr. Johannes said he did not want me behind a steering wheel for more than twenty minutes, so I only drove for short bursts. Charles was exhausted, but he was pushing himself for Tania.

I had phoned my parents from a phone box in Francis Town on the way to South Africa to let them know we would be stopping over at their house for a meal and break before setting off again. We pushed hard, hour after hour, and got to my parents' house at about ten o'clock that evening.

It had been a long, hot, twelve hours of despair. I had never seen Charles so tense before. My heart was breaking for him and I did not know what to say. As he walked into my parents' house, he went straight to the phone.

My mom looked at me and said, "Michele, Charles looks exhausted."

I remained outside after my mom had gone back inside. I looked up to the stars and cried out to God for Tania and Charles. The Holy Spirit said to me, *If Charles gets behind the steering wheel now, he will fall asleep and you will have a fatal accident.* Even though I was messing up with my bulimic addiction I knew it was Holy Spirit warning me.

"Oh, Lord, Charles won't listen to me. I don't know what to do."

Charles came outside to let me know Tania was in a coma, but hanging on. I knew he wanted to get back in the car. I just burst out and told him what the Holy Spirit had told me. He wanted nothing to do with that. I did not know what to do. The Holy Spirit had made it clear he would fall asleep and there was still another 600 kilometers (372 miles) of driving to do.

Charles made it clear he wanted to get back behind the wheel after eating. I had never seen him so adamant and defiant. He stormed back inside the house. I knew if I stopped him, he would never forgive me. But then I realized that if Charles did get behind the wheel, we would not live. So I did not follow Charles inside but locked the main gate, then went into the house, got hold of all the gate keys and hid them.

Charles was livid.

I was angry at myself. I had let Charles and Tania down because of my addiction. It was because of the bulimia and not the pregnancy that my legs were permanently numb and I was not able to assist with the driving.

"Oh God, what have I done? Please forgive me. Please be with Tania. Let her live, in Jesus' Name."

I hoped Tania would understand and even agree with what I had done.

After three hours of sleep, we were back on the road. Charles was still fuming and the 600 kilometers were spent in silent hostility.

We did not make it in time. The decision I had made is something I will have to live with every day. I do not regret having made Charles sleep for three hours; he would have fallen asleep behind the wheel, as he was exhausted. However, I do regret that my bulimic addiction made it impossible for me to drive and allow Charles three hours of sleep while the car took him closer to Tania.

Tania was truly loved. When they closed the curtain as the coffin went in, something in Charles' eyes died. He is known for keeping his feelings deep and to himself but his eyes never lie.

He told me, "I will never forgive you for making me sleep." Since we were teenagers, I had instinctively known I should never try to keep Charles away from Tania. He did not think what I did to prevent us from having a fatal accident was needed.

Throughout their life, Tania had always been the one to express things for Charles. I knew I would never be able to fill that spot. Charles made it clear to all of us that he did not want any birthday wishes and did not want his birthday mentioned ever again.

When we returned home, we went through the motions. It felt as if our special connection had also been cremated. I knew Charles remained with me because he had committed himself to the baby and me but he had emotionally disconnected himself from me.

My binges increased and the stress on my baby also increased.

Dr. Johannes said I could not stay in Sowa Town. It was not safe. He wanted me to be under his watchful eye. This was July. Tests and scans predicted that Baby Pulford would be due in November. Because I had never ovulated in my life, Dr. Johannes was not able to use this information to predict a precise due date.

Charles was falling more and more in love with our baby and he was sad I had to go and stay with my parents in Johannesburg because he could not place his hand on my stomach every day. But I think he was relieved he did not have to see me and deal with me every day.

Twenty-One

Miracle Babies and Bulimia

SOWA TOWN WAS GROWING AT an amazing rate. More telephone lines had been put in giving Charles more access to phone. This made it easier for necessary communication, but it still did not take away the widening wall that was rising between Charles and me.

The weeks went by quickly. Even though I had decreased the amount of my binges by 50 percent, I had not stopped altogether. The stress contractions increased so I knew my baby was not happy. At times my right leg went beyond feeling numb—it felt dead.

I was open about being a bulimic addict and that my medical problems were caused by my addiction, so I was not the most popular person around. Someone even told me, "You are going to be a disastrous failure as a mother." I did not blame her, because I believed it.

I had let down those who had believed in me and given me another chance. Charles and Baby Pulford were in the front of the line.

One night I was on my knees crying out to God, "Father, in Jesus' Name, I have messed up so badly. Please forgive me. Forgive me for hurting Charles and Baby Pulford, for hurting my mom and dad again. And worst of all, for letting You down."

I immediately heard the still and gentle voice saying the words of 1 John 1:9 to me. "If you confess your sins, He is faithful and just to forgive us our sins and purify us from all unrighteousness." *Michele, God loves you with an everlasting love. He has forgiven you and desires the best for you.*

"Oh, Holy Spirit, I have put our baby at risk. The wall between Charles and me is expanding. He will never forgive me for Tania. It is not going well at all." I was filled with so much guilt and despair.

God's love is deeper than any ocean. He has not given up on you. Do not give up on Him. He is mighty. Put your faith in Him. Stand on His promises to you. Hope in God Almighty. He never disappoints.

"Thank You, Lord."

As I said this, I raised my hands to the heavens and gave God praise in song and dance. I had not done that for a while. Not because I did not want to, but because I felt I was not worthy to do so.

Michele.

"Yes, Lord."

You must never stop praising God. Praise God because of who He is and what He has done for you. Don't stop praising God because of what you are guilty of, but in spite of it.

"Oh, Holy Spirit, thank You."

Go and phone Charles and tell him how much you love him.

I did. And Charles told me the same. A lot of the wall between us came crashing down. I knew this was God Almighty's work of reconciliation. That night I made a commitment to never stop praising and believing in the Lord God, no matter what the circumstances.

The next day, the 1st of October 1991, was my check-up appointment with Dr. Johannes. Given my addiction, my pregnancy was going as well as it possibly could. I had just over a month left to carry my baby to full term.

Dr. Johannes smiled and jokingly said, "When you were a baby, your fever was so high. I was called out of an important rugby game. This Saturday coming is another big rugby game; be good so your baby does not have to call me out."

He was like a second father to me and I know he was telling me to work hard at not bingeing. I smiled back, "My family never stops telling me the story about the big rugby game you had to leave because of me. Enjoy the rugby, doctor. See you in two weeks' time for my next check-up."

My spiritual and emotional breakthrough the previous night had been personal, between me and God and Charles and me. I felt hopeful once again, also grateful to Dr. Johannes.

I hugged him and said, "Thank you, doctor."

He smiled and with his usual steady and quiet voice said, "See you in two weeks' time."

That Friday, my mom took me to one of her favorite coffee shops for a cappuccino and salad. She had been declared medically unfit to work at age fifty with chronic, crippling arthritis. Being able to go out for a treat was something she cherished. My dad would take her to eat out every Saturday or Sunday, traveling for hundreds of miles just to go to their different favorite restaurants.

The coffee shop she chose was in Stuttafords, a prestigious clothing department in East Gate Mall. Whenever we went to the coffee shop, my mom would always go into the store itself. That day, my mom said she wanted to go to the baby department to get Gareth, Sonja's little boy, a summer outfit and to see what they had for newborns.

My mom had picked up an outfit and as she did this, she dropped another one she was holding onto the floor. As she bent down to pick it up, she started to giggle as she got stuck on the way down. Her arthritis did that to her sometimes. Whenever my mom started to giggle, she did not stop. I knew she was stuck, so I went over to help her. Her giggling had turned to uncontrollable laughter. I began to laugh too and after a time we were crying from laughter on the floor. My mom was holding her tummy from all the laughter and I also wanted to, but with my pregnant tummy I did not know where or what to hold. My mom saw this and both of us started laughing and crying even more.

A security guard came over and asked us, "Is everything alright? He then bent down to try to help us up.

I then looked at my mom wide-eyed and said, "I am not going to make it to the toilet."

She thought this was even funnier than us rolling on the floor, but the security guard did not. I felt some moisture, but thought it was just a weak bladder from the pregnancy. We eventually made it to the car and kept on giggling on the ride home.

Before this, there had been so much tension between us because of the bulimia. All the laughter had really helped break the tension.

I went to my room thanking God and went to bed.

The next morning I told my mom I was having a very weird pain.

"Michele, you are in labor."

"Impossible, Mom."

She demanded we check to make sure. After examining me, she said, "Michele, pack your bags. We are taking you to hospital."

I heard her on the phone to Dr. Johannes, "Doctor, I have checked. It looks like Michele has dilated about two centimeters."

Dr. Johannes had been my mom's obstetrician as well and had brought us into the world. He was still my mom's GP at that time so they had a very long standing and direct doctor-patient relationship.

After finishing on the phone, she said, "Michele, phone Charles. You are in labor."

I silently obeyed and phoned Charles immediately. "Hello, Charles. My mom says I'm in labor, but I don't know. I have had these contractions before and they usually pass. Mom says

I've dilated two centimeters. She has arranged with Dr. Johannes to meet us at the hospital."

"I'm on my way."

"But Charles, what if my mom is wrong? Maybe I should just go have it checked out and then I'll phone you and let you know."

"And what if your mom is right? I'm on my way. See you in twelve hours."

"But . . ."

"Michele, it's all going to be fine. Now go with your parents to the hospital. I love you."

"I love you, too, Charles. Drive safely."

"Always. See you."

When Dr. Johannes walked in, he was smiling. "At least it isn't during the rugby match."

"Oh, Dr. Johannes, I am so sorry." I had not realized it *was* the rugby day.

"It's fine, you've never done anything according to the book. Let's check and see if your mom is right."

Dr. Johannes looked at the nurse and told her to call my mom in. I think she had been waiting right at the door because she was there in a shot.

"Michele, your mom is right. You are about two centimeters dilated. When did your water break?"

"It hasn't," I said and my mom confirmed this.

His slow gentle smile appeared again and he said, "Michele, many miracles have taken place with you, but every pregnancy requires fluid to break free when it is time for the birth of a baby and the period of labor to begin. Your water did break."

This was when we realized it was my water that broke when we had been laughing so much the day before in the clothing store.

"But doctor, why didn't I go into labor then?"

"Michele, you did, but remember, there is no specific period of time for labor."

His demeanor changed as he went out to speak to the nurse and then there was a whole lot of hustle and bustle. I was hooked up to a machine and Baby Pulford was also hooked up to a machine. It was so unreal when I heard the beautiful little heartbeat.

I began to pray silently, *O Lord God Almighty, in Jesus' Name, Charles is not here. He is still about ten hours away. Please let our baby be safe. Please be with Charles on the road and help him to get here safe and sound. Father, I am scared.*

I heard the Holy Spirit's gentle voice, *Michele, God is in control. Trust Him. And don't forget, praise Him.*

Dr. Johannes walked in and said, "The baby is fine and is now in safe hands. You have no need to worry."

"Thank You, Lord. Thank you, doctor."

I put my hands on my tummy and said, "Baby, your daddy is still ten hours away. Please stay in there just a little bit longer. Ever since your Aunt Tania died, he's been dreaming about helping to bring you into the world."

"Oh, Father God, please don't let Charles miss this. Please!"

I had always been free to talk to God in front of Dr. Johannes so he heard my every word.

"Michele, you have got good nurses taking care of you. They will keep on checking. They will let me know when you are five centimeters dilated. You must remain calm. This could take thirty minutes or three hours . . . or even longer, like ten hours. If I am not called, I will come and check on you in two hours' time. Is that okay?"

"Yes, doctor."

He placed his hand over mine and squeezed it like a loving dad, smiled and said, "See you later."

With nothing further happening, every now and then I would ask the nurse, "Are you sure I am in labor?"

"Yes, you are. It is just that you have only dilated to three centimeters and it has just halted. Let us wait and see what Dr. Johannes says when he comes."

I breathed a sigh of relief. I believed God was in control of everything, including halting the dilation process. He knew Charles wanted to be there for the birth of our baby.

Dr. Johannes came mid-afternoon. The baby was not in any stress or danger and my vitals were fine.

"Doctor, I am trusting God to get Charles here in time. I do not believe I am going to dilate further until he gets here."

"I know. I believe that too. God is mighty and He has heard you. I am going to the rugby match and will come here straight afterwards."

Dr. Johannes truly believed God would let Charles arrive on time. When he walked back into my labor room at about 8:30 p.m. after enjoying his rugby match, the contractions had become tighter. After he had spoken to the nurse on duty, he asked me, "Have you heard from Charles yet?"

"No, not yet, but I am sure he will walk in soon."

Charles walked in at about eleven that evening. I was so happy and relieved to see him and Charles was happy he had not missed the birth of our baby. We immediately held hands as Charles prayed, "Thank You, God Almighty, in Jesus' Name, for protecting Michele and our baby and for getting me here safely. We continue to look to You, Lord, for the birth of our baby."

Charles was exhausted. He had been on the road for twelve hours and, as usual, had been doing many extra hours at work. I could see how tired he was.

"Charles, you need to get some sleep," Dr. Johannes told him. "The nurse will phone you if anything happens." He also told Charles that the baby and I had been hooked up on the machine for thirteen hours already and he wanted me and the baby to try to get some sleep before the intensive labor and birth process began. If I had not progressed by 6 a.m., he would induce me.

Charles sat with me for an hour and then he went for some much-needed sleep.

Before I shut my eyes, I held my tummy and spoke to my baby, "Your daddy is here. You can come."

Charles and I had chosen not to find out the baby's gender. This pregnancy was a miracle and we only wanted to know the sex of our child at the time of birth.

After being induced the next morning, I learned what intense labor pains were all about. Charles stayed right with me. When our baby was born, Charles looked at me smiling from ear to ear.

"It's a boy!"

The nurse wrapped our son in a sheet and gave him to Charles.

"He's perfect. He has ten fingers and ten toes and lots of hair." Charles wanted to give him to me, but the nurse said I could not take him yet and took him from Charles.

Charles was so excited that he ran out to go and phone his parents.

I was in immense pain. My right leg was not doing well so I was given more drips and injections.

Dr. Johannes said to the nurse, "She needs to be carefully monitored."

He looked at me and said, "Congratulations, Michele. Your son is beautiful and as strong as can be. I was not sure if you would be able to handle a natural birth, but you and Charles did great. The sister is going to put your son under the lights for a few hours. It's just standard procedure for babies who have been born before their full term."

He paused. "Your right leg has just had a burst thrombosis and it doesn't look good. We've already started the medication and treatment will begin as soon as you get to your bed.

"Michele, I know you. You are going to want to walk and will try to sneak a step or two when no one is around. Don't! You are at the risk of having your leg amputated. You have to stay put. Don't even think of taking your leg out of the straps. Keep it high."

It felt as if a red light was flashing in my heart. This was my own doing. I was guilty of this.

"I'm sorry, doctor! I have messed up badly."

"It's okay, Michele. Let us concentrate on saving your leg."

God had blessed us with a perfect, beautiful baby boy, Cyle-jay Pulford. Charles was head over heels in love with his son. As I watched his celebration of excitement and bursting joy as he ran between being with Cyle-jay and then with me, it brought my spirit low before God. Once again God had blessed me, despite my foolishness.

A week later, I was blessed further when I was able to walk out of the hospital with Charles and our beautiful son. Cyle-jay represented the miracle of life and hope to both Charles and my family.

—m—

I would love to tell you that the bulimia was over and done with, but I can't. I am ashamed of this and wish I could hide this part away forever and pretend it never happened.

I had managed to cut down to craving and having only one binge a day. There were times when I would slip up and have two binges a day. I do not have an excuse for this; what I was doing was unacceptable. When I was bingeing, I could not care for Cyle-jay and the nanny had to.

When I admitted I was a bulimic addict, some responded, "Oh! Like anorexia!" And they would just brush it off as if I had issues with my weight and almost be apologetic for me.

"No, not anorexia. I have an addiction to bingeing and purging. I don't have an eating disorder because of my weight."

And they would say something to the effect, "Oh, that's a shame! Don't worry, it will all be okay."

I knew they did not understand what I was trying to tell them; my cry for help was hitting a dead end. I was not bingeing and puking because I had issues with my weight. I was happy with my weight. I had not lost any of the weight I had put on. Since giving birth, I had only put on two kilograms and Dr. Johannes had said it was better to let them remain. I was still slender in build but this did not worry me because I was within the acceptable weight requirement range. My weight was stable and I had no need or desire to get rid of the meals I ate or the kilograms I weighed.

I binged and purged because I craved it. The bingeing itself would put me on some form of a high and bring immense satisfaction. The purging brought such an emotional sense of relief from stress. After a high there was always a low; when the low came, it would hit in full force.

So though I had managed to cut this addiction to once a day, Charles and Cyle-jay had to go on this rollercoaster ride with me every day. A baby can sense what the mom and dad go through. Cyle-jay would cry the minute I started having the jitters from craving a binge and purge, even though the nanny would be with him. He would not let up until I had finished this two-to-three-hour process. Charles would know what I was doing, but he was so tired and just wanted peace, so he would allow the binge-purge episodes.

I was truly trying to fight and stop this selfish addiction. The stronghold had changed since the birth of our son. Before giving birth, I had pushed the Holy Spirit away from my ugly scenes. However, since I had first held Cyle-jay in my arms, I had asked my Best Friend to walk this path with me. I shared every single step with Him, even the very ugliest.

I also made sure to do what I had committed to do—praise and worship God because of His greatness, despite my addiction. Every morning Holy Spirit was there when I woke up with all His love and strength. Without fail, He would always place a new hope in me that this would be the day I would not binge and purge. I had once again started looking to and having faith in God Almighty to be set free from this curse I had allowed to shadow us.

Another shadow that came over us, especially Charles, was the news that his father, Dad Pulford, had cancer of the spleen and gall bladder. It was suspected that it had already begun spreading to his stomach.

This all happened within a year of Tania's death. We knew we had to take Cyle-jay to meet his granddad so we planned a trip to Durban to spend some time with him and the family.

We also knew I needed an operation to strip the varicose veins in my legs as circulation in them was dangerously bad. This was planned to take place after our Durban trip.

My mom was in the same small hospital at the time for my planned surgery. I was in the surgical section and mom in the non-surgical. I had been sitting with my mom when the nurse came in and told me it was time to start prepping me for the operation. I told my mom, "I'll see you later."

Dr. Johannes came in the operating room with that familiar smile on his face. He placed his hand on my arm as he usually did when he wanted to say something of importance. I immediately took notice of this and looked at him with a question in my eyes.

"Don't look so worried, Michele. I just came to tell you that the nurse is going to wheel you out. You are not having the operation."

"What have I done wrong now, doctor?"

"Nothing! It is what God has done right. Dr. Oliver, the anesthetist, did some tests after he consulted with you this morning." He once again smiled as he said, "You and Charles are going to have another baby. You are pregnant!"

This was just as much of a surprise as the first time, but I just smiled.

"I don't know how you keep doing this without any ovulation. God really wants these children of His to be born. He has got something mighty for them to do. Go tell your mom. She could do with some good news. I will come and see you."

After they wheeled me out of the operating room, I jumped off the cart and ran to my mom's room. After celebrating with her, I ran to phone Charles from a public telephone. He was ecstatic.

When Dr. Johannes came to see me, he told me he was not qualified and experienced enough to help me with this pregnancy because of the state of my legs. He had already contacted Dr. van der Walt, a gynecologist who would be able to help me with the pregnancy. "Please understand, Michele, there is a real possibility of you losing your right leg, especially because of the addiction."

Dr. van der Walt also had a gentle voice and was a patient gynecologist. Even though I had overcome my fear and hatred of men, God knew how important it was for me to have a doctor who I would feel safe with. He calculated our baby would be born in the first week of July 1993.

I had to inject my legs twice a day, every day, for the rest of the pregnancy, but they still became permanently numb and the stress contractions also began.

I was not able to stay in Sowa Town, Botswana so I went back to stay with my parents in Johannesburg.

Twenty-Two

Deliverance from the Giant

A FEW MONTHS LATER, IN April 1993, Charles picked me up from my parents' and we went to visit Dad Pulford. It was not only so he could see his son and grandson, but so Charles could see his father. Charles was very aware that his dad was not well at all.

After our visit, Charles went back to Sowa Town and I remained in Johannesburg. By the last week of May, Dr. van der Walt and Dr. le Roux, my gynecologist and surgeon, had both determined that our baby and my legs would not be able to hold out until July.

Then my dad was diagnosed with cancer in his lungs and had to have surgery. Charles' father's cancer had been getting worse since we had visited him at the beginning of that year, so this was another blow. My dad had the operation immediately and the lower part of his left lung was removed. The operation was a success, but we had been told the healing process was going to take a lot of care and time.

Because of my dad's operation and me being on almost 24-hour bed rest, Charles had to come down to help with Cyle-jay. He also helped drive my mom to and from the hospital where my dad was still in ICU.

On the 2nd of June, Charles got a call saying his father had taken a turn for the worse and the family was called to gather. When he put down the receiver, I could see on his face it was not good news. We cried and we prayed together before Charles and Cyle-jay left for Durban.

When he phoned me, I could hear great relief in his voice as he had made it in time. Two days later, Dad Pulford had passed away with Charles holding him. He told me all the deaths he had seen while with the SADF in Angola had not come close to watching his own father breathe out his last breath. He passed away on the date of Tania's funeral two years earlier and was buried the day after Charles' and Tania's birthday on June 7, 1993.

As soon as the funeral and remembrance tea were finished, Charles and Cyle-jay got in the car and came back to Johannesburg. Our baby was in high stress in my womb and I was having continuous contractions. Charles got back to Johannesburg that evening and booked me into the hospital by 10 p.m.

At sunrise the next morning, the 8th of June, I was induced and our daughter was born after just one hour of labor. There was tons of water all over. What a big difference from my previous dry birth after twenty-seven hours of labor. Brontii-ann represented new life and joy for both our families.

Even though Brontii-ann was premature, she was surprisingly strong and the pediatrician gave her a clean bill of health. We took our daughter home to my parents' house twenty-four hours after her birth. After Brontii-ann was settled in, Charles took me to another hospital by 4 p.m. that afternoon because Dr. le Roux wanted to operate on my legs immediately.

As I went, I was very aware of the guilt I felt for all the chaos my selfish addiction had created. Following this successful operation, I was released. Charles had to return to work in Botswana. We agreed I would remain at my parents' with Cyle-jay and Brontii-ann until she was six weeks old. By that time, I'd have her birth certificate and papers for my passport and would have grown accustomed to caring for a two year old and a newborn.

Everyone close to us knew that, of the two of us, Charles was the better baby parent. He was so confident and always knew what to do with a baby. Tania and Charles, and their younger sister, Tracey, had a passionate love for babies and children. When they were young children, Mom Pulford had her own day care center when they were living in Zambia. Charles, Tania, and Tracey helped her after school. Watching them with children or babies was like seeing a magnet drawing steel to it.

When Brontii-ann was three weeks old, her lips turned blue and I immediately took her to Dr. Johannes. He gave her oxygen and arranged for her to go to a pediatrician, Dr. da Silva, at our hospital. I winced when I had to help hold her flat on the x-ray table. *Lord, what have I caused, what have I done?*

After many x-rays and tests, it was discovered that Brontii-ann had no anti-allergens in her system. This was causing a major build-up of slime-mucous around her lungs and prohibiting total oxygen flow to her lungs. She was allergic to all grasses, twenty-two tree types and all animals except horses. She was immediately hospitalized to break this slime-mucous barrier with antibiotics. After being discharged, Brontii-ann had to be brought to the hospital every morning and afternoon for physiotherapy. As the physiotherapist worked on her, she would writhe and cry out in pain. She was on six pumps a day. I knew that this was a result of me being a bulimic addict during my pregnancy. Many times it is the loved ones around the addict who suffer the most.

What kind of mother am I, Holy Spirit? What kind of wife am I? What kind of Christian am I? Please forgive me for what I have done! These thoughts were always with me in my waking hours.

The Holy Spirit would say, *Brontii-ann is safe; she is healed. You are forgiven. Jesus loves you with an everlasting love, but now you must stand firm and resist bulimia. God is faithful to His Word and He will meet you where you place your faith in Him. Always! Slay this giant in your life, before this giant plunders more from Cyle-jay and Brontii-ann's life.*

Falling down, I committed myself to doing this. I began to declare as David did before going to slay Goliath, "The Lord will deliver me from this giant." I declared that God would break me free from this sin I had indulged as I turned from my evil ways.

My part of slaying my addiction was not to give in to my desires and cravings to binge and purge. Having to watch Brontii-ann go through the pain of physiotherapy twice a day was enough to make me determined to stand firm. Every night, at around 10 p.m., I would literally strap my hands in a belt because the withdrawal pains and violent cravings would get me sweating and shivering so bad that all I would want to do was go raid the kitchen.

I would just cry out to the Holy Spirit for strength.

There were times when I allowed my craving to win. I am ashamed to tell you I was worse than a pig. On those nights, I went to sleep riddled with guilt because of my weakness. I knew I had to stop. I also knew I could not just stop eating and stay away from food because that would make me head back down the road to anorexia.

I cried out, "Oh! Abba Father, in Jesus' Name, if I can't stop this, I can't stay around my babies. It is not fair on them. Please help me, Lord!"

The Holy Spirit reminded me, *The Lord will deliver you from this giant.*

Brontii-ann began improving. Within a month from treatment, she no longer had a blue mouth and blue lips and the physiotherapy was down to once a day. Dr. da Silva told us she did not suffer from asthma, but from slime around the lungs. The slime acted as a thick liquid that could literally drown her lungs. Because of this she would need daily physiotherapy throughout her early childhood. He also informed us that the pumps would be a lifetime requirement as is with asthma patients. Brontii-ann would be allowed to go home to Sowa Town, Botswana when she was three months old if there was a certified physiotherapist close on hand.

We were so grateful because one of the men who worked for Soda Ash Botswana was married to Alison, a qualified physiotherapist. They had been living at Orapa Mine, Botswana before coming to Sowa Town so Alison had already received her work permit. She said she would definitely take Brontii-ann under her wing. I still bow down in thanksgiving and awe before our Almighty God when I think of how He placed a qualified physiotherapist in such a small remote community.

Brontii-ann was only two months old when Mom Pulford phoned and asked if she could fly us down to Durban before we went back home. She wanted to meet her granddaughter and give her grandson a birthday party as Cyle-jay's birthday was coming up. I knew this would help her deal with Dad Pulford's death. Durban had many physiotherapists so Brontii-ann's treatment was not a problem.

Watching Mom Pulford with Cyle-jay and Brontii-ann was one of the precious pearls in my life. How rich I was! I had a husband who was a living jewel of forgiveness and unconditional love. God had blessed me with a son who was living evidence of the miracle of life and hope and a daughter who was a living miracle and pearl of new life and joy.

But I knew I had to tell Mom Pulford why Brontii-ann was suffering the way she was.

The Pulford family thought I had a simple eating disorder as Charles had always covered up for me. I told Mom Pulford everything about my bulimic addiction and the nightmare I sometimes made it for Charles. I felt so ashamed at what I had done and what I was guilty of. I was so scared she would chase me out of her house, but she did not. Instead she looked at me with tears running down her cheeks.

"I am so sorry, Mom. I would never intentionally harm your Charles, Cyle-jay or Brontii-ann."

She lovingly looked at me and said, "I know you would never. It's fine."

"No, Mom, it's not fine. This is not an eating disorder. It's an addiction. This has also caused a lot of pain for Charles. Please, will you forgive me?"

"Michele, you have made my son the happiest man alive and he loves you with all his heart. Of course, I forgive you. And I know Charlie will help you with this problem. You are always praying and so God will help you."

With a sigh of relief and joy, I gave Mom Pulford a big hug. She did not have to forgive me, yet she did.

"Michele, it is time for me to ask you to forgive me."

I did not understand why she was asking me this.

"Michele, Tania gave me a message to give you, when she was still coherent a few days before she died. I still don't understand what it means, but I am so sorry I never told you."

I could see Mom Pulford was in great emotional pain as she spoke.

I gently said, "Mom, it's okay! I forgive you." I paused a while and then continued, "What is the message Tania wanted you to give me?"

After she told me, I just burst out crying. I turned my face and raised my hands up to the heavens and said, "Thank You, Lord!"

Now Mom Pulford was confused. I let her know what the message from Tania meant to me and she burst out crying too.

(The message has to do with the great victory story of Tania's salvation by Jesus Christ, to be shared at another time).

Mom Pulford then started speaking about Tania and Dad Pulford. After we exhausted this, she spoke about Charles, Tracey, and Leslie and then herself. We spent the whole afternoon talking. She thanked me for allowing her to give Cyle-jay his second birthday party and for letting her sleep with Brontii-ann in her arms.

I was the one who was more grateful to Mom Pulford for flying us down to Durban for the two weeks. Even though he was not there, this meant so much to Charles. I had been so blessed with the message from Tania that was so important, and a friendship between Mom Pulford and me had also been birthed.

After our visit to Durban, Dr. da Silva, Brontii-ann's pediatrician, gave us the required permission to take her home to Botswana.

By then, my dad was recovering well from his operation. He still had to go for regular check-ups to see if all the cancer had been removed, but at that moment he felt positive about his healing.

Charles came to fetch us. We were both grateful and excited because we would be together again with Cyle-jay and Brontii-ann. I told Charles about the newfound friendship with his mom and that her love and support had helped me recommit to zero tolerance with my bulimic addiction. I needed him to give me firm support.

Peter tells us in 1 Peter 4:8, "Above all, love each other deeply, because love covers over a multitude of sins." It covers all wrongs. This was and still is a value and code by which Charles lives. Charles had always looked for the best in people and lets their weaknesses slip by. That is why Charles would forgive me every single time I had slipped up with my addiction and asked for forgiveness. He forgave me and threw my wrongdoing into the deepest sea. He would literally forget what I had been guilty of and never bring it up again. He didn't tell me my addiction was selfish and destroying him and the children.

Eventually, after explaining it to him again and again, I convinced him that his firmness would be the ultimate love and kindness he could give to me, Cyle-jay, and Brontii-ann. He agreed to be firm.

I don't think you have to be cruel to be kind. Being cruel means purposely withdrawing love from the addict to make them want to stop what they are doing. This does not help or build and strengthen the person. It brings the addict into the punishment of rejection, breaking them down even further.

Being firm to be kind means not withdrawing love, but standing firm in love while setting boundaries, conditions, and punishment as consequences for actions—and refusing to compromise because of love.

Charles felt being firm was just as bad as being cruel.

I had already made a big step forward with the bulimia, but every day I would go through cravings and suffer withdrawal symptoms. In this recurring nightmare, I clung to God's promises of His Word that said he would break these chains and set me free.

There were days when I lost and the pig-hyena would reappear ending with the elephant seal.

Charles would be extra loving then and so forgiving. I told him, "I need you to be firm," and asked him to discipline me, but he could not bring himself to do it.

"I can't be so cruel," he said.

Eventually, one night in November that year, I told him, "I can't do this to you or our precious babies anymore. If I enter the new year as a bulimic addict, I will have to remove myself from you and the babies. Either my addiction goes or I will have to go out of your lives."

Charles and I knew what I was doing with this addiction was selfish, destructive and not acceptable. I did not want our children growing up with this consuming shadow looming over their lives.

Charles was not happy to hear this, but I told him, "This is the only way to give our children and you an abundant life." It was not God's will that Cyle-jay and Brontii-ann grow up without their mother, which meant I had to be set free from this addiction.

Determined, I recognized that on my own I would never be strong enough to step away from this addiction. I needed strength from God Almighty, the maker of Heaven with all its heavenly hosts and Earth with all its inhabitants, who is also my Abba Father and loves me so much that He gave me His Son, Jesus. He had given me eternal life and He also gave me the Holy Spirit to strengthen me and cause me to get the victory.

The Holy Spirit reminded me, *Michele, God is an ever-flowing fountain of grace. He already has forgiven you and your faith in His grace always pleases Him."*

I repeated back to Him, "And He will meet me where my faith is. Oh, thank You, Holy Spirit."

Remember, if you stand firm and resist this addiction in the Name of Jesus, it will leave you. According to God's Word, it has to bow down to the Name of Jesus.

"Holy Spirit, I refuse to begin 1994 as a bulimic addict. I cannot do this without You, Lord."

You won't have to Michele. You won't have to.

I fell on my knees and bowed down, "I believe this. Thank You. I know it is You, Lord, who has given me the strength and boldness to believe this and not doubt it."

Charles and I and our two beautiful little darlings celebrated Christmas together as a family and then I set off with Cyle-jay and Brontii-ann to spend New Year's with my mom and dad. Charles was going to be on standby at work over this period and usually that meant more hours at work than at home with us. My parents also wanted to see their grandchildren and give them their Christmas gifts.

When Charles kissed me good-bye, I reminded him, "Charles, I will only come back when my chains of addiction are broken and I am set free. I will not carry on doing this to you or the children."

I ended New Year's Eve of 1993 and entered 1994 crying in desperation and guilt because of my weakness. Shivering and sweating and on my knees, I'd roll while clutching my knees. For three days, I had been craving and going through major withdrawal cramps and pains. For the first time in five years I had not binged and purged for three whole days and nights, going onto four. The longest I had ever lasted before had been two days. The three days had already felt like years, and I was really in a desperate state.

"Oh, Father God, Jesus, please forgive me. I am such a weakling. Please forgive me."

You have already been forgiven.

"Oh, Holy Spirit, I don't deserve this. I am not going to make it. Please help me. If I cave in now, it's over. I will never be with my family again."

Michele.

"Yes, Holy Spirit?"

Stop looking at your sin and your weakness, and start looking at the Christ in you. God is a God of grace. He doesn't see your sin, He sees His Son in you. He loves you; you are forgiven. Forget about yourself, receive His love and praise Him.

In my desperation, I sat on top of my hands and began singing all the songs of praise and worship I could think of.

I fell asleep in that position. Brontii-ann's cry for feeding woke me up. The sun was rising.

"Thank You, Lord! I would not have made it through the night without your help."

Michele, you must go to Nolene later on today and ask her to pray for you.

"But they will have over one hundred people over at their house to celebrate New Year's Day."

God has already set your visit in place.

"Thank You, Lord."

I phoned Nolene mid-morning to ask if I could come over.

"Of course you can! I'm having a few people over for New Year's celebration and you are most welcome to join us. Are you going to bring your beautiful babies with?"

"No, not this time. My mom and dad are taking them for a treat."

"That's fine. Looking forward to seeing you!"

Nolene was the most loving, kind person I knew. She had taken me under her wing from around the time I became a Christian and was like a spiritual mom to me. I knew I could trust her and she would never say no to helping a child of God, any time of day.

When I arrived at her house, I smiled as I saw about twenty cars there. "Lord, maybe I should come back tomorrow."

No, Michele! God called your hope into being now. Faith is now! Do you want to go through another night like last night?

"No. I am not strong enough."

Then trust God. Go and find Nolene and ask her to pray for you. She will. I will lead her.

"Oh, Holy Spirit! What would I do without you?"

Once again, I felt His loving, gentle smile. *You don't have to do things alone, Michele. I am always here for you.*

"I know. I am sorry I have grieved You with this for all these years now. Please forgive me?"

You have been forgiven. Now walk in this grace from God. Jesus died to set you free and give you the victory.

"Oh! I love You, Lord Jesus."

Hearing my best friend's divine encouragement gave me the determination to stand firm, walk forward, and believe.

I walked around, greeting and talking to people at the party, and noticing all the delicacies and cakes and sweets and savories all around me. As I looked for Nolene, I was tempted more and more by the food. It felt as if everyone was luring me to eat the delicious food in front of me. I could feel my strength crumbling and my craving lusts increasing to binge on all of the alluring food.

Then I heard a loud thought cross through my mind, *Go on! Just have one more binge. There is so much delicious food here. You can come back tomorrow for Nolene to pray for you.*

I immediately heard the Holy Spirit say, *Michele, don't listen to this thought. God loves you and has planned and purposed this specific time for Nolene to pray for you. Don't look at or think of all the food. Think of Jesus and how He has set you free from being a slave to all this food. Stand firm in Him.*

I had a decision to make and I made it.

I said silently, *Get behind me bulimia and addiction. Jesus is my strength and my refuge and it is in His Name that I stand firm. I refuse to give into these cravings. What I see is no longer delicious food, but be-damned food.*

I knew that only half a teaspoon of anything could trigger a massive, pig-purge session that would never end. I knew this could be the binge that could bring about my death and the destruction of my family.

No more pig-purging, do you hear? No more! Get behind me! Now! In the name of Jesus.

Instantly, my attraction to the food that had been luring me and calling my name just disappeared. All the delicious meats, breads, puddings, cakes, sweets, chocolates, and savories were still there, but they had just become food on platters and nothing more.

Not so tempting anymore, hey addict-demon? Now leave me alone! I had never spoken to this addiction with a voice of total authority before. I had always been the one begging.

God did not want to continuously bless me in my mess of bulimic addiction. He wanted to take me out of the mess completely.

The Holy Spirit reminded me, *Now go and find Nolene. I have anointed her to bring forth your total release.*

I rushed because I did not want this moment of boldness and authority in me to die out. I found her in the kitchen with her friends. There had always been something special about Nolene's kitchen. Everyone seemed to socialize in her kitchen; it had always had such a relaxed and joyful atmosphere. On that day, it was packed to capacity and buzzing with excited woman's laughter and joy.

I spotted Nolene and walked directly to her. She saw me and welcomed me. We blessed each other for New Year's and then it went along the whole line of ladies.

Lord, I can't pull Nolene away from this.

You don't have to. Go tell her God is asking her to pray for you.

I went over and whispered this in her ear and she responded immediately.

She said, "Ladies, please excuse me. I am just going to pray for Michele," and she led me to the other side of her kitchen. She placed her hand on me and prayed in the Name of Jesus. I felt the anointing that God had placed on her being released into me.

This is no mystical phenomenon. Many people accept it when I say "divine energy" is transferred from person to person so that they can transfer it to others. We Christians call this an "anointing" from God, according to His Word. This supernatural occurrence happens when the Name of Jesus is called out.

Nolene had no idea what to pray for. But she understood that God's Word tells us to pray in Spirit and in truth, and that the Holy Spirit will help us pray when we do not know what to pray. This is exactly what she did.

"Oh! Thank you, Nolene! You have just saved my life." I knew she did not completely understand I meant this literally. Her eager obedience to God's call to pray for me, even though she was in the middle of celebrating the new year with her friends, had just brought abundant new life for me—and Charles, Cyle-jay, and Brontii-ann.

The Holy Spirit had directed the stone from the slingshot through Nolene's prayer in the Name of Jesus. This had given the giant of bulimia, harboring its soldier called addiction, a fatal blow. The giant had been slain, once and for all.

"It is a pleasure, my sweetheart." Her kind eyes and beautiful smile shone out as she asked, "Now! Are you going to join us?"

"No, thank you. I want to go back to my parents and give my children a massive big kiss and hug and also phone Charles and give him my news of total victory!"

Nolene gave me a hug and said, "Then just stay for a cup of tea."

As we walked back to the crowd, one of her close friends of many years popped a big dessert in my face. "Michele would like a bowl of this with some custard? We have just taken it out of the oven. We call it Pudding Revenge. It is made from condensed milk, syrup, chocolate, fudge and caramel. It is really a revenge pudding!"

Before, this would have been my downfall and started a week of piggish bingeing. But I looked at the dessert and it was dead to me. No taunting temptations called out to me to guzzle it all up and then go and look for more. I had no cravings. No more torment in my mind. It was all gone. The cake was just a warm cake that smelled very sweet, too sweet.

I hugged her. She was surprised because a yes or no would have covered it. I hugged her because I felt no temptation at all and it felt so exhilarating and great and victorious.

"No, thank you. I am an ex-bulimic addict."

"But you can afford it. You are nice and slim."

"No, I can't. I am an ex-bulimic addict."

I could see all the questioning eyes. "I am not saying no because of my weight. A recovering alcoholic can never take a sip of alcohol because that could be a trigger to alcoholism. This is how it is with me. Even a teaspoon of Pudding Revenge or the like can trigger me and get me back to that addiction."

As I said this, I literally felt this giant's shadow, its stronghold, its spirit, fall right off me. Its power no longer had a hold over me.

Smiling, I looked up and quietly said, "Thank You" to God.

I stayed for my cup of tea. I was laughing and sharing in all their joy and enjoying my own. The shackles that had been locked around my ankles since my very first binge and purge had been cut off. The chains were loosened. The God of grace had set me free. I was free. Charles was free. Cyle-jay and Bron-tii-ann were free.

It has been well over twenty-odd years since this giant fell, and I have never looked back. I say it again, "Thank You, my Lord God Almighty."

The veil I had brought into my relationship with God was torn into shreds and it allowed God's shining glory through. God is always faithful to His Word. He met me where I placed my faith.

Twenty-Three

The Curse of the Witchdoctors

I WENT TO SEE DR. Johannes to let him know of my victory before going back to Sowa Town, taking Cyle-jay and Brontii-ann with me. Once again, he had played a major role in my victory.

He gave his usual gentle smile. "You know, Michele, when you were first pregnant, I was really doubtful about what kind of mother you were going to be. I felt more weary than excited, but I began trusting God for you, Charles, and your family that was still to come.

"When Cyle-jay was born and Charles had to bring him to me to be circumcised, you were still in the hospital because of your leg. You could not join him. It was then I knew. I saw how at home Charles was with the baby and what an amazing father he already was. I knew God had answered my prayers. You have a wonderful husband and your children have a very special daddy."

"Yes, Charles is a super parent. I don't even come close."

"Michele, I have watched you. You are a great mom."

"Doctor, I was a bulimic addict until now. When was I ever a great mom? I was the worst mother that existed."

"Never talk like that, Michele. You would not have overcome this addiction if you were the worst mother. You wouldn't have cared."

"Thank you for believing in me! Thank you for always showing me God's persevering love."

"It is a pleasure, Michele, but it is I who must thank you. I am going to retire soon. You were already one of my victory patients. Now you have come to tell me the giant that has been disrupting you and your family's life has been slain. This is a victory for me, too. Thank you." As he came and gave me a fatherly hug, I could see the tears in his eyes behind his glasses.

I felt my own tears welling and tried to shut them off by saying, "At least when you retire, there won't be any patients calling you away from very important rugby matches."

A chapter in my life had closed in that year of 1994. There is one very special pearl of wisdom I have carried with me. How you end an issue in life will be the way you start the next issue. I had ended this walk with Dr. Johannes's blessing. Since then, we have always been blessed with God-appointed doctors and specialists, and I know we always will be.

When the giant in my life fell, many of its soldiers fell with it. God's glory that pierced through the torn veil enabled Charles and me to enter a brand-new extra-blessed season in our marriage, which also flowed over into Cyle-jay's and Bron-tii-ann's lives. Nehemiah 8:10 tells us, ". . . the joy of the Lord is your strength." The joy that had been produced in our lives strengthened every area of our lives. We rose from glory to glory together as a family and as individuals. And it is the same to this day.

My mom did not share this victory with us. She thought I was lying and said, "I'll have to see it to believe it." This hurt me deep, deep inside. This was not the first time my mom had falsely accused me of being a liar . . . and it was not the last time either, even when I had proved her false accusations wrong so many times in my life.

Mom Pulford shared in our joy as she understood what a miracle this was. I knew I was totally healed and was encouraged to have Charles' mom believe it and support me.

Mom Pulford had always suffered with water on her lungs, which created heart problems. There were times when she had to be rushed to the emergency room because of this. This increased after Dad Pulford passed away. Mom was always casual about this and would say, "It's nothing to be overly concerned about."

Whenever she was taken to the emergency room, treated, and sent home, she always allowed me to pray for her over the phone. The freedom of discussing Mom's walk with God made our calls very special.

One night in February of that year, Tracey phoned telling us Mom Pulford had passed away. We were all devastated. Tracey said when the ambulance had taken her to the emergency room, she had thought it would the same as other times. She sat in the waiting room expecting the doctor to come and tell her everything would be fine.

This time the doctor came with different news. They were not able to save Mom Pulford. We all thought she would be with us for a long time, even with this problem. Charles and I once again packed, got in the car, and traveled the many miles for the funeral. She was so loved by her family and circle of many friends. Tracey hurt and mourned the most as she had been with her mom every day for a long time.

On returning to Sowa Town, we knew how important it was to keep the ties strong between Cyle-jay and Brontii-ann with my mom and dad and their cousins. Charles never denied me any visits to stay with my family in Johannesburg. Both our children needed regular medical attention, which we'd do in Johannesburg. With Charles' blessing, it was as if the children and I had two homes: one in Sowa Town and the other in Johannesburg.

Both Cyle-jay and Brontii-ann had suffered from the consequences of my addiction. I had been totally forgiven by God and Charles, but seeing what I had caused my children, I didn't know how I could forgive myself.

I did everything in my power to ensure that Cyle-jay and Brontii-ann received the best medical treatment available. The most important thing I could do was to go on my knees day and night, declaring their healing. I stood firm and expected nothing less than their full healing because God's Word promises us this. The Bible tells us that by Jesus' wounds, the stripes He endured, we are healed.

I had told them from a very young age why they were suffering and always asked them to forgive me. They were young and always said yes. Because of their love and forgiveness, they allowed me in. I taught them how to expect and call in the promise of healing. From the time they could speak their first words, I taught them to say, "Jesus, only You can heal me and I thank You."

Did they receive their healing? Of course, yes. They both have powerful testimonies of how God brought their healing, but it is not for me to tell but their stories. Not only were their births a miracle, their lives, sufferings, walks, victories, and faith are a continual daily miracle.

God is so faithful! Charles and I bow down in absolute surrender with thanksgiving for His mighty favor, blessings, and purpose for both Cyle-jay and Brontii-ann. I learned never to speak failure and disaster over my children, but to declare destiny, greatness, and speak only the best for them. We watch in awe as they grow in stature, fixed in the destiny, calling and purpose that God has created them for.

We settled down in Sowa Town as we secured our roots as a family in this world. I would go stay with my mom and dad for ten days every second month or so. Both Sonja and Gavin did not live far away, so the cousins would always visit with each other. My mom would always take Gareth, Cyle-jay, Jade and Brontii-ann on outings over the weekends when we were visiting. There are only four years separating the four of them so they became good friends, a further blessing to our family.

—◊◊◊—

Having been freed from the bulimic addiction and the stigma of this label, I was able to stand even more boldly for God's Son and His Kingdom.

I began a godly friendship with a woman who had just arrived in Sowa Town. Rica was a beautiful fifty-two-year-old woman who had recently married Henny who had already been working at Soda Ash Botswana and had lost his first wife.

Rica was very passionate about helping the local Botswana women become empowered in skills development and had started a garment manufacturing training course. As I was a qualified fashion designer, it was natural thing that I would help. She also began a choir with the same group of ladies who signed up for the garment course. The training and products had done exceptionally well from the very start. The choir did just as well. We used both the training group and the choir to show them the love and victory of Jesus Christ. This, and our friendship, filled us with joy.

All we wanted to do was help teach the ladies a skill they could use to sustain themselves. At the same time, we wanted to encourage them to use their gifts and love for singing and dancing to preach and teach God's Word.

We did not know we were making the local witchdoctors very angry. Six months had not even passed by when Rica and I received a warning from the local witch doctors. Neither of us had been exposed to anything like this before. We did not know witchdoctors not only existed but ruled.

We soon learned that though many of the locals said they were Christians, in reality they were not. They went through all the outward Christian motions, but they would do what the witchdoctors instructed them to do.

The witchdoctors used fear to rule and gain power. Watching the women being enslaved to the commands of these men and women and doing what was demanded of them for fear of being cursed made Rica and me dig our heels in even further.

One day the women came in for their training, wailing. When we asked, "What's wrong?" we were given a final warning from the witchdoctors. We were told to stop trying to influence and brainwash the locals with our white man's ways or else our husbands and children would be taken from us and we would die.

To say that we were shocked would be putting it mildly. Our first reaction was a half-hearted laugh, but then the women told us it was true and warned us the witchdoctors would attack through their curses.

One morning two very somber looking women came with the ladies we were working with. They would not greet us but kept babbling in their tribal language.

Even though I did not understand the words, I immediately knew they were releasing curses. Rica and I grabbed hands and prayed for the blood of Jesus over us. Afterwards, we kept saying, "In Jesus' Name."

This immediately got a reaction from the two women. They scowled, pointed at us, and walked away. The wailing ladies told us to follow.

Rica and I lived on different streets, but, because of the town's layout, we were connected through "rat roads" and a big open piece of bush land. These narrow dusty rat roads ran between the houses to shorten the walking distance for pedestrians and were also used to transport cows through the town.

The two mumbling women marched off through the rat road next to Rica's house and into the bush. They then went to a certain spot and started digging with their bare hands. The dirt was flying and their mumbling had changed to chanting. Both Rica and I immediately responded by starting to pray out aloud in tongues.

The other poor wailing women were looking from the chanters who were frantically digging up dirt to the Spirit-tongued prayer warriors who were lifting their arms and looking to Heaven. They did not understand what was going on. As their fear increased, the wailing turned to high-pitched hysteria.

Rica and I did not know what was going on either. We just knew we had to continue praying.

Suddenly the flying dirt stopped and so did their chanting. The two scowling women turned and pointed to us. The other women stopped wailing.

Rica and I lowered the volume of our prayers, but we did not stop praying.

The women then pulled out of the hole two dirt-infested dolls made of burlap. They turned and pointed to Rica and me. Quickly, the group of hysterical women ran away. The two somber ladies held up the hideous dolls as they walked up to us. They spat on the dolls and then threw one doll at Rica and one doll at me and left.

We had no idea what this meant. It was like a horror movie. We also had no idea what to do or to whom to go to for help.

There were no pastors or ministers in Sowa Town. I went to bed that night asking myself, *What am I doing in this land? What do the dolls buried in the ground mean?* It felt like a bad dream.

Charles and I would take Cyle-jay and Brontii-ann for a walk in their strollers every night for about twenty minutes. In that time we could walk around our whole small town.

Rica and I had asked around and found out this small town had *six* witch doctors living on its outskirts. At night, we could hear their drum rolls. We were told what drum roll belonged to what witch doctor. The locals said the witch doctors were passing on messages sent from their ancestors.

We knew the blood of Jesus covers and protects us from the enemy so we had no reason to fear. We just had to make sure we were always living with the full armor of God protecting us and were operating through the fruit of the Spirit.

I also found out from some pastors in the area that the witch doctors operate using the spirit of fear to blind, manipulate, and control to get power. We learned the devil cannot create; he can only use what is there.

God is the mighty Creator. The devil needs a doorway to be left open, even if it's just slightly open. Only God Almighty holds the keys to open and close doors, and He does this through His Son Jesus Christ. He has given us this authority. God is the only one who knows all our comings and goings.

The Bible also tells us the devil prowls around "like" a roaring lion. It does not say that he *is* a roaring lion. There is a big difference between being *like* a lion and being a lion. What he does is roar and hope this will create fear within us. This fear opens the door into our lives and the protection God gives us is compromised. Instead of seeing this fear as sin and confessing it to close the door, we reason and justify this fear and allow it to remain and make itself at home. Fear is not content unless it is able to devour and destroy and steal more of the target's territory.

> Finally, be strong in the Lord and in His mighty power. Put on the full armor of God so that you can take your stand against the devil's schemes.
>
> (Eph. 6:10–11)

> Be self-controlled and alert. Your enemy the devil prowls around like a roaring lion looking for someone to devour.
>
> (1 Peter 5:8)

We had understood the witch doctors' message clearly and were on guard for any more roaring lion attacks. Even though no more dirty dolls were thrown at us, I never anticipated their next strategic step.

Twenty-Four

Assignment to Kill

ONE AFTERNOON I RECEIVED A telephone call from a mysterious woman with a local accent. She said, "I want your husband. Soon he will leave you and the children and he will be mine!"

That instant, all my preparing, declaring, and praying flew out the window. My anger boiled over and I lost my self-control. I screamed back at the woman. This opened the door of insecurity inside me, perfect grounds for fear to move in.

When I put the phone down, I did not run and share it with the Holy Spirit and ask Him to help me. Instead, I let it boil and brew inside me as I waited for Charles to come home. When he did, I attacked him. Suspicion and false accusations entered our home.

Even though I knew Charles was nothing like Lawrence and would never look at another woman, I allowed my insecurities and old wounds to resurface. The fear of being completely rejected and abandoned had cast another shadow over our marriage.

Each day, I would wait anxiously to see if Charles would come home, fearing he may have decided to leave me and take the children with him. Charles continually assured me of his commitment to me, but I couldn't believe him. This brought immense stress into his life as well.

The fear began to eat at me. Then one evening I had a very weird attack. I was told it was an allergy attack, and I did not take it too seriously until I had another one.

The second time, I got itchy lumps under my chin. Then my face and my whole body broke out into massive itchy hives as big as golf balls, which would burst into a blazing heat, causing my body to burn red as if on fire. My throat closed and my tongue blew up making breathing almost impossible. My face would swell and contort as if someone was inside pulling it from one side to the other. As the swelling traveled through me, it felt as if there were little men inside me, kicking and trying to break out of my skin, at any cost to my body.

I would have to have ice packs rubbed on my skin and my hands literally tied to stop me from scratching my skin raw. Then I would become slowly paralyzed until I could not move, speak, or even blink my eyelashes. I'd stay in this paralyzed state anywhere from half an hour to a couple of hours. Afterwards, I would be left with a contorted, heavily scratched, bruised, and bashed-up looking face and body, as if I had been attacked by a lioness with her claws.

This scared me, Charles, and the doctor as well. I went down to Johannesburg for tests and more tests . . . and then some more. Not even the specialists knew what was causing this analgesic, anaphylactic allergy attack. My medic alert bracelet read: idieopathic recurrent analgesic anaphylaxis uticaria angioedema!

This meant if my allergy attack was not immediately treated, I could die. I was no longer allowed to travel alone or go for walks or runs by myself.

I was not afraid of death. I already knew I would go to Heaven and be put in an eternal, heavenly body. But I was afraid of being a prisoner. I felt the shackles grip and chain my soul. It was as if I was once again in solitary confinement at the SADF army hospital, as I had been all those years ago.

Because the tests did not show what triggered my allergies, I never knew when, where, or why the allergies were going to appear. I did not know if they were going to attack with full force or just pass in a light phase. I could be inside, outside, sitting, standing, laughing, crying, eating, or not eating. I did not know when to expect them. To make matters worse, we still did not have a clinic in the town.

The fact that they could not find what was causing these attacks was proof to me that the battle was found in the spirit realm and was just manifesting through medical symptoms. I believed this to be psychosomatic and that it needed medical as well as spiritual treatment. I had learned the root of allergies in the spirit realm is fear. Fear can only enter in if we open a door of sorts, as I had done.

I no longer had any self-control to stop this as I had blown all my emotional gaskets in that telephone call. The devil knew this was a very clever tactic to use, and I fell for it.

It is understandable and reasonable that I would be shaken after having received that phone call from a strange woman telling me she was going to steal my husband. But the way I handled it was wrong. Screaming back at her was letting the armor of God down; I was operating out of the flesh and not the fruit of the Spirit. And I allowed this to taunt me and bring up all my old hurts and failures.

I had still not gained victory over my fear of Charles rejecting and abandoning me. When the Holy Spirit showed me this, I immediately repented and began standing firm against the allergy attacks. The shackles did not fall from me immediately, but I continued to stand firm and persevere in holding onto Charles' reassurances that we were married, we were one, and nothing could separate us.

I had also begun to fear what would happen if I would be alone with Cyle-jay and Brontii-ann when I had an anaphylactic attack? This would put them in danger; without any help, they might have to watch me leave this earth. In my past attacks, they had been close at hand and had always started screaming. Watching what was happening to me was totally terrifying for them.

The progression from the start of the first hive to my eventual paralysis was happening at an accelerated pace. When this occurred, I needed someone to get my adrenalin, open it, and then inject it into my stomach area. In those days, the injection was a lot more complicated and took more time to administer than the adrenalin injections today.

Charles also feared our children would be alone with me one day. He would never speak about the fear he felt the instant the allergies would attack, but I could see it in his eyes. He had to administer the injection and then get me to the doctor for the other emergency treatments required, besides caring for a baby and a toddler. This fear brought a major shadow of fear over our family.

Charles and I immediately began praying for complete breakthrough and healing. We placed our trust in God. We took a step forward, determining not to allow this stronghold of allergy to rule our lives. The truth was, I could have an allergy attack at any time! But we refused to let this linger at the back of our minds. We planned our daily lives ensuring I was never alone with the children.

We had a very special next-door neighbor, Christine, a qualified nurse from Australia. She had taught Cyle-jay, who was not yet four years old, to always react when he saw his mommy holding her throat and when her eyes became smaller and her head seemed to grow bigger. She told him he had to run to the fence and begin banging and shaking it. The dogs would hear and this would alert her. She showed him she would hear the noise and come and help him right away.

I praise the Lord that never happened. But just knowing the stress it was putting on our babies, I stood firm and declared every day that the allergies had lost the battle. I knew Jesus had given me the victory. If I did have an attack, even in my paralyzed state, I would declare with my inner voice and thoughts that Jesus is Lord and the allergy would have to bow down to Him.

I had let people know if I did have an allergy attack, and they could see the paralysis settle in, they were to sing or play

Jesus songs around me. I worked hard at refusing to let any fear in. The children were to be taken to play at one of their friend's homes. Eventually we got to the victory point where that shadow was never ever allowed to control. It tried to settle in, but we firmly took the joy of the Lord as one of our weapons against it. That would always break and shatter the shadow, causing it to disintegrate.

This mysterious woman who was working with her witchdoctor to covet Charles from us then sent me another message.

One evening we arrived home at dusk after a few days away visiting my parents. We pulled into the driveway to find Shalom, our collie, with his throat cut. We ran to phone Dave, an animal lover in our tiny village who had experience helping distressed animals. He arrived within a couple of minutes and immediately started putting stitches in Shalom's throat. The blood was gushing out all over the place, but the stitching helped get air into him.

Charles and I put him in the car and drove off to Francis Town, just over two hours away. I drove because Charles was trying to help Shalom breathe, and had just finished driving for a good eight hours.

When we arrived at the vet, Charles was soaked with Shalom's blood that was dripping off him. The vet looked at us and she began to cry. She said, "This is one of the cruelest things I have ever seen." She advised us to put Shalom down immediately as that was the kindest thing to do.

This attack sent us reeling. The witchdoctors would stop at nothing to try to manipulate and control and to induce fear.

I went before the Lord and asked Him, "What am I doing here in the bush with witchdoctors?"

That night I dreamed I saw a big, black, evil dome over Sowa Town. Then I saw a small tiny window being opened in this dome. The sunlight from outside pierced its way through. As it did, the dome started falling apart, allowing more and more sunlight in. I immediately understood. I bowed down and asked for forgiveness for my shortsightedness.

I also asked God to give me the strength for what lay ahead. I was ready and knew the witchdoctors would try to do something else to me.

The next attack was calculated and strategic.

Around this time my domestic worker became very, very sick with AIDS and had to go home. We had already lost a garden worker and now our domestic lady. After tons of prayer and many no answers, I eventually got the go ahead from the Holy Spirit to appoint a new woman to help us around the house.

The morning Rose started working was one I will never forget. Within ten minutes of her being there, my washing machine caught fire and my main fridge shook violently and then died. As if that were not enough, Rose then "accidently" stuck a knife into the smaller fridge. She said she was cleaning it!

I went into the sitting room and asked, "Holy Spirit, what does this mean?" But I already knew the answer. The sick feeling in my gut was shouting it out loud and clear. "She has been sent here by one of the witch doctors, hasn't she?"

He gently said, *Yes.*

I could not believe it. Had I heard wrong about hiring Rose? The relationship between me and the Holy Spirit was very sound and clear and I had always heard His counsel correctly. This was a first. I was so sure He had told me that Rose was the right one.

I immediately wanted to charge through and ask her to take her things and get out of my house.

But then the Holy Spirit said, *No, Michele, do not go. Stay right here.*

"I don't understand! What must I do then?"

The Holy Spirit spoke clearly and loudly, *Nothing! Keep her and show her the true love of God. She won't be here for a long time.*

"Did I hear You correctly?"

Yes. It is God's will that Rose is here.

"Holy Spirit, she was sent by the witchdoctors. She has just somehow caused the washing machine to be set on fire and both fridges are totally dead!"

God will provide for you by the end of the day.

"What about Cyle-jay and Brontii-ann? She could harm them."

The firm, gentle voice answered, *She won't, Michele, the blood of Jesus will not let her. God is far greater than any intention of the enemy. My hand is over them, just as it was over you when you were in the fiery flames of Hades. Rose cannot touch them. It is not the witch doctors who have sent Rose here. It is God Almighty who has sanctioned and purposed for Rose to be here. His glory always reigns.*

When she comes in your home, play worship songs and have TBN on without ceasing. Pray for her always. This, together with your acceptance and making her feel she belongs, is all Rose will need. This is going to bring the fear of God Almighty upon her.

After that, I made sure she heard either worship songs or Christian TV programs blaring out of the television.

From that moment on, Rose seemed petrified because of the joy flowing through our home. She did not know what to do when I shouted, "Glory, hallelujah!" and raised my hands to the heavens to wave. Or when I dropped down onto my knees in reverential fear before the Lord God.

One morning I went over to her with a cheerful demeanor and said, "I never want to see you near my children. If you ever come too close to them, my Almighty God, who lives in Heaven, will send fire down to stop you."

I knew this sounded extreme, and when I did this, it surprised even me. But these were my babies, I had become a lioness looking after her cubs.

Rose understood the message clearly. She knew that, though I was smiling and twirling around the house, I would not hesitate to strike out if she got too near Cyle-jay or Brontii-ann.

I also told her, "You better not try leaving any *mutie* anywhere in my house." (Muties are cursed objects that are commonly left in households.) "If you do, my Lord God, who sees everything, will show me where you hide it."

I then told her she must go and tell the witch doctor who sent her that Jesus Christ is Lord and the witch doctor would always only be a footstool at His feet.

I did not know where all these words came from because I had not thought about any of them. But I stood firm in my newfound boldness.

Rose ran out. I was not sure if she would return, but it did not matter. I knew my Lord God is far greater than her god. At that point, so did she.

God is *always* faithful. Many times, people are not happy because He does not do things their way. Isaiah tells us that God's ways are higher than our ways, and His thoughts are higher than our thoughts. He is the omniscient, all-knowing God.

I was most surprised to see Rose back on my doorstep the next morning. This was when I knew for sure she had been sent on a mission by those witch doctors. I also knew, deep within, that the Lord God Almighty already had this covered. It suddenly struck me that this was a mission He had given me.

I smiled at her and said, "Rose, I am also on a mission."

She did not understand what I meant, but it did not matter because I knew the devil and his demons had heard, and they would tremble. With all of this taking place, I felt purposed by Lord God. I was on a mission as a wife, as a mother, and I was also to lead Rose to Jesus Christ—snatch her out of the claws of the witchdoctor and put a stop to his plans and intent.

Rose lived with her uncle who was the controlling witchdoctor of that territorial part of Sowa Town. I knew he was at war with me. It was so strange. I had no fear of this battle at all. I knew it was an evil, greedy, deceptive, manipulating, and controlling spirit operating through the function of this witch doctor. But he would lose and be chained up forever.

But I had never ever imagined I would go to battle against a witch doctor. Dying and going to Hades seemed a more normal thing to do than this. However, what I had learned in the different levels I had been to in Hades was a source of great benefit that I drew from in this battle.

I then found out another reason why Lord God had sent Rose to me. Within two weeks of her starting date, she found out she was pregnant. She had gone to the nurse at the temporary, prefab office clinic because of a major pain in her leg. Through tests, they discovered she was pregnant. The local doctor was very worried because her leg had already started to give problems at this early stage in her pregnancy.

This was my chance to help Rose and show her the love of God. I had suffered the very same problem and the possibility of losing my leg during both my pregnancies. I had been issued special stockings from Switzerland to wear throughout my pregnancies and was supposed to wear them for the rest of my life. But, with the heat in Botswana, I just could not wear them. I gave them to Rose and told her to take it to the nurse and doctor and ask them if they would help her.

The local doctor and nurse told Rose that these stockings were a miracle. There were no other special stockings like mine available in the whole of Botswana. The local type of stockings were not half as good as the ones from Switzerland were and they were convinced the stockings would definitely help save her leg. "Only God in Heaven could have sent these stockings," the nurse told Rose.

The news spread like wildfire among the locals in Sowa Town and the surrounding areas. Who would have thought that the Holy Spirit would use Swiss medical stockings to bring such a breakthrough in the spirit realm over such a widespread territory?

From that moment on, wherever I went, locals would greet me. Rose became open to all I could give her from Lord God. She allowed me to pray for her, to read things from the Bible to her and teach her things of God's Kingdom. Unfortunately, her leg just started getting bigger and bigger and in her fifth month she was put on bed rest. I did not see her from this point onward because I was not welcome or allowed to go and visit her.

While she was still with me, her uncle said the stockings were just a white man's trick and there was an evil spirit in her leg. She needed to go to the ancestors for cleansing and healing rituals to get rid of it.

I told her she had no evil spirit in her leg, and that it was a lie trying to make her fear so the liar could get complete power over her. I said, "You have an abscess that has formed into a blood clot in your leg. You must trust God Almighty in Heaven and not some dead ancestors for healing."

When she told her uncle this, he became so angry that he cursed her and kicked her out of his house. She was immediately offered a place to stay by the nurse who had been looking after her pregnancy. I knew God had provided this new home and environment for Rose.

Rose gave birth to a boy and came by to show me her son and to say thank you for helping her. I reminded her it was not me, but Lord Jesus, God's Son, who had blessed me with the stockings, which made it possible for me to give them to her.

She said, "But your God is so great."

I replied, "He is not only my God. He is your God, too. He loves me and He loves you just as much."

As I hugged her and her son, her tears flowed and she said, "I am so sorry."

"What do you have to be sorry for? You have done nothing wrong."

"No. I came to work for you because my uncle the witch-doctor sent me." I think she had expected me to be surprised.

"I know he sent you Rose. It is fine."

"He sent me to kill you!" Now that was one small, yet very vital point I had not known. It caused me to shake.

I immediately heard the Holy Spirit's voice, *Michele, greater am I in you, than he who is in the world.*

I smiled at Rose and said, "When you took a knife and stabbed my fridge, I knew you were sent on a mission from a witch doctor. That is why I started praying, singing, and dancing." I did not want Rose to know I had not known how deadly serious her mission had been.

She looked at me and said, "But I could see your God is much bigger than mine."

I smiled, and inside said to Holy Spirit, *Greater are You, Lord.*

"Yes, God is, and He is not my God but the Almighty, living Lord God. He can be your God, too, Rose. All you have to do is accept His Son. Would you like to?"

She was crying as she told me, "I already have." We embraced and prayed. After we said good-bye I went inside and fell on my knees in thanksgiving as the tears flowed. Rose knew Jesus Christ as her Lord, and I was alive.

For God did not give us a spirit of timidity (of cowardice, of craven and cringing and fawning fear), but [He has given us a spirit] of power and of love and of calm and well-balanced mind and discipline and self-control.

(2 Tim. 1:7 AMP)

And you will know the Truth, and the Truth will set you free.

(John 8:32 AMP)

Georg + Cherry

with their

Grandson

Twenty-Five

Paralyzed

OUR DAYS WENT BACK TO being normal after this, until we were made aware that Cyle-jay was 100 percent deaf, after he had gone for major tests at Wits University. After well over a year of intense prayer and warring, he was later healed and the same team at Wits University declared him healthy with 100 percent hearing. They advised us that Cyle-jay should go for extensive, daily speech therapy over a six-to-eight-month period. If we did not take him for this, they said it would cause major side effects when he started school. This is another one of God's divine miracles.

Around this time, Dr. Chris, our doctor in Sowa Town, met with us. He feared the next anaphylactic allergy attack could leave me paralyzed for life. He also said there was a growing chance that my lungs could collapse at any time during the paralysis, making it fatal. He advised us to move to a place where there were hospital facilities, unlike Sowa Town that was still in the process of building facilities.

I could not work toward victory and complete healing with a doctor who feared the worst instead of believing and trusting Jehovah *Rophe*, the Lord God who heals. Dr. Chris was the only doctor I had who did not believe in God's greatness and divine miracles. He was extremely cynical about the truth of the Bible, and displayed such cynicism when Cyle-jay was healed from deafness.

We had been blessed with six fruitful and colorful years in Sowa Town, but both Charles and I knew our season there was drawing to a close. God immediately opened doors for Charles and he signed on with a company whose plant was on the eastern side of Johannesburg.

We left the children with my mom and dad for the last two weeks of our stay in Sowa Town to enable me to prepare for the big packing up and removal day.

Charles and I enjoyed our time together and on the last evening in town, decided to take an extra long walk to say good-bye. Halfway back to the house, the attack started.

"Charles, the bump is under my chin," I said as calmly as I could because I refused to allow fear to gain control.

Charles also calmly looked at me and then grabbed my hand and said, "Run! Run to the house as fast as you can." We did not realize running was the worst thing to do!

Charles had always been a sprinter and his lightning pace was just too fast for me. Eventually, he had to carry me. By the time we got into the house, my tongue had blown up completely, my face was already contorting and I was on fire. Charles got my Epipen, thrust it into my chest and injected me, then got a spoon and placed it in my mouth. He went to the phone, telling Dr. Chris to get over to our house immediately because I was in too serious a condition to go to him. He grabbed all the ice blocks we had and dispersed them over my entire body. (I had wanted to turn the fridges off earlier, but Charles had said he would do it when we went to sleep. Thank You, Lord!)

My heart felt as if it was going to burst open as I started gasping for breath. I knew this was a major attack and it was not going well. The paralysis had already started, but this time it was different. It felt as if someone had taken my lungs and squeezed them flat. I thought about what Dr. Chris had said about my lungs collapsing and now it felt as if they were in the process of doing just that. Eventually I was totally paralyzed and struggling to breathe.

Dr. Chris arrived. He threw his case open and started injecting me with what seemed like endless little bottles.

I looked up and saw Charles and Dr. Chris looking at me and could not believe what I was seeing. Their faces were saying good-bye. I didn't know why Dr. Chris was not trying to resuscitate me. I needed oxygen in my lungs! He knew this and yet there was no oxygen with him or in the town itself. The closest oxygen was at the work clinic, which was too far to help me. I needed it right then.

Then I heard the Holy Spirit say, *Michele, remember: "All things work together for the good of those who love the Lord and are called according to His purpose."*

I immediately thought of Cyle-jay and Brontii-ann, *Oh Lord, thank You that they are safe with my mom and dad. Bless them, Father.*

Immediately I saw their faces as if they were right there. I realized this was not good at all. I was dying, but I felt no fear.

Holy Spirit, hold me tight.

I am, He spoke to me softly.

I am in too much pain. I can't feel You.

Look and you will see Me.

It was at this moment when I literally could see and smell what seemed like immense, glorious light enter into our sitting room. I just knew that this was part of Heaven's porthole that had come down to fetch me.

Twenty-Six

Heaven

I LOOKED AND SAW HIS dancing flame, the same flame that had been placed in me when I was rescued from hell. The split-second I saw Him, and Heaven along with him, I no longer felt any more pain.

I am going on a journey, aren't I?

Yes. I will never leave you, Michele.

I know.

Can you feel My comforting arms around you?

Yes. Thank You. The pain was gone and peace was in its place.

I began trying to tell Charles with my eyes that I loved him with all my heart. I also tried to tell him to smile, because then his beautiful, deep blue eyes would light up with laughter. I loved looking into them and taking that trip of joy with him. We communicated so much with our eyes. But his eyes were dull and serious.

My eyelids had already become paralyzed together with everything else in my body. There was no communicating at that very moment. I so wanted to reach out and just love him, but I could not even release a tear from my eye; even my eye ducts were paralyzed.

But my spirit and soul were not paralyzed! They were leaving my earthly body. This time I already knew, beyond any doubt, they would be taken to Heaven and placed in my new heavenly body.

Oh, Holy Spirit, please let Charles know how much I love him! And stir him up to put on some worship music for me as I leave.

The instant I had said this, I began hearing the most beautiful music, music like no other music I had ever heard. With this music came an array of dancing angels that were beautiful, magnificent, and glorious. I felt the Holy Spirit tighten His grip around me and we enjoyed this array of splendor and music together.

I had forgotten I was totally paralyzed and my breath was slowly leaving me. Instead, it felt as if I was on a mountaintop with my arms and heart wide open, singing with this music about the majesty of our everlasting great and mighty God.

As the music started getting louder, I could see a brilliantly bright-white light appearing out of the array from the porthole of glorious life.

I knew this Light—He was Jesus, my Lord.

Michele, I am right here. I will never leave you and I am bringing you a song just as you have asked.

I knew I was not alone. I felt so safe and protected. There was no fear.

My body had started to black out because it could not get any air. As my lungs were dying, my body jolted, I knew the moment had arrived when I would leave my earthly body. There was still no fear in me at all. I could see the big hand that had placed me in my body the first time was coming down to fetch me. I knew I was going to be taken out of my body of flesh.

Jesus.

Michele, I am here. He took my hand.

I could feel my spirit and soul leaving my body. I looked down from the ceiling at Charles and Dr. Chris who stood as if frozen. I went and stood before Charles and said, *I love you. Please tell Cyle-jay and Brontii-ann that I love them.* But I knew he could not hear me.

Oh, Holy Spirit, hold him tight in your arms, too. Hold our babies tight in your arms, too.

As I said this, I could feel myself being carried and placed into the glorious, divine splendor of light. I felt myself traveling in this porthole at an accelerated speed. The intensity of this light was increasing in its magnificence, glory, and splendor.

The number of worshiping angels and the volume of their song increased. I could see a group of angels singing and dancing, flooding the light with joyous praise and bubbling laughter. There was another group who were standing tall, raising their angelic voice in worship, releasing waves of serene peace. There was a group who were bowing and waving, releasing waves of declarations of God's holiness. All of this was done in beautiful melodious unity with their eyes and actions fixed on this divine splendor of worship upon worship beyond human understanding.

I felt the timelessness of eternity. It seemed my senses had intensified as Jesus began to lead me through a mist. I was not scared because I could see and hear the music and the glorious splendor of light. The dancing flame held me tight. The mist that covered me was not like a black and empty void of permanent isolation and fear that I had felt when the consuming black monster stole my life. Instead it was a tranquil, peaceful, restful state of complete surrender. It was so beautiful and pure and had such consuming love.

There was no darkness, but a mere shadow; not the shadow that places shackles around you and chains you up. No, it was more like a living, moving shadow of going from one earthly life into life eternal.

Oh, my Lord, this is the shadow David wrote of. As I said this, I was now able to see what was on the other side of this shadow of mist.

> Even though I walk through darkest valley, I will fear no evil, for you are with me; your rod and your staff, they comfort me.
>
> (Ps. 23:4)

> Yes, though I walk through the [deep sunless] valley of the shadow of death, I will fear or dread no evil, for You are with me; Your rod [to protect] and Your staff [to guide], they comfort me.
>
> (Ps. 23:4 AMP)

I was not alone. The love of God engulfed me. I had never experienced His love like that ever before.

Leaving the shadow, I entered into a glorious light out of which the angels were singing. I could clearly see the magnificent glorious and holy light of divine splendor we were going into. It was by far more magnificent than the brilliant light I and the singing angels were already in.

The most amazing thing was how I became aware that Jesus had become this light and so had the dancing flame. Oh! It was a glorious, magnificent, brilliant splendor. They were a part and yet separate. I was also able to see mighty angelic beings around this divine splendor of light. They were different from the angels who were making the heavenly music. These magnificent angels were singing, "Holy, Holy, Holy."

I had seen angels on earth since I was given a second chance at life. However, these angels were even more exquisite and graceful, mighty and majestic. They carried a holiness I had never before encountered. It blew me away and I felt my spirit and soul falling face down.

When I was rescued from hell, I had seen the brilliance of this light, the forgiving love and amazing grace emanating from out of the essence of this light. But now I was facing the righteous splendor and holiness, the lordship that was emanating from out of this light.

I said, *Jesus, You are holy. You have not only forgiven me but have made me holy too.*

As I said this, the angels, both those carrying the music from heaven and the angels declaring the holiness of God, all bowed down and worshipped Jesus in harmonious praise.

Angels eyes are glorious. As with God's splendor, angelic beings are breathtaking. They are mighty like living gem stones. Each angel has a unique personal and militant beauty. As they looked at me, their eyes deepened and started drawing me to the love of God as if to a running river. Their eyes reflected the music and firm declarations coming from them. As they bowed in unity, their eyes stayed fixed, locked on the divine splendor that stood in front of us.

The joy, peace, and righteousness that flooded my soul then was more life than I had ever known on earth. The eternal words of Jesus came into full totality at that very moment.

> I have come that they may have life, and that they may have it more abundantly.
>
> (John 10:10)

This life, like the love of God, was like no life here on earth. This was true life. There was absolutely no evil in it whatsoever. It was a living water of love, joy, peace and holiness.

Imagine life with no evil. A life that just loves.

It is so divine and magnificently beautiful in all its glorious splendor.

Even though we were in a heavenly array and magnificence, we were still not in all of it yet!

I could see we were approaching the Kingdom of Heaven. The porthole of light we were in was just a taste of what lay ahead of me. It was as if I was looking at a massive, shiny diamond. The light emanating from this Kingdom was a brilliant, gleaming, white light. This brilliant Kingdom also had an array of magnificent colors that were piercing their way through the diamond rays.

Then I saw at the end of the porthole of light what looked like shining pearls. I immediately thought of the white pearl gates the Bible describes.

Jesus, is that the entrance to Heaven?

Yes.

I knew that beyond those shining pearl gates stood the throne of the King of kings and the Lord of lords, my Savior, Jesus Christ. Beyond those pearl gates I would be able to stand face to face with Jesus and speak to Him for eternity. I was bursting with an anticipation, an expectation bubbling over with inexpressible joy, and yet a reverent, holy fear at the same time.

As I stood awestruck in my praise and worship, I sensed something had been gently, lovingly infused deep within me—an awareness of what I had not completed on earth.

Lord, I have not successfully completed any of the tasks God has given me. I have only started being a mommy and still have so much growing to do with Charles. And I am not even forty yet. I haven't even started writing my book.

I felt the gentle flame, the Holy Spirit's familiar loving smile. He said to me, *God will meet you where your faith is. You can stop this allergy attack right now.*

I don't understand.

Michele, you are in Heaven as we speak, but once you pass these gates you will be in the Kingdom of Heaven and then there is no turning back.

Holy Spirit, I can't die now. I still have to finish my God-given destiny and the purpose I was created for.

I will not die but live, and will proclaim what the Lord has done.

(Ps. 118:17)

I press on toward the goal to win the prize for which God has called me heavenward in Christ Jesus.

(Phil. 3:14)

My gentle, faithful friend said, *You know what to do.*

I took one more look at the divine Kingdom of Heaven that stood in front of me.

Oh, Lord, this is a life beyond life, so much better than the happiest moments I have ever had on earth. The love, the peace and the joy—it is all so alive!

It is magnificent with the divine splendor and holiness of Yaweh—the Lord our God! It is so real and so, so thirst-quenching!

I don't want to go back to the evil and the fighting and the pain and the death of earth. But I have not finished my destiny, Lord. I have not won my race. Lord Jesus, I want You to say to me, "Well done, Michele, my good and faithful servant."

I felt myself crying, not only in sadness but with the immense love, joy, and peace that was engulfing me. Then I stood up and joined the angels in praise and worship unto Jesus. I sang what my whole being had been singing all the years since Jesus had rescued me out of hell—"Jesus, You are Lord."

I knew, beyond any doubt, going back was the right thing. There was a sadness to leave, but I was joyful to be given another chance to hear those words from my first love.

I said, *Jesus, I want to go back. I want to go back and make sure I lead Cyle-jay and Brontii-ann to You, my Lord. I want to help them know their God-ordained destiny, their God-anointed purpose. I want to finish my life with Charles. I love him so much, Lord.*

Once again, I felt His understanding smile of true mercy and grace wrap around me even tighter.

My Lord, I want to go back and write the book You have told me to write. You did not rescue me from hell for nothing. I have a God-destiny to finish. I am not yet finished on earth.

I was very aware I was outside of the pearl gates of Heaven.

Lord Jesus, beyond these gates must be a million times more than what I am experiencing now.

I felt His encompassing smile as He lovingly said, *No, Michele, it is a whole eternity more. It is Me.*

Oh, if only I could express what I was experiencing at that very moment, but there are not sufficient words to describe it in its fullness. John Bevere explains eternity as "infinity times infinity, times infinity, times . . ." It is endless. The human mind cannot comprehend this. Jesus is endless. The Kingdom of Heaven is endless.

My basking in Heaven's glory and pure essence was coming to an end for *the time*. I stilled myself to capture as much as I could of the divine splendor, the worship, and the true abundant life of the Kingdom of Heaven I was standing before. The sights, sounds, smells and tastes of the pure love and holiness, joy and peace that I was experiencing were endless. The human mind cannot imagine and comprehend all of this—from the splendor and glory of the running waters of the River of Life to the endless worship of the angels. At that very point, I was so glad I was spirit and soul so I was free from the restrictions of the flesh. Jesus is the center. Holy Spirit flowed from Lord Jesus as the Living River carrying and releasing the essence of Heaven. He is endless. Jesus is endless. The Kingdom of Heaven is endless. All of this is in Abba Father.

I took in all that I was capable of one last time. My soul and spirit once again fell down in grateful worship. This was where I would return and walk again when my life was completely fulfilled. Strangely, I began crying along with my praises.

Holy Spirit, I don't want to forget this when I go back.
You don't have to.
Really?
Yes, take Heaven with you and share it all over the earth wherever you go.
Can I?
Always. That is why you have Me in you. Jesus said the Kingdom of Heaven is here.

I said what the Holy Spirit continually told me, *It is Christ in you.*

He smiled as He said, *Yes, Jesus was the first to carry Heaven on earth and now all those in Him do so as well.*

Over all my years as Christian, I had declared the Kingdom of Heaven is at hand because of Jesus. It is here. But this was the first time I really understood it. I could see it! The Kingdom of

Heaven is here. Jesus carried the Kingdom of Heaven to earth. *Oh, my Lord Jesus, You brought Heaven back down to earth.*

The Holy Spirit affirmed this. *Yes, Michele, that is why He has given you the keys and His Name. Use them wherever you go.*

> I will give you the keys of the Kingdom of Heaven; whatever you bind on earth will be bound in heaven, and whatever you loose on earth will be loosed in heaven.
>
> (Matt. 16:19)

As He told me this, I was once again reminded that the kingdom of darkness has no option but to bow down and submit to Jesus as He is Lord of all. He carries the Kingdom of Heaven and the gates of Hades shrink back from Him in complete fear, knowing the final hour of complete destruction is drawing closer. I had read this in the Bible and had experienced it firsthand when Jesus came and rescued me out of hell.

I immediately knew what to do.

With the boldness and strength I had received from drinking from the river of Heaven, I then shouted with my whole being: *You spirit of allergy, demon of fear, in Jesus' Name, I command you stop this attack right now. I resist you! I bind you! I loose my full healing and the fullness of God's destiny over my life. I will run my full race and run it well. I do not fear you! Devil, you cannot take my life, do you hear? Now get behind me!*

Immediately the big hand took me and carried me back down. Once again, I traveled back down the porthole of light and I was gently returned to my flesh body again. I felt the same warm feeling as when I had been returned to life the first time.

I am back. Thank You, Lord God.

Once again, I felt the Holy Spirit smile and say, *Michele, we love you with an everlasting love. We will never leave you, nor forsake you. We will always meet you at your faith.*

Oh, Lord, I love You.

I knew that this time I was not unconscious, but I could feel the complete restrictions of my body, so I knew I was still completely paralyzed. I did not care because God would meet me at my faith. I knew the paralysis would have to go, whether it took one hour or one week or even one month. God was in control! This strengthened me and with my whole inner being I shouted out, *Glory, hallelujah!*

Even though it was only the inside of me that could hear, that was all I needed. I still was not able to see through the shadow yet, but I knew I was already out of the shadow.

Holy Spirit, help me run this race and finish it in such a way that it will please the Father. I want to fight this good fight and receive my crown of righteousness from Jesus. I want to hear Him say, "Well done, my good and faithful servant." This is a crown no one other than He can give.

> Do you know that in a race all the runners run, but only one gets the prize? Run in such a way as to get the prize.
>
> (1 Cor. 9:24)

> For I am already being poured out as a drink offering, and the time of my departure [from this world] is at hand *and* I will soon go free. I have fought the good *and* worthy *and* noble

fight, I have finished the race, I have kept the faith [firmly guarding the gospel against error]. In the future there is reserved for me the [victor's] crown of righteousness [for being right with God and doing right], which the Lord, the righteous Judge, will award to me on that [great] day—and not to me only, but also to all those who have loved *and* longed for *and* welcomed His appearing.

(2 Tim. 4:6–8 AMP)

Full of cheer and boldness, I eventually felt myself coming out of the shadow of darkness that had engulfed me. I was once again able to see Charles and Dr. Chris again. I felt the death around my lungs being released and I took a deep breath through my nose and exhaled with such gratefulness. Ah, oxygen, the necessity of life on earth. I was back on earth so I could finish my destiny!

As I inhaled, I saw Charles and Dr. Chris release big sighs of relief too.

Even though I could not move anything due to the paralysis, I connected with Charles' eyes which were flooding with tears. I did not need to move my lips to say what I had to say, neither did Charles. The love flowing in our eyes was what we had shared so many times before, but this time it was so very much more, so very precious and intense.

In my mind I said, *Thank You, Lord. I love Charles so much.*

I then heard Dr. Chris saying to Charles, "I will arrange for a plane first thing tomorrow morning. Make arrangements for which South Africa hospital where your GP will want to receive Michele. Also arrange for an ambulance to pick her up and take her directly there. She is going to need intensive care for quite a while."

I saw Charles nod.

Because I was still totally paralyzed, I could not share my joy and excitement with them and reassure them everything was absolutely fine. I was free and alive, or as alive as life on earth is possible.

I remained completely paralyzed for several hours and the rest of the paralysis took about a week to leave. This did not worry me because I knew God was in control.

Charles and I continued to communicate with our eyes all those hours I was completely paralyzed. He was so tired, so drained, and eventually I watched him drift off to sleep. Even though I remained alone in my physically-imprisoned body, it did not stop me from celebrating within my innermost being.

Holy Spirit, I love Charles so much. We still have so much love to share and together help our children grow. I am glad to be back . . . Heaven is real, just as hell is.

Holy Spirit then said to me, *Michele, you cannot tell people about hell unless you tell them about Heaven.*

I then felt His familiar smile within me and my soul and spirit joined Him as He said, *Since you were born, you have always wanted to know what happened on the last page. Once you knew the ending, you would then turn to the first page and start reading.*

I know, Holy Spirit. I would always love seeing how the princess marries her prince and they live happily ever after. I never tired of it. I still don't.

His answer brought a new understanding, one that I will never let go of.

The whole church is the bride of Christ. This is better than happily ever after; it is a victorious and glorious eternal life with Him.

Holy Spirit, please help me with this.

I already am.

Even though I still had major paralysis, I fell sound asleep after going through both of my near- death experiences. Still to this day, there are some nights I lie in bed and go over the experiences I have been through. I then never cease to fall on my knees before God Almighty in praise and thanksgiving for all He has done for me.

The first was a terrifying, horrific death that left my soul and spirit paralyzed with eternal death and damnation as I begged and screamed God to forgive me and save me from death and its torturous, fiery flames devouring me. I stood guilty of everything, every sin the devil and his demons accused me of.

The powerful truth that only Jesus could save me as He is eternity only hit me as I stood in that burning pit of hell. I did not deserve to stand before Him and expect His forgiveness. I had ignored and stomped upon the sacrifice He had endured for me.

Yes, I had acknowledged him as God's Son. Yet I had never truly accepted Him as Jesus the Christ, God's only begotten Son and Lord and Savior of all.

Eternal damnation had been my lot, and this is the lot for all who do not accept Jesus as the Christ.

A person might be able to hide and deceive other people about who they really are, but no one can ever hide who they are from God Almighty. He sees right into our hearts, every split second of every single day we are on earth.

In the second death I had just come out of, I had fallen prey to complete physical paralysis from the top of my head to the tips of my toes, yet not in my spirit and soul at all. My spirit and soul were more alive, freer than I had ever known could be possible.

It had not been death as people think. My physical death was not the end of my abundant life, but the beginning of it. My life in heaven was filled with the presence of Jesus Christ, as He and His whole entourage of heavenly beings took me through a mere shadow of death that was completely free of fear.

Instead, it was filled with the true abundant life flowing and feeding me with the living river. I had been immersed in the Kingdom of Heaven, and God's righteousness and His grace. This river is unexplainable; it is the River of Life.

I felt so free, despite having died and come back into a totally paralyzed body that was being pumped full of medicated drips. I had found such pure and holy love, joy, and peace through the Holy Spirit who is Jesus Christ's special gift to us.

As I lay there I could feel this river within me rising. From within my innermost being, I cried out, *Death you have no victory, you have no sting. Not only am I saved, but I have eternal life. The Kingdom of Heaven is living in me! And one day, when my God destiny is finished here on earth, I will go and join my*

King and Lord Jesus Christ. But know this, He is living in me and you have no hold, no power over me.

I knew no one on earth could hear me as I lay voiceless and motionless, but I also knew the whole spirit realm had heard me. So I shouted out, *Jesus has come to give abundant life!*

Glory, hallelujah! has a whole new ring of eternal praise to it. I will never stop saying it and living in the light of eternity.

Jesus replied, "If anyone loves me, he will obey my teaching. My Father will love him, and we will come to him and make our home with him."

(John 14:23)

Their destiny is destruction, their God is their stomach, and their glory is their shame. Their mind is on earthly things. But our citizenship is in heaven. And we eagerly await a savior from there, the Lord Jesus Christ, who, by power that enables Him to bring everything under control, will transform our lowly bodies so that they will be like His glorious body.

(Phil. 3:19–21)

Afterword

IF YOU HAVE READ UP to this point, you will never be able to say to God our Father, "I never knew."

Now you do know.

God does not need to take us all through near-death experiences to shake us into the reality that Heaven and hell are real.

My story shows you that we are all born with eternity in us. One day our earthly bodies will die. The choices that we make while here on earth will determine to which eternal kingdom we will go.

Either we will go through a mere fearless shadow that is full of the brilliant light carrying Jesus, His singing angels, and His abundant life. Together they will carry us to the pearl gates of Heaven. When we go through them there is eternal, glorious life awaiting us in the magnificent splendor of the Kingdom of Heaven. Oh, the love, joy, peace, and righteousness! The glory and grace are beyond description.

This is eternal life.

If you do not go to Heaven you will die in agonizing pain because you will be all alone and in fear as you are swallowed up by the black consuming monster of eternal damnation. The end of this monster's tunnel leads you to hell, the kingdom of darkness, where there is a fiery burning torture, filled with the gnashing of teeth and the screaming agonizing howls of hate, fear and regret.

This is eternal death.

It is one way or the other. We all have to face this and decide. I tell you this because I do not want any one to go to hell. I am known to be straight. When I see the devil trying to blind someone with his lies, or use them for one of his lies against someone else, I just have to tell them straight out.

I shudder when I hear people say there is no hell. The one who wants you to believe there is no hell is the devil, Satan, Lucifer. It is his sick kingdom to come and he desires for you to be trapped in it. He hates you because you are created in the image of God Almighty with the capacity enabling you to choose to be with Him in Heaven.

God planned and created earth for us because of His mercy and grace. He sent His only Son, Jesus Christ, to die for us here on earth. This is the qualification, the accepted, once-and-for-all sacrifice that allows us into Heaven.

That is why the devil wants us. He wants to destroy that capacity within us, *the spirit and the soul*, which in turn will destroy God's plan of us living with Him in Heaven for eternity.

Most people accept and agree we are spirit beings. However, many people do not know or understand that what also separates us from all other creatures on earth is the gift of our free will.

Because of this free will we can have the priceless gift of faith. Yes, God has given us the gift to choose by faith.

God does not force Himself and His Kingdom upon us. He loves and values us way too much to ever do that.

Allow His amazing grace in. When you do, you will forever see His amazing splendor. God Almighty loves you beyond measure.

The Holy Spirit told me, *Michele, you cannot tell people about hell unless you tell them about Heaven too.* Heaven is real, and so is hell.

My hope is that my story has caused you to ask yourself, "Where am I heading?"

We are all climbing into eternity. Only we, ourselves, have the power of free will and free choice to decide which one it will be.

Don't leave this question unanswered any longer. Will it be Heaven or hell? Eternal life or eternal damnation? The River of Life or the burning lake of fire?

Father God, in Jesus' Name,
I pray and ask You to be with the very precious ones who are weighing and deciding the above question. Holy Spirit, we need You. I ask You to help them see the truth that Jesus is the Son of God who has died for them on the cross; that He went to hell and on the third day rose again. He then ascended into Heaven and is on the right hand of Abba Father. Help them get to know and accept Jesus as Lord of their life as He is the way to eternal life. Amen.

Order Information

To order additional copies of this book, please visit
www.redemption-press.com.
Also available on Amazon.com and BarnesandNoble.com
Or by calling toll free 1-844-2REDEEM.